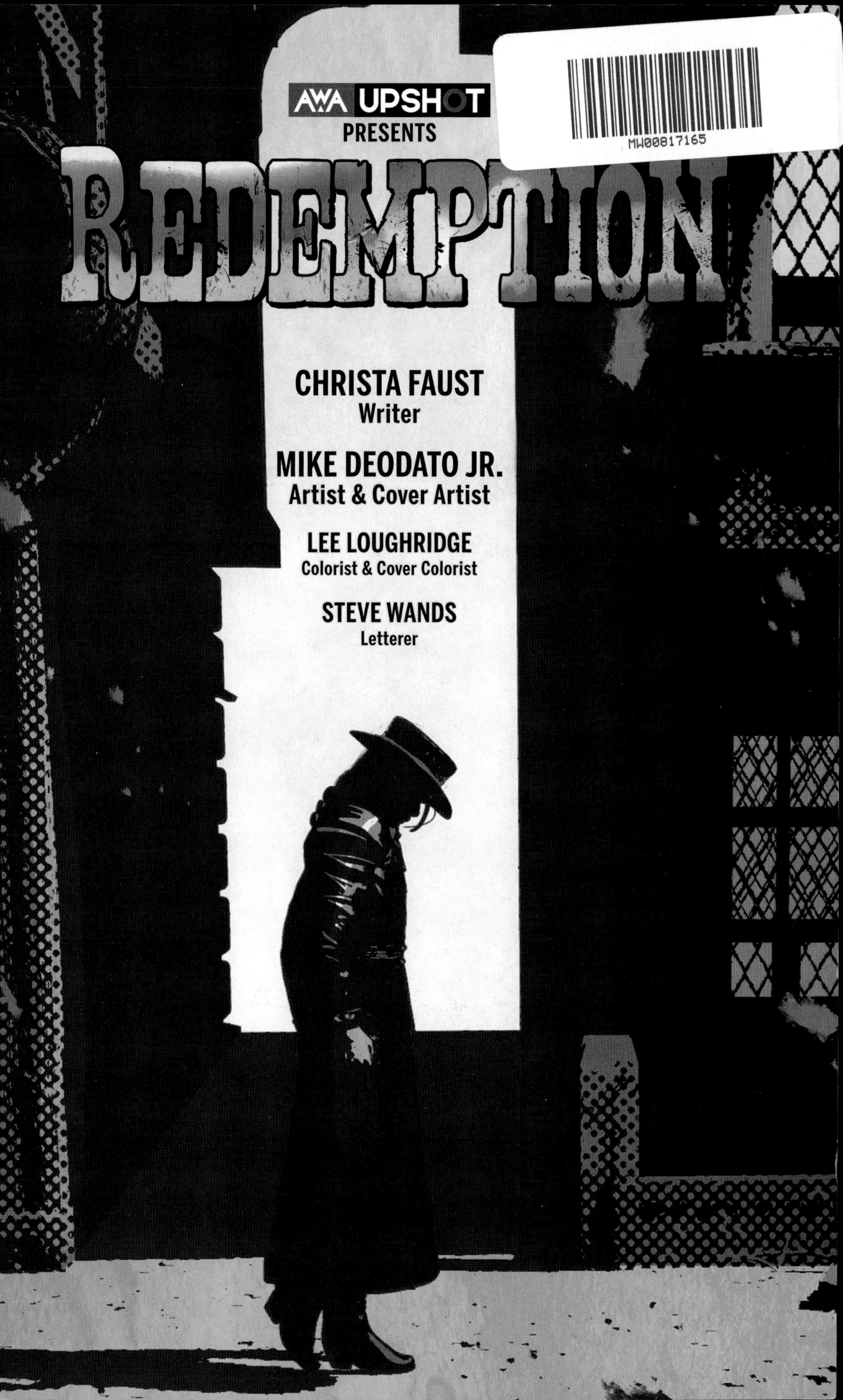
AWA UPSHOT
PRESENTS
REDEMPTION
CHRISTA FAUST
Writer
MIKE DEODATO JR.
Artist & Cover Artist
LEE LOUGHRIDGE
Colorist & Cover Colorist
STEVE WANDS
Letterer

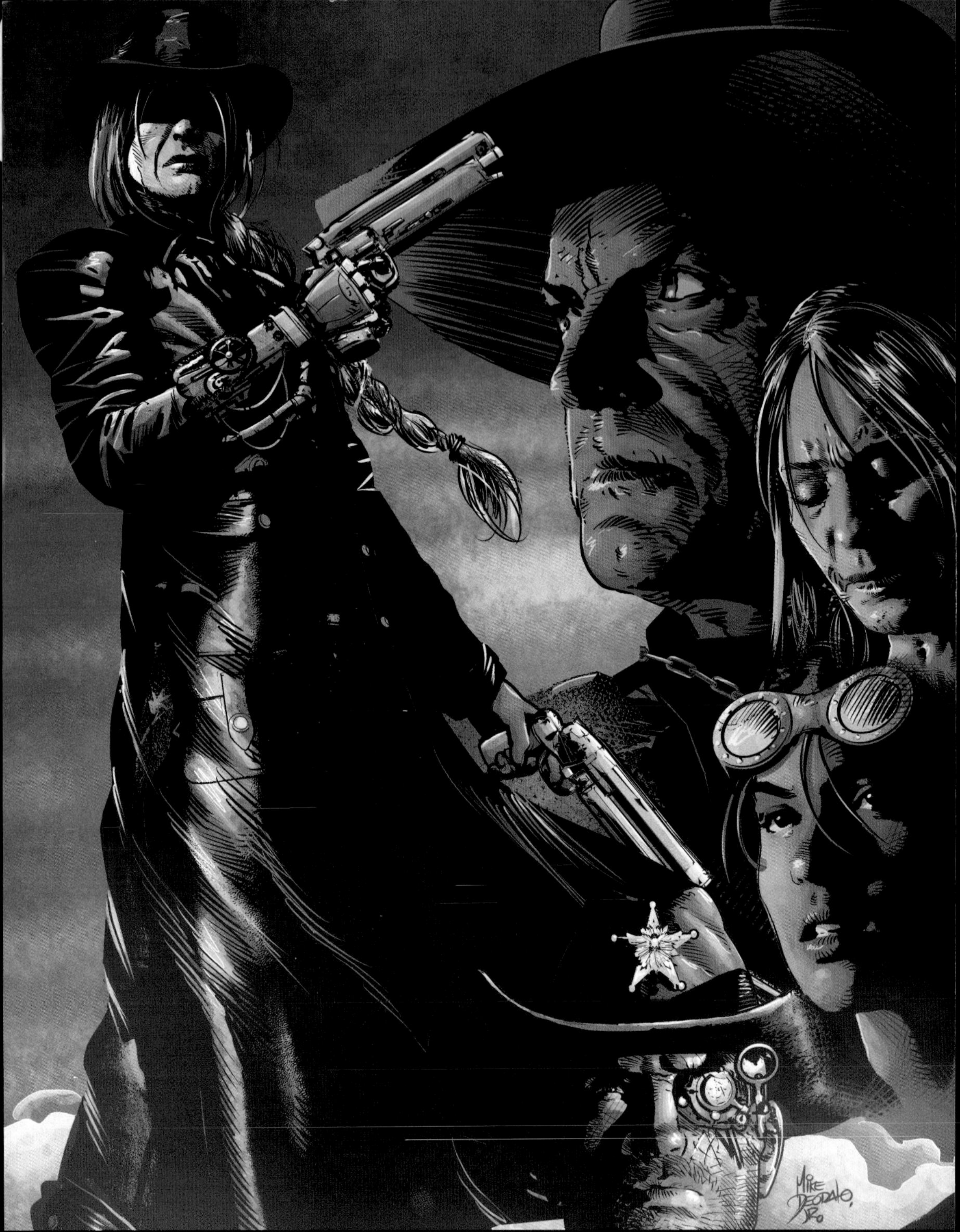

AWA UPSHOT AWA_studios AWAstudiosofficial UPSHOT_studios UPSHOTstudiosofficial

Axel Alonso Chief Creative Officer
Ariane Baya Accounting Associate
Chris Burns Production Editor
Ramsee Chand AWA Studios Assistant
Thea Cheuk Assistant Editor
Stan Chou Art Director & Logo Designer
Michael Coast Senior Editor
Frank Fochetta Senior Consultant, Sales & Distribution
William Graves Managing Editor
Bill Jemas CEO & Publisher
Jackie Liu Digital Marketing Manager
Bosung Kim Graphic Designer
Allison Mase Project Manager
Dulce Montoya Associate Editor
Kevin Park Associate General Counsel
Daphney Stephan Accounting Assistant
Zach Studin President, AWA Studios
Harry Sweezey Finance Associate
Lisa Y. Wu Marketing Manager

REDEMPTION VOL.1 TPB. September 2021. Published by Artists Writers & Artisans, Inc. Office of publication: 178 Columbus Avenue #237194 New York, NY 10023. **Printed in Canada.**

10 9 8 7 6 5 4 3 2 1

Mike Deodato Jr. Concept Sketch for Cat Tanner

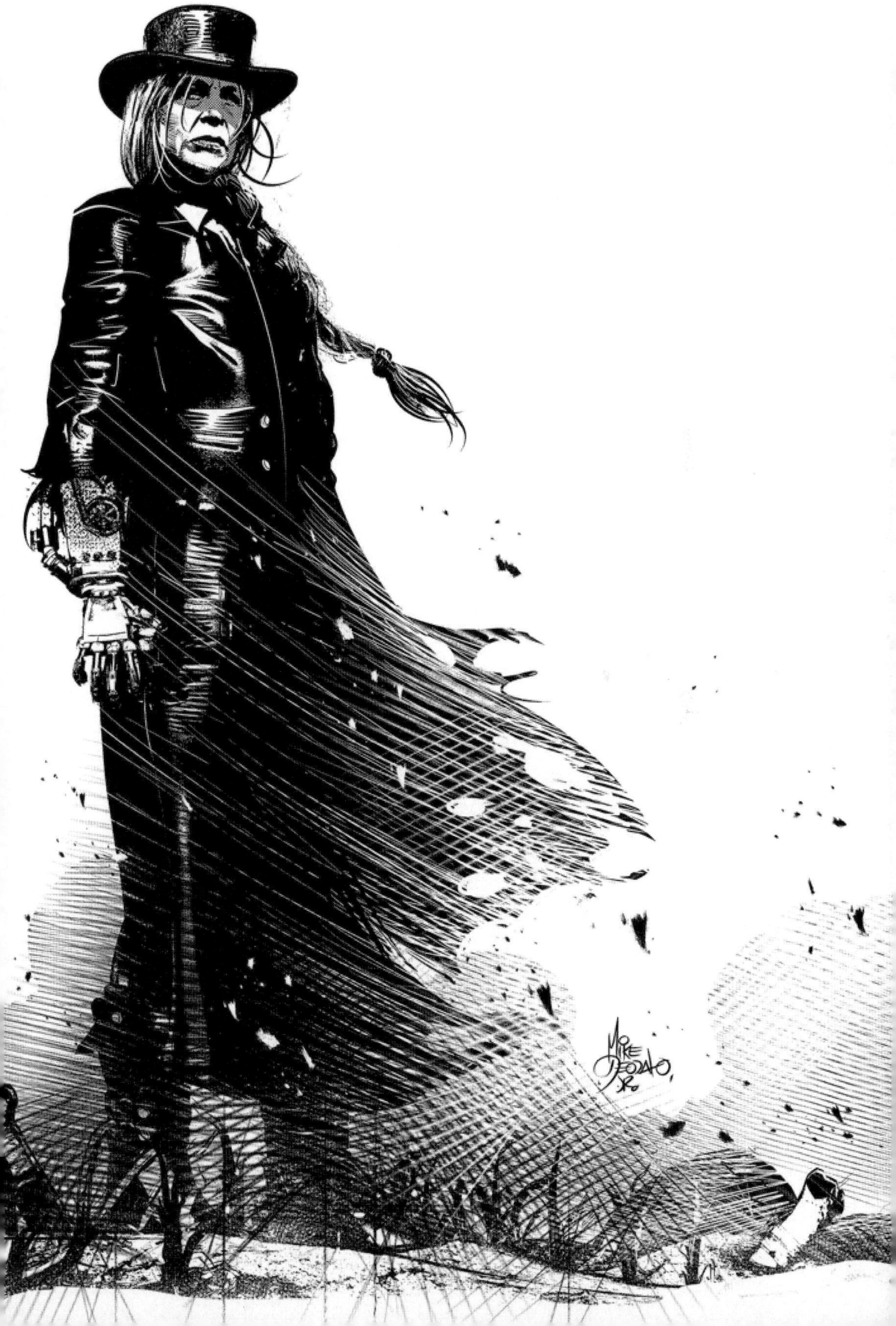

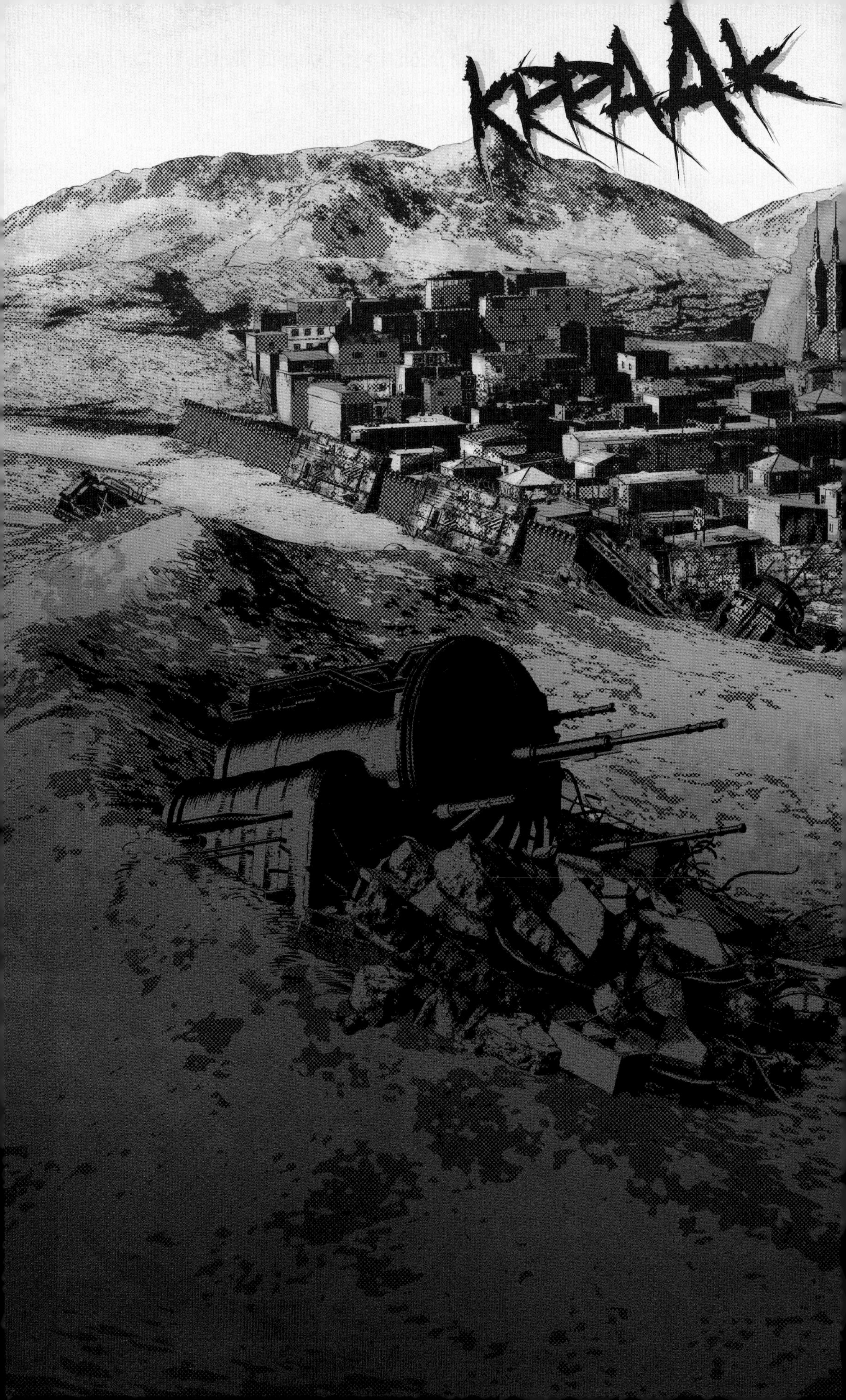
KRAAK

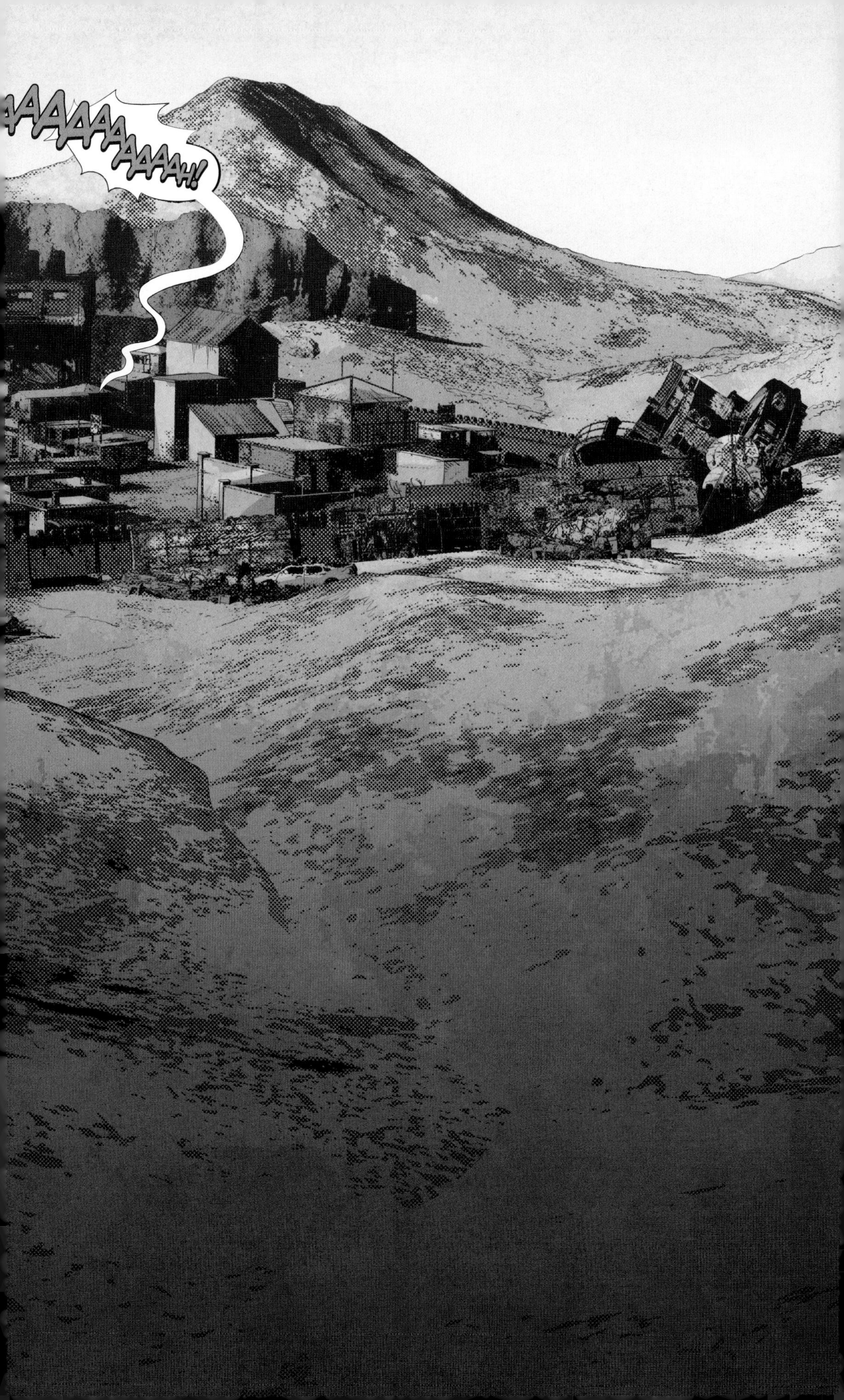
AAAAAAAAAH!

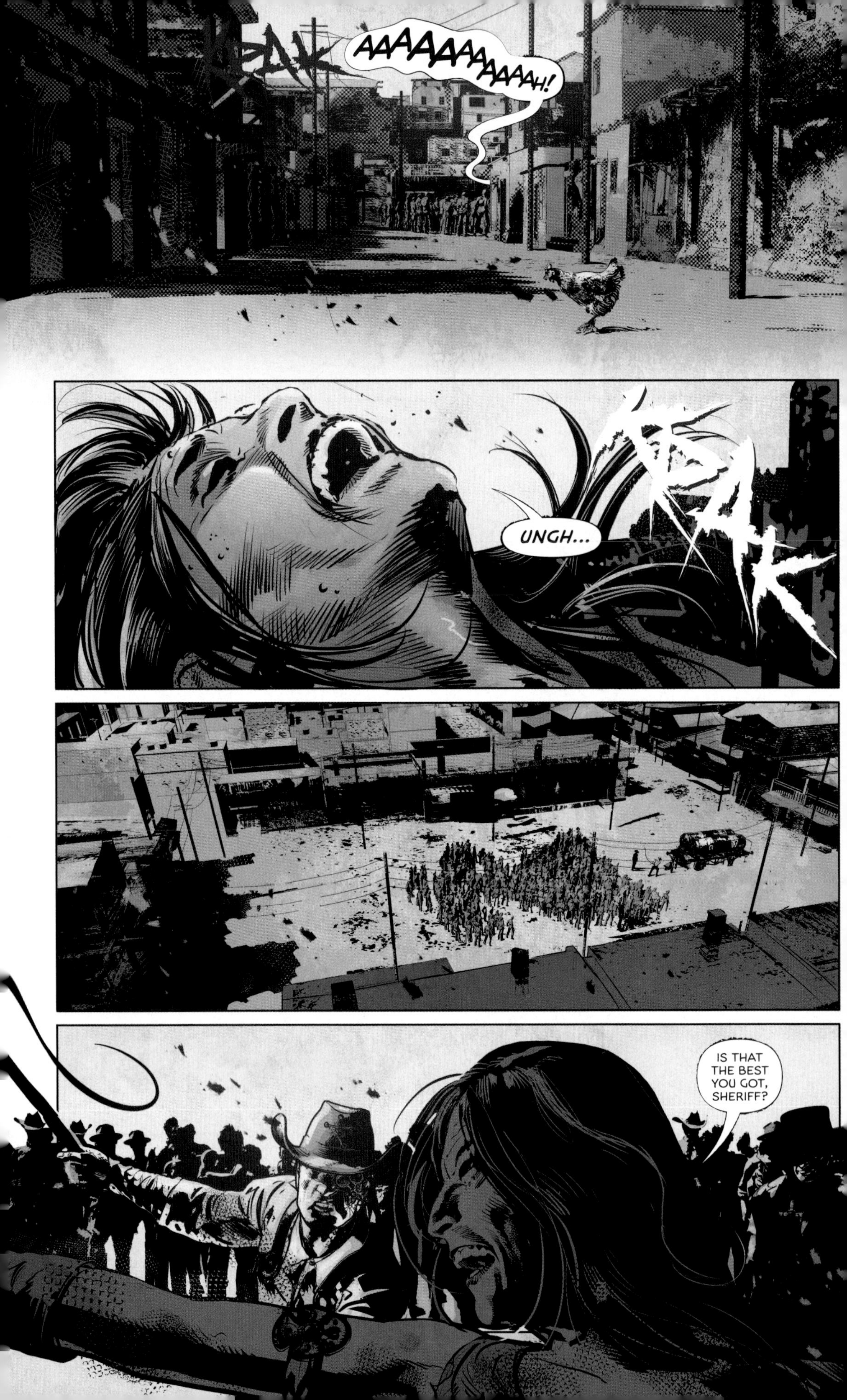
AAAAAAAAAAAAH!
UNGH...
IS THAT THE BEST YOU GOT, SHERIFF?

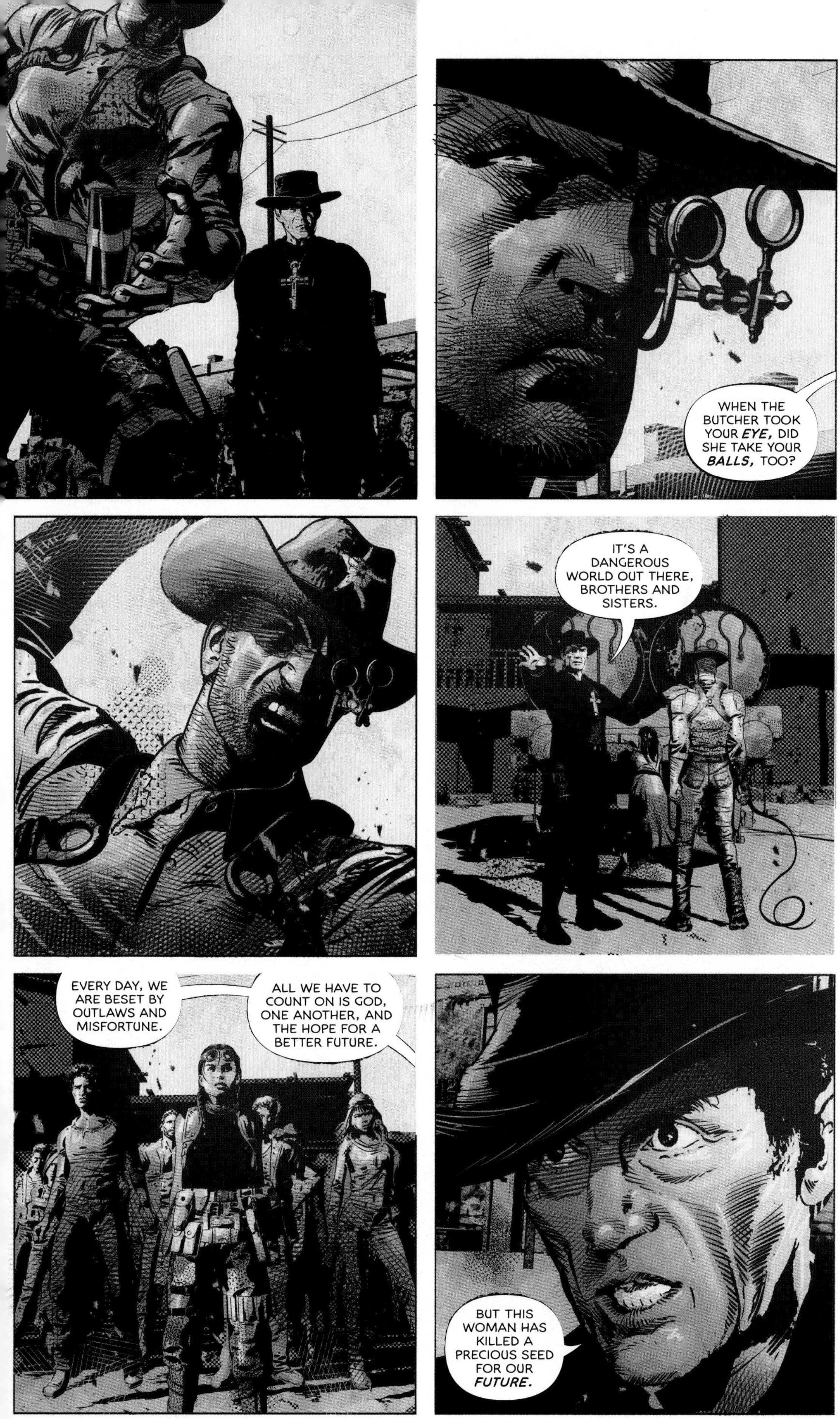
WHEN THE BUTCHER TOOK YOUR ***EYE,*** DID SHE TAKE YOUR ***BALLS,*** TOO?
IT'S A DANGEROUS WORLD OUT THERE, BROTHERS AND SISTERS.
EVERY DAY, WE ARE BESET BY OUTLAWS AND MISFORTUNE.
ALL WE HAVE TO COUNT ON IS GOD, ONE ANOTHER, AND THE HOPE FOR A BETTER FUTURE.
BUT THIS WOMAN HAS KILLED A PRECIOUS SEED FOR OUR ***FUTURE.***

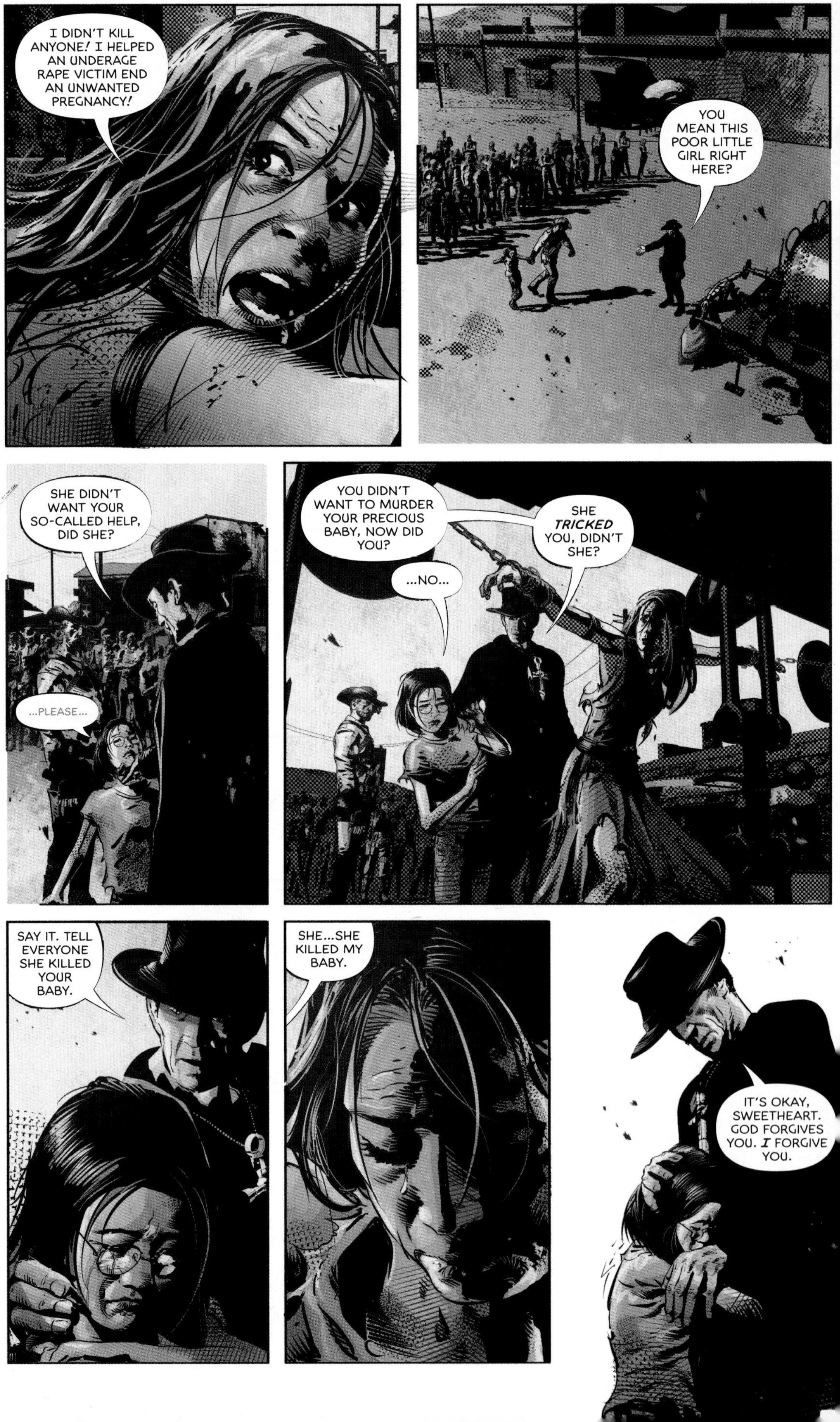
I DIDN'T KILL ANYONE! I HELPED AN UNDERAGE RAPE VICTIM END AN UNWANTED PREGNANCY!
YOU MEAN THIS POOR LITTLE GIRL RIGHT HERE?
SHE DIDN'T WANT YOUR SO-CALLED HELP, DID SHE?
...PLEASE...
YOU DIDN'T WANT TO MURDER YOUR PRECIOUS BABY, NOW DID YOU?
...NO...
SHE *TRICKED* YOU, DIDN'T SHE?
SAY IT. TELL EVERYONE SHE KILLED YOUR BABY.
SHE...SHE KILLED MY BABY.
IT'S OKAY, SWEETHEART. GOD FORGIVES YOU. *I* FORGIVE YOU.

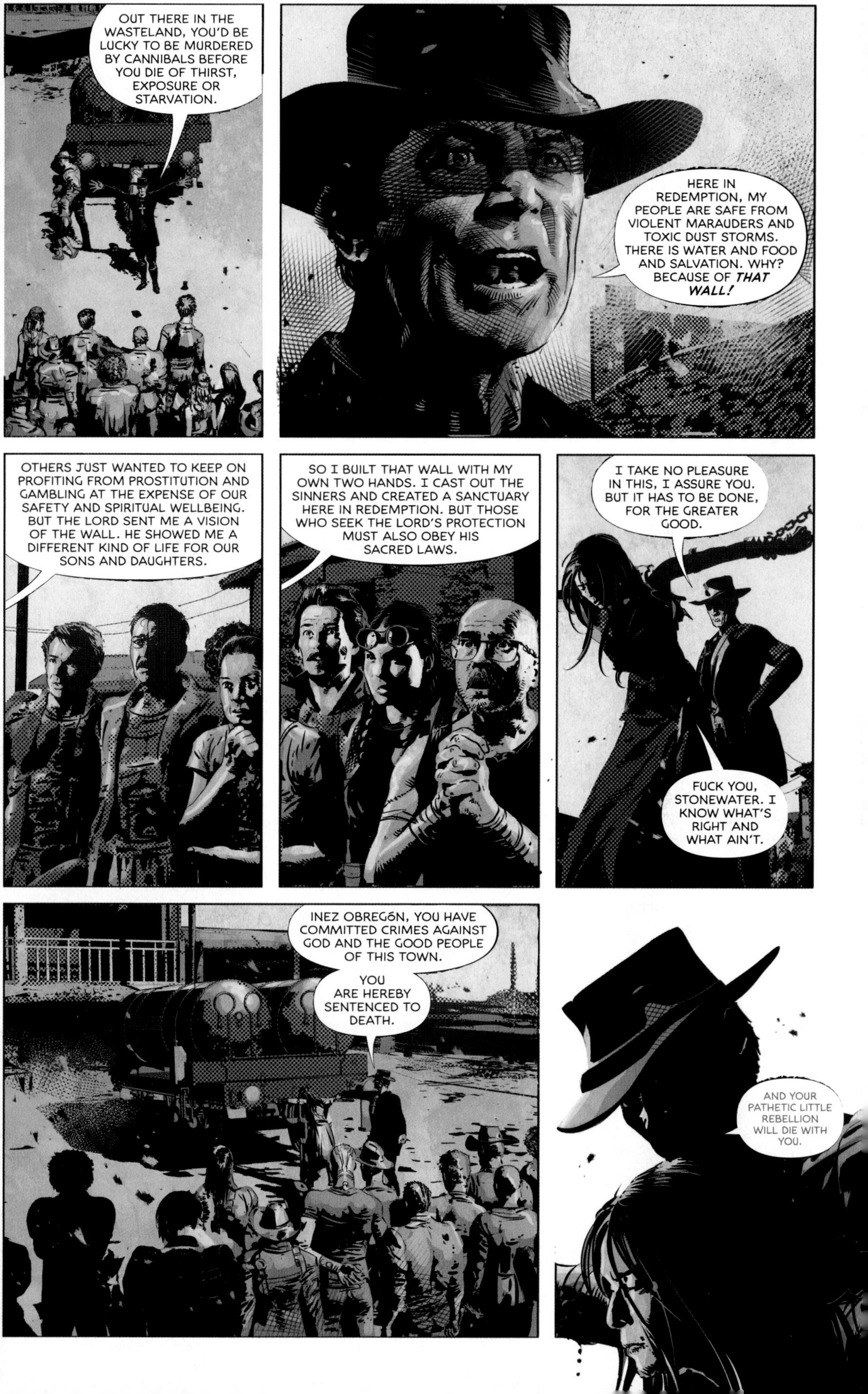
OUT THERE IN THE WASTELAND, YOU'D BE LUCKY TO BE MURDERED BY CANNIBALS BEFORE YOU DIE OF THIRST, EXPOSURE OR STARVATION.
HERE IN REDEMPTION, MY PEOPLE ARE SAFE FROM VIOLENT MARAUDERS AND TOXIC DUST STORMS. THERE IS WATER AND FOOD AND SALVATION. WHY? BECAUSE OF *THAT WALL!*
OTHERS JUST WANTED TO KEEP ON PROFITING FROM PROSTITUTION AND GAMBLING AT THE EXPENSE OF OUR SAFETY AND SPIRITUAL WELLBEING. BUT THE LORD SENT ME A VISION OF THE WALL. HE SHOWED ME A DIFFERENT KIND OF LIFE FOR OUR SONS AND DAUGHTERS.
SO I BUILT THAT WALL WITH MY OWN TWO HANDS. I CAST OUT THE SINNERS AND CREATED A SANCTUARY HERE IN REDEMPTION. BUT THOSE WHO SEEK THE LORD'S PROTECTION MUST ALSO OBEY HIS SACRED LAWS.
I TAKE NO PLEASURE IN THIS, I ASSURE YOU. BUT IT HAS TO BE DONE, FOR THE GREATER GOOD.
FUCK YOU, STONEWATER. I KNOW WHAT'S RIGHT AND WHAT AIN'T.
INEZ OBREGÓN, YOU HAVE COMMITTED CRIMES AGAINST GOD AND THE GOOD PEOPLE OF THIS TOWN.
YOU ARE HEREBY SENTENCED TO DEATH.
AND YOUR PATHETIC LITTLE REBELLION WILL DIE WITH YOU.

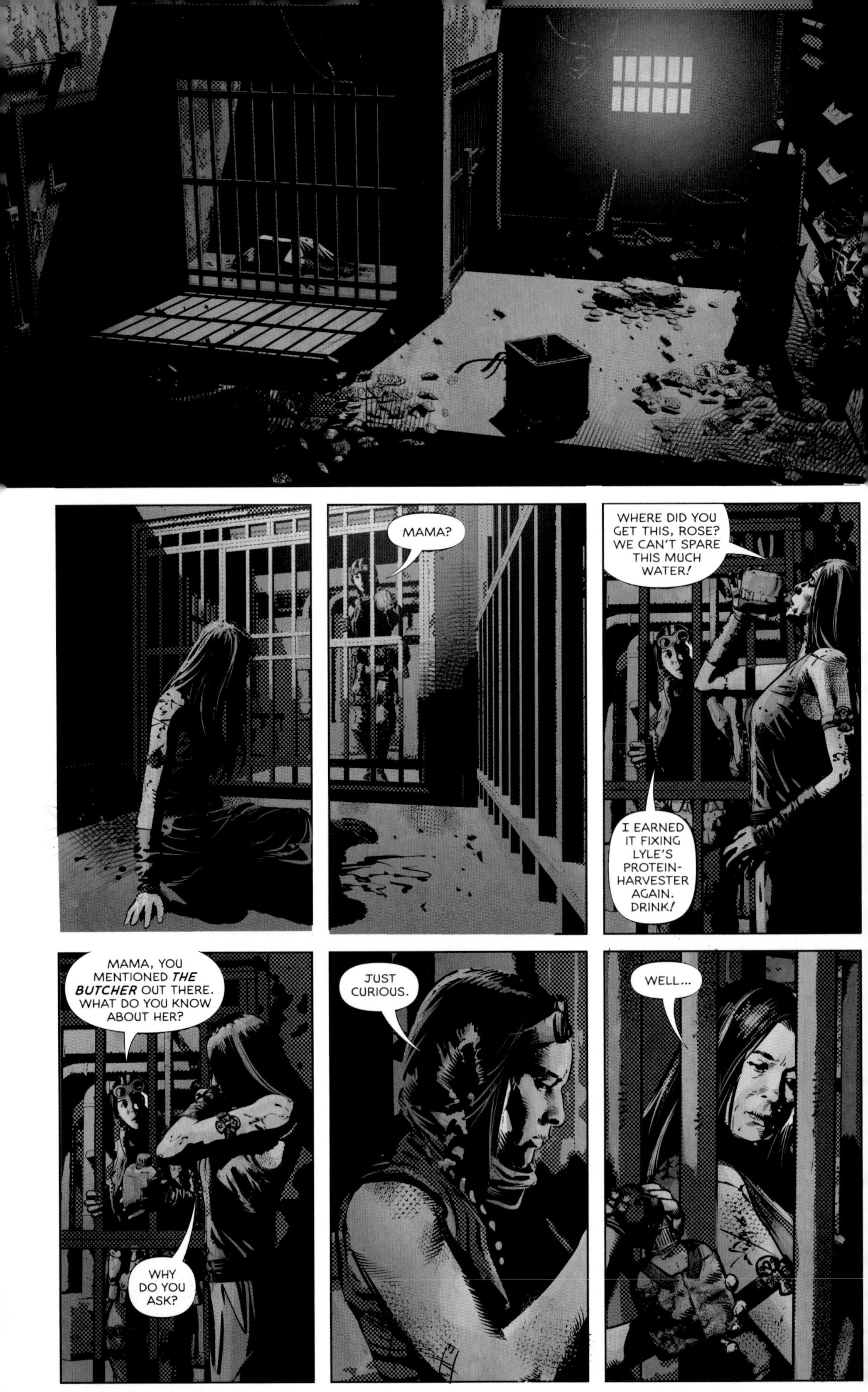
MAMA?
WHERE DID YOU GET THIS, ROSE? WE CAN'T SPARE THIS MUCH WATER!
I EARNED IT FIXING LYLE'S PROTEIN-HARVESTER AGAIN. DRINK!
MAMA, YOU MENTIONED THE BUTCHER OUT THERE. WHAT DO YOU KNOW ABOUT HER?
WHY DO YOU ASK?
JUST CURIOUS.
WELL...

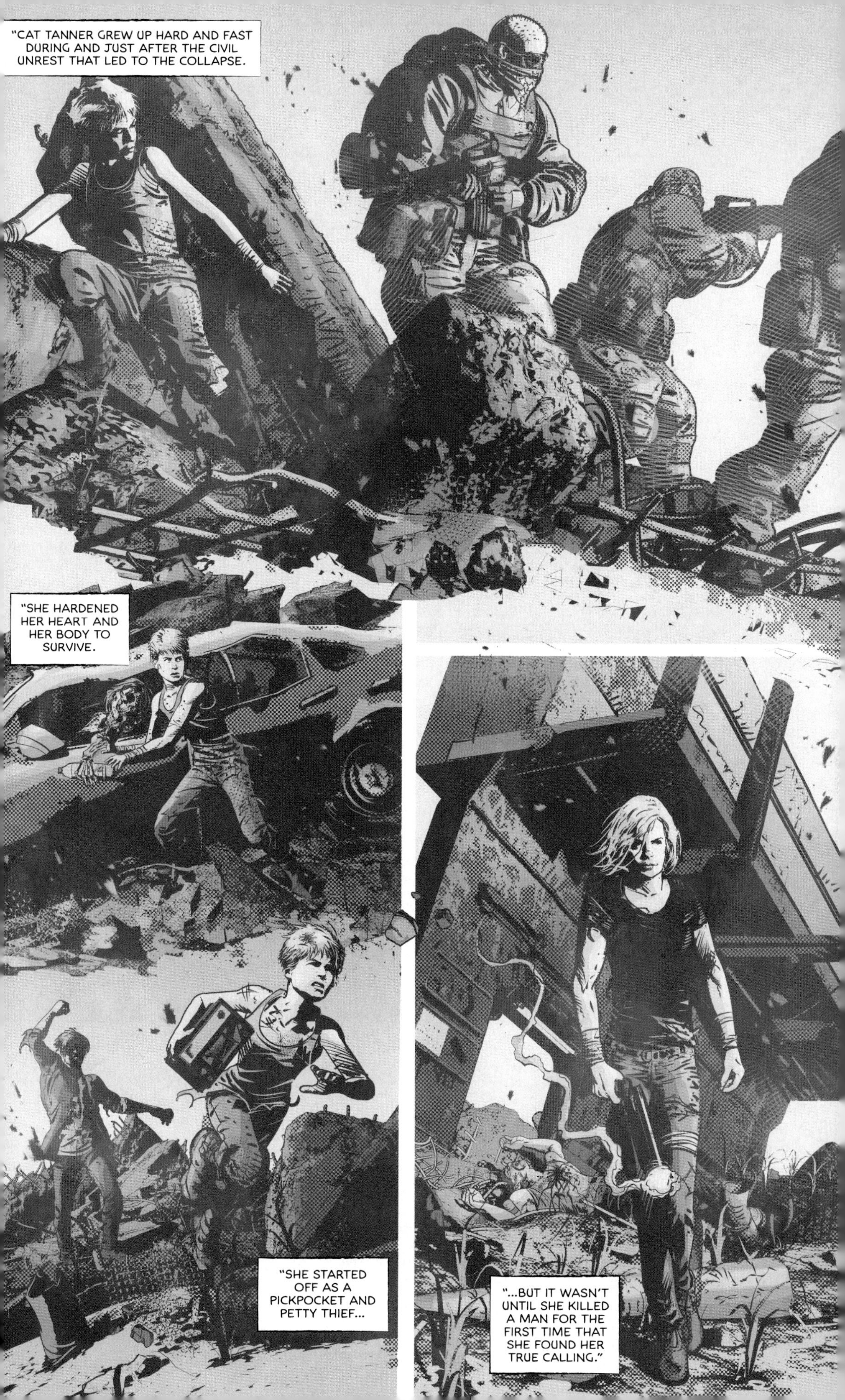
"CAT TANNER GREW UP HARD AND FAST DURING AND JUST AFTER THE CIVIL UNREST THAT LED TO THE COLLAPSE.
"SHE HARDENED HER HEART AND HER BODY TO SURVIVE.
"SHE STARTED OFF AS A PICKPOCKET AND PETTY THIEF...
"...BUT IT WASN'T UNTIL SHE KILLED A MAN FOR THE FIRST TIME THAT SHE FOUND HER TRUE CALLING."

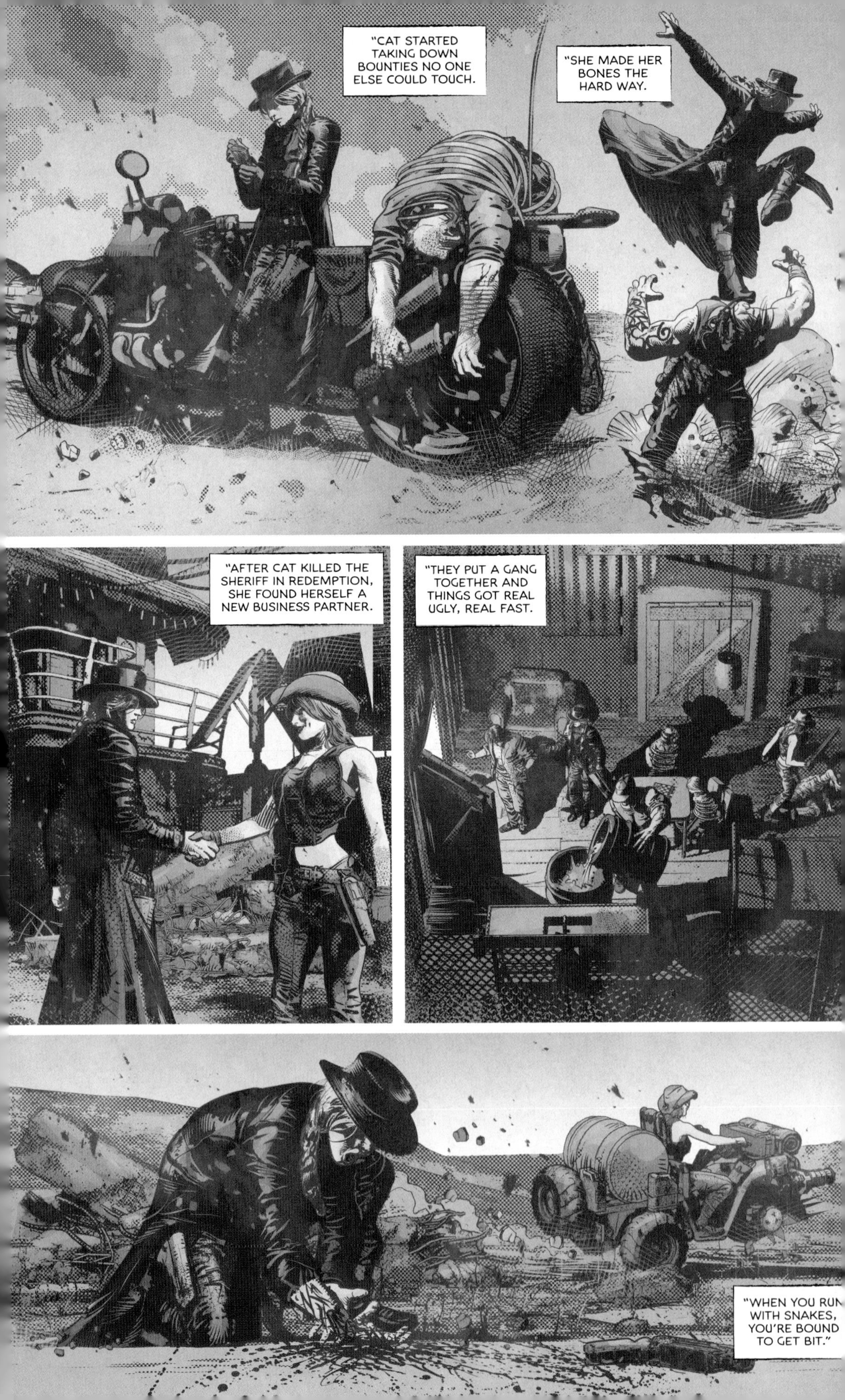
"CAT STARTED TAKING DOWN BOUNTIES NO ONE ELSE COULD TOUCH.
"SHE MADE HER BONES THE HARD WAY.
"AFTER CAT KILLED THE SHERIFF IN REDEMPTION, SHE FOUND HERSELF A NEW BUSINESS PARTNER.
"THEY PUT A GANG TOGETHER AND THINGS GOT REAL UGLY, REAL FAST.
"WHEN YOU RUN WITH SNAKES, YOU'RE BOUND TO GET BIT."

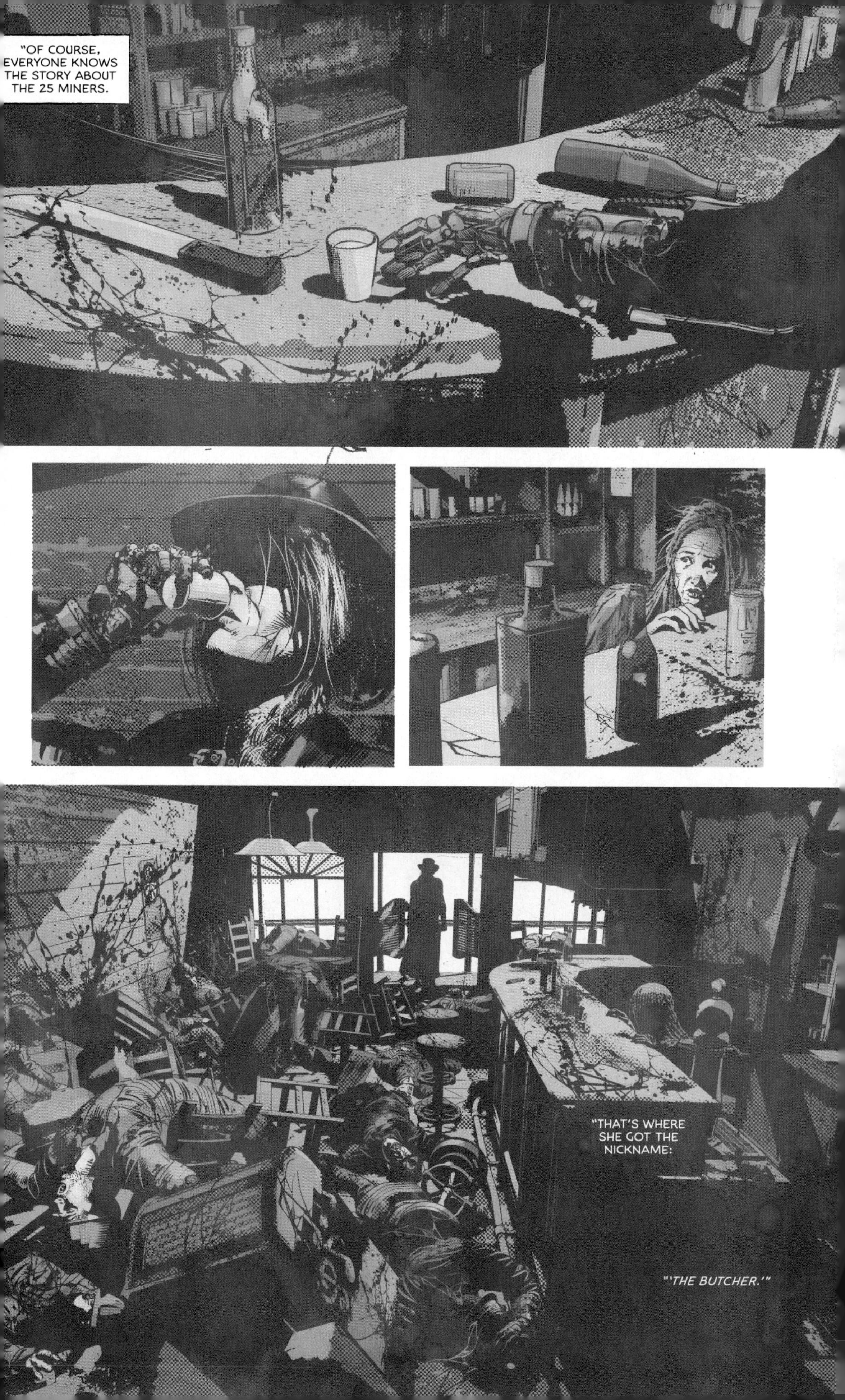
"OF COURSE, EVERYONE KNOWS THE STORY ABOUT THE 25 MINERS.
"THAT'S WHERE SHE GOT THE NICKNAME:
"'THE BUTCHER.'"

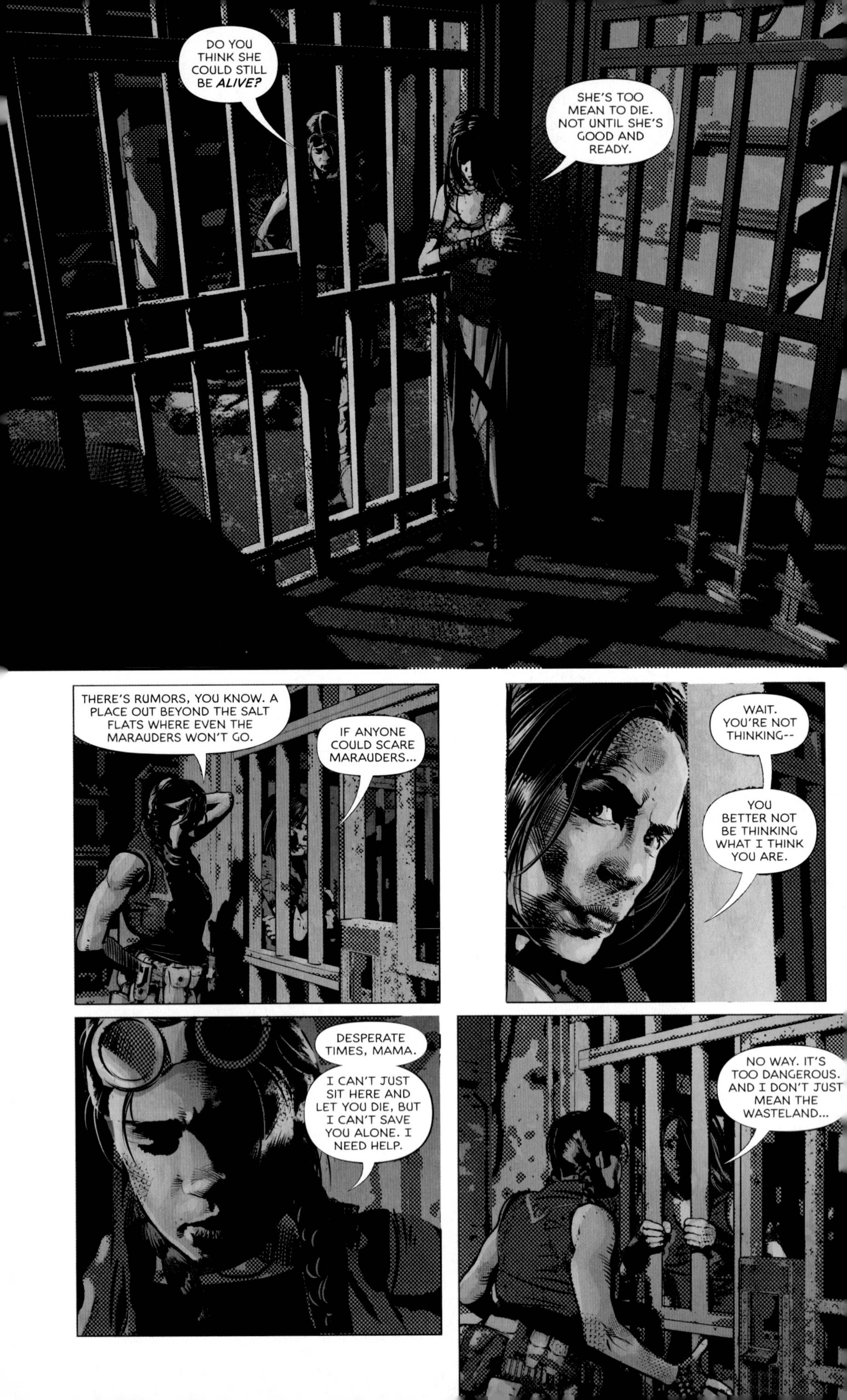
DO YOU THINK SHE COULD STILL BE *ALIVE?*
SHE'S TOO MEAN TO DIE. NOT UNTIL SHE'S GOOD AND READY.
THERE'S RUMORS, YOU KNOW. A PLACE OUT BEYOND THE SALT FLATS WHERE EVEN THE MARAUDERS WON'T GO.
IF ANYONE COULD SCARE MARAUDERS...
WAIT. YOU'RE NOT THINKING--
YOU BETTER NOT BE THINKING WHAT I THINK YOU ARE.
DESPERATE TIMES, MAMA.
I CAN'T JUST SIT HERE AND LET YOU DIE, BUT I CAN'T SAVE YOU ALONE. I NEED HELP.
NO WAY. IT'S TOO DANGEROUS. AND I DON'T JUST MEAN THE WASTELAND...

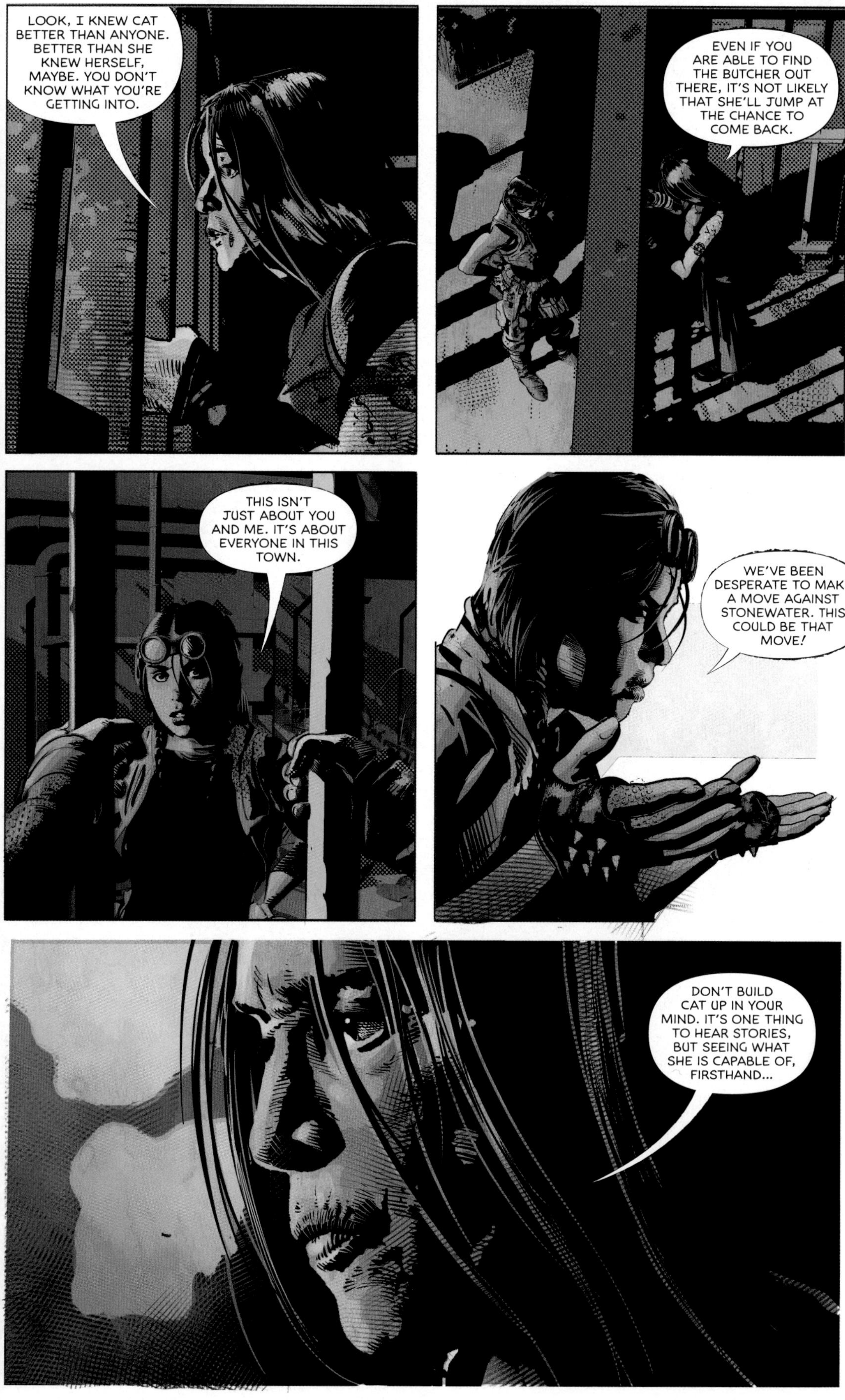

LOOK, I KNEW CAT BETTER THAN ANYONE. BETTER THAN SHE KNEW HERSELF, MAYBE. YOU DON'T KNOW WHAT YOU'RE GETTING INTO.
EVEN IF YOU ARE ABLE TO FIND THE BUTCHER OUT THERE, IT'S NOT LIKELY THAT SHE'LL JUMP AT THE CHANCE TO COME BACK.
THIS ISN'T JUST ABOUT YOU AND ME. IT'S ABOUT EVERYONE IN THIS TOWN.
WE'VE BEEN DESPERATE TO MAKE A MOVE AGAINST STONEWATER. THIS COULD BE THAT MOVE!
DON'T BUILD CAT UP IN YOUR MIND. IT'S ONE THING TO HEAR STORIES, BUT SEEING WHAT SHE IS CAPABLE OF, FIRSTHAND...

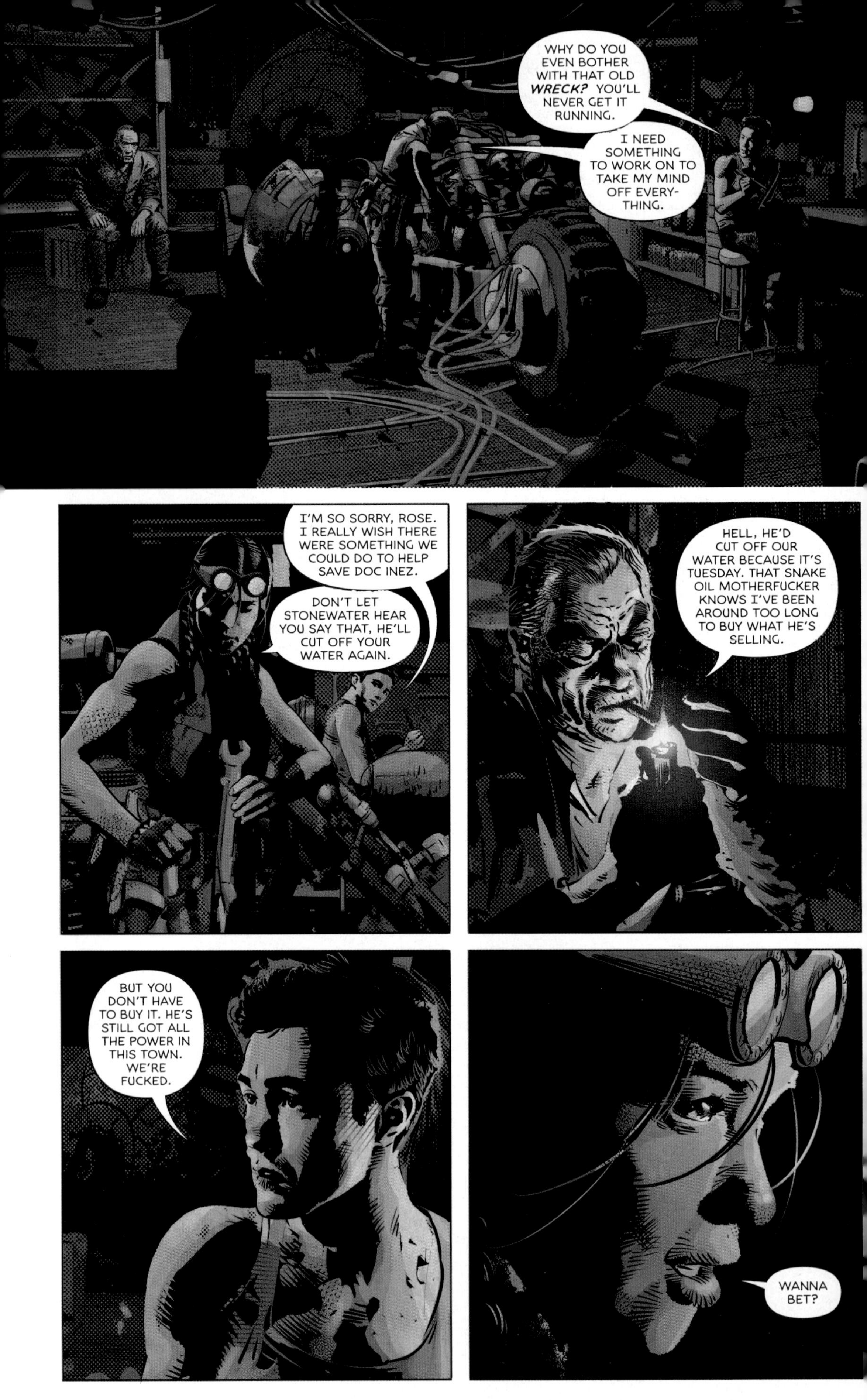
WHY DO YOU EVEN BOTHER WITH THAT OLD WRECK? YOU'LL NEVER GET IT RUNNING.
I NEED SOMETHING TO WORK ON TO TAKE MY MIND OFF EVERY-THING.
I'M SO SORRY, ROSE. I REALLY WISH THERE WERE SOMETHING WE COULD DO TO HELP SAVE DOC INEZ.
DON'T LET STONEWATER HEAR YOU SAY THAT, HE'LL CUT OFF YOUR WATER AGAIN.
HELL, HE'D CUT OFF OUR WATER BECAUSE IT'S TUESDAY. THAT SNAKE OIL MOTHERFUCKER KNOWS I'VE BEEN AROUND TOO LONG TO BUY WHAT HE'S SELLING.
BUT YOU DON'T HAVE TO BUY IT. HE'S STILL GOT ALL THE POWER IN THIS TOWN. WE'RE FUCKED.
WANNA BET?

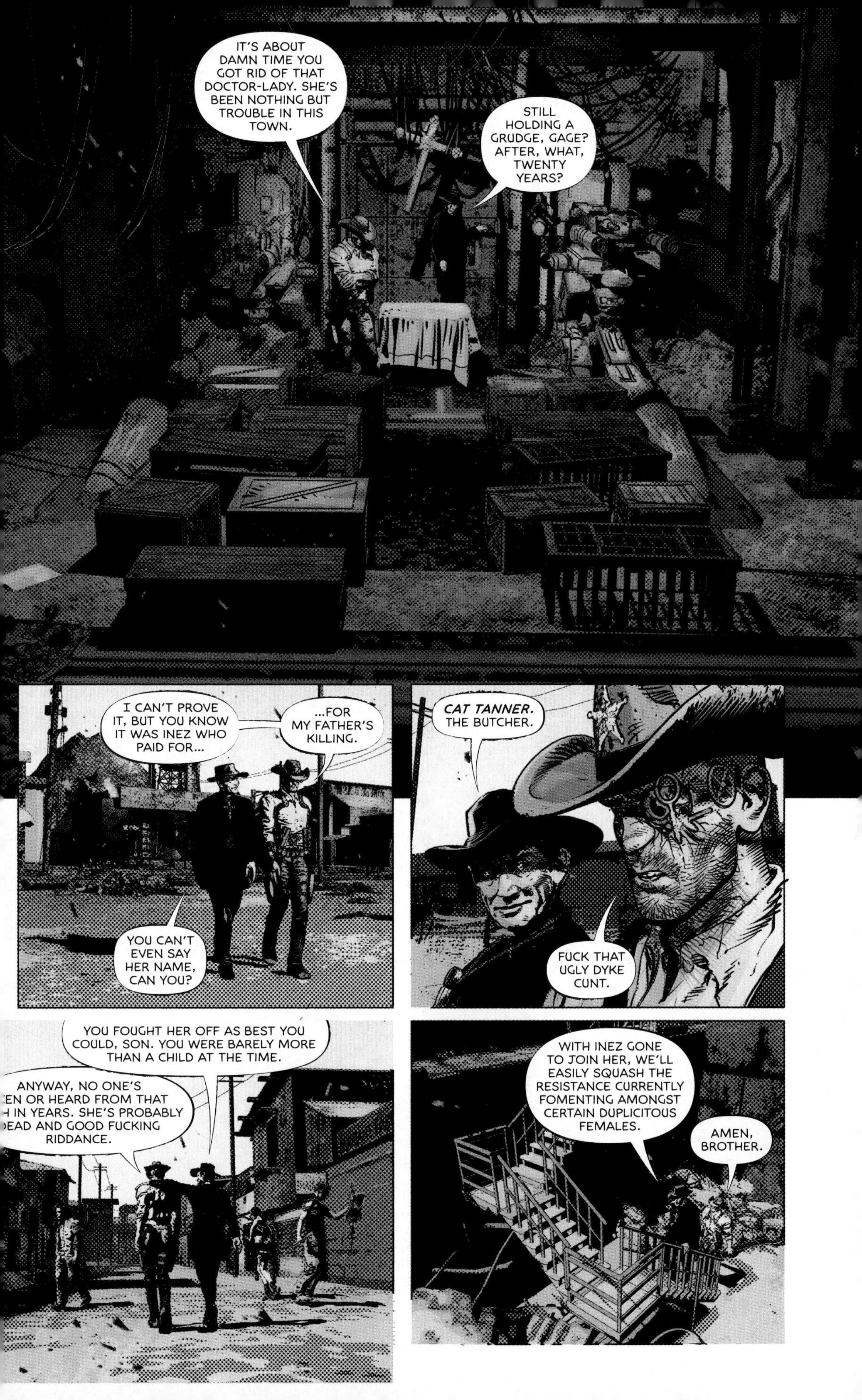
IT'S ABOUT DAMN TIME YOU GOT RID OF THAT DOCTOR-LADY. SHE'S BEEN NOTHING BUT TROUBLE IN THIS TOWN.
STILL HOLDING A GRUDGE, GAGE? AFTER, WHAT, TWENTY YEARS?
I CAN'T PROVE IT, BUT YOU KNOW IT WAS INEZ WHO PAID FOR...
...FOR MY FATHER'S KILLING.
YOU CAN'T EVEN SAY HER NAME, CAN YOU?
CAT TANNER. THE BUTCHER.
FUCK THAT UGLY DYKE CUNT.
YOU FOUGHT HER OFF AS BEST YOU COULD, SON. YOU WERE BARELY MORE THAN A CHILD AT THE TIME.
ANYWAY, NO ONE'S
EN OR HEARD FROM THAT
H IN YEARS. SHE'S PROBABLY
DEAD AND GOOD FUCKING
RIDDANCE.
WITH INEZ GONE TO JOIN HER, WE'LL EASILY SQUASH THE RESISTANCE CURRENTLY FOMENTING AMONGST CERTAIN DUPLICITOUS FEMALES.
AMEN, BROTHER.

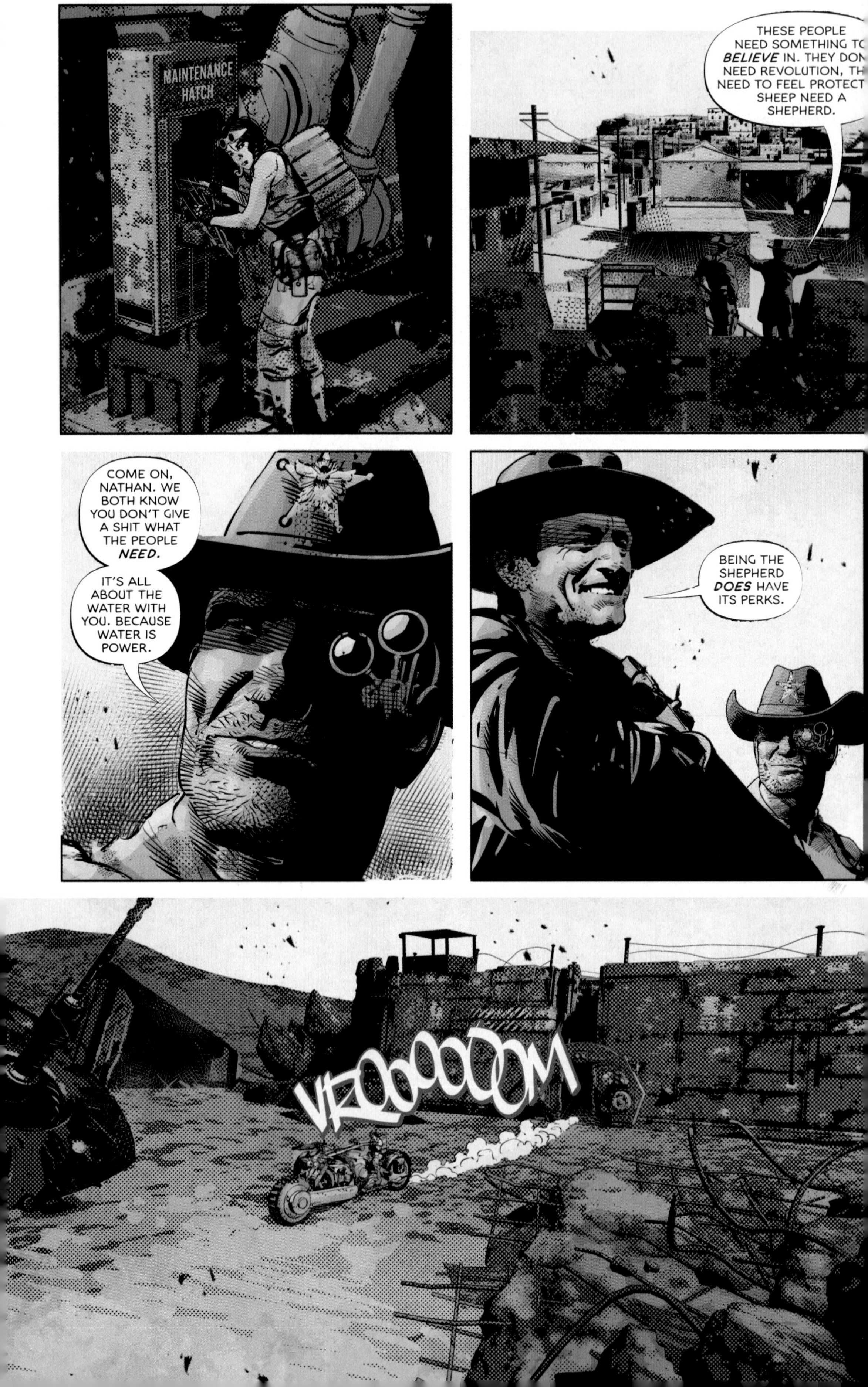
MAINTENANCE HATCH
THESE PEOPLE NEED SOMETHING TC BELIEVE IN. THEY DON NEED REVOLUTION, TH NEED TO FEEL PROTECT SHEEP NEED A SHEPHERD.
COME ON, NATHAN. WE BOTH KNOW YOU DON'T GIVE A SHIT WHAT THE PEOPLE NEED.
IT'S ALL ABOUT THE WATER WITH YOU. BECAUSE WATER IS POWER.
BEING THE SHEPHERD DOES HAVE ITS PERKS.
VROOOOOOOM

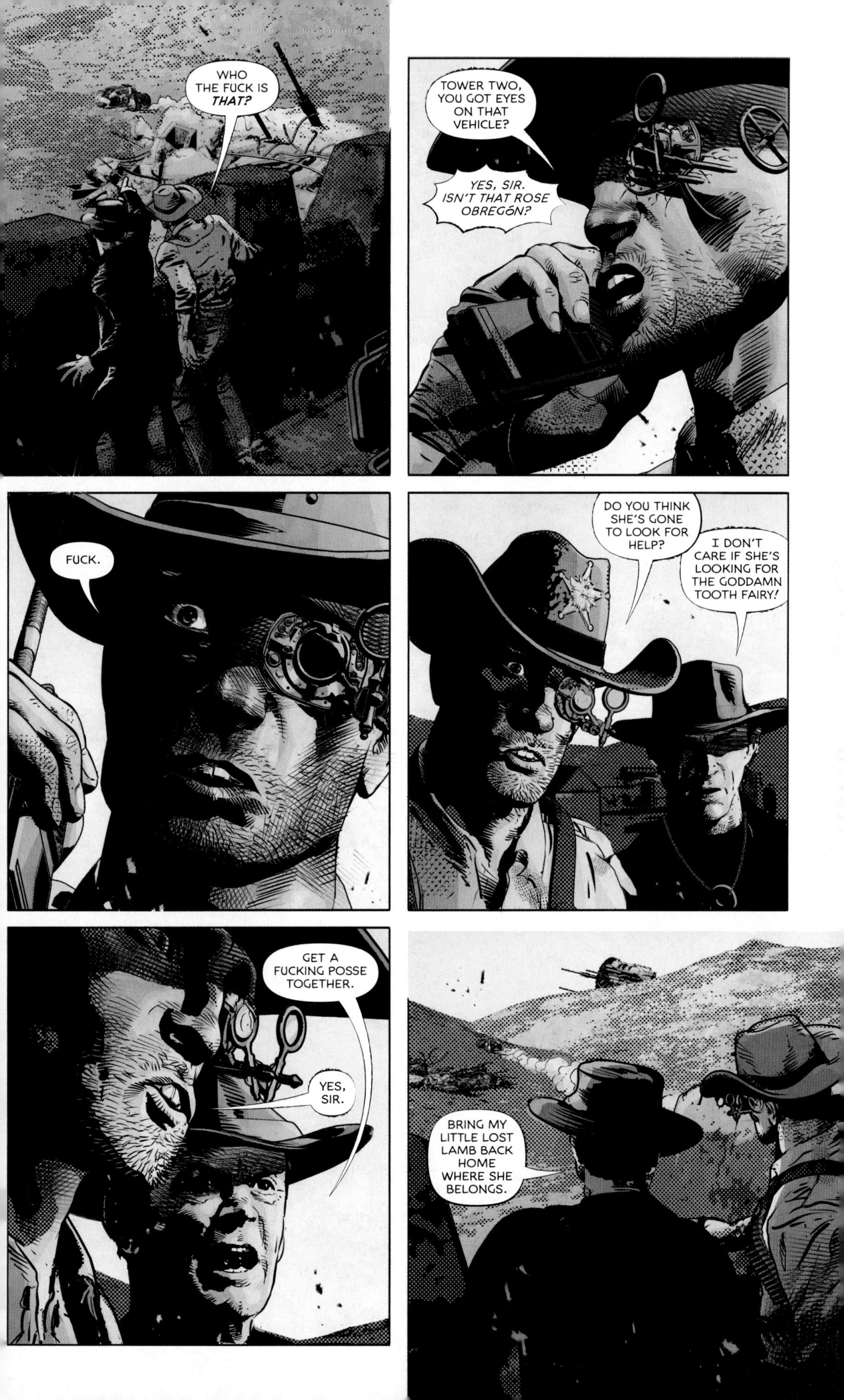
WHO THE FUCK IS *THAT?*
TOWER TWO, YOU GOT EYES ON THAT VEHICLE?
YES, SIR. ISN'T THAT ROSE OBREGÓN?
FUCK.
DO YOU THINK SHE'S GONE TO LOOK FOR HELP?
I DON'T CARE IF SHE'S LOOKING FOR THE GODDAMN TOOTH FAIRY!
GET A FUCKING POSSE TOGETHER.
YES, SIR.
BRING MY LITTLE LOST LAMB BACK HOME WHERE SHE BELONGS.

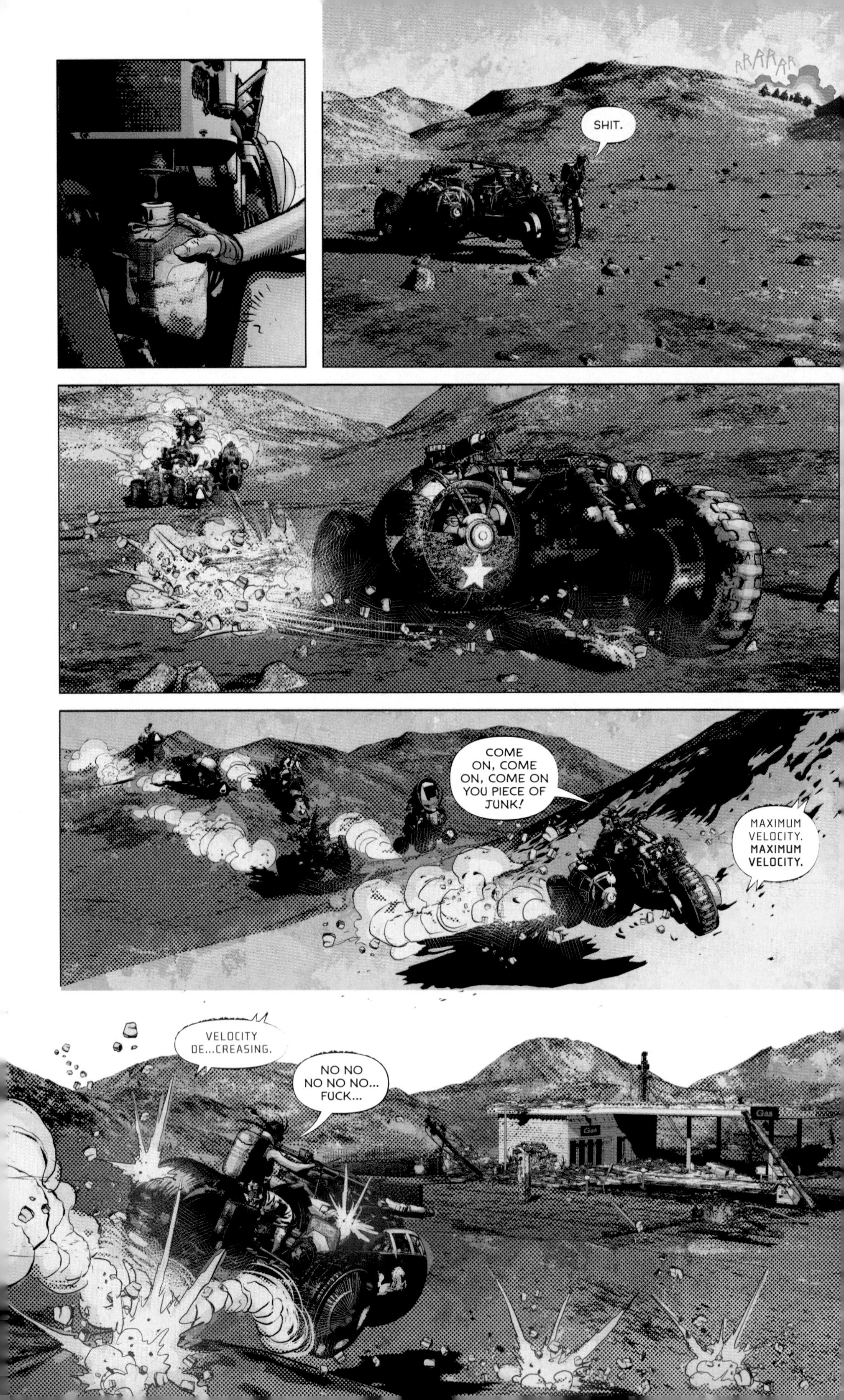

RRRRRR
SHIT.
COME ON, COME ON, COME ON YOU PIECE OF JUNK!
MAXIMUM VELOCITY. MAXIMUM VELOCITY.
VELOCITY DE...CREASING.
NO NO NO NO NO... FUCK...
Gas

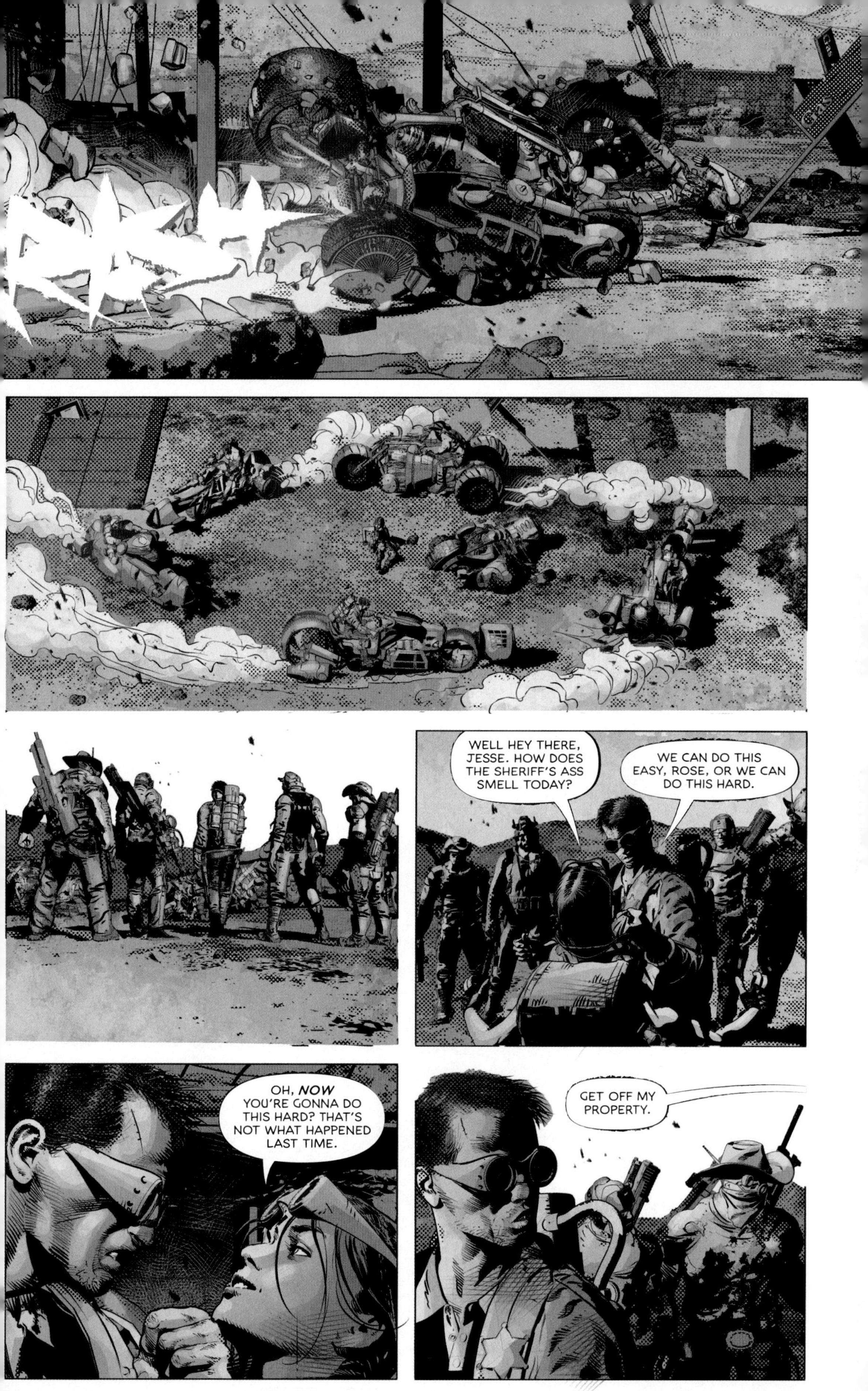

WELL HEY THERE, JESSE. HOW DOES THE SHERIFF'S ASS SMELL TODAY?
WE CAN DO THIS EASY, ROSE, OR WE CAN DO THIS HARD.
OH, NOW YOU'RE GONNA DO THIS HARD? THAT'S NOT WHAT HAPPENED LAST TIME.
GET OFF MY PROPERTY.

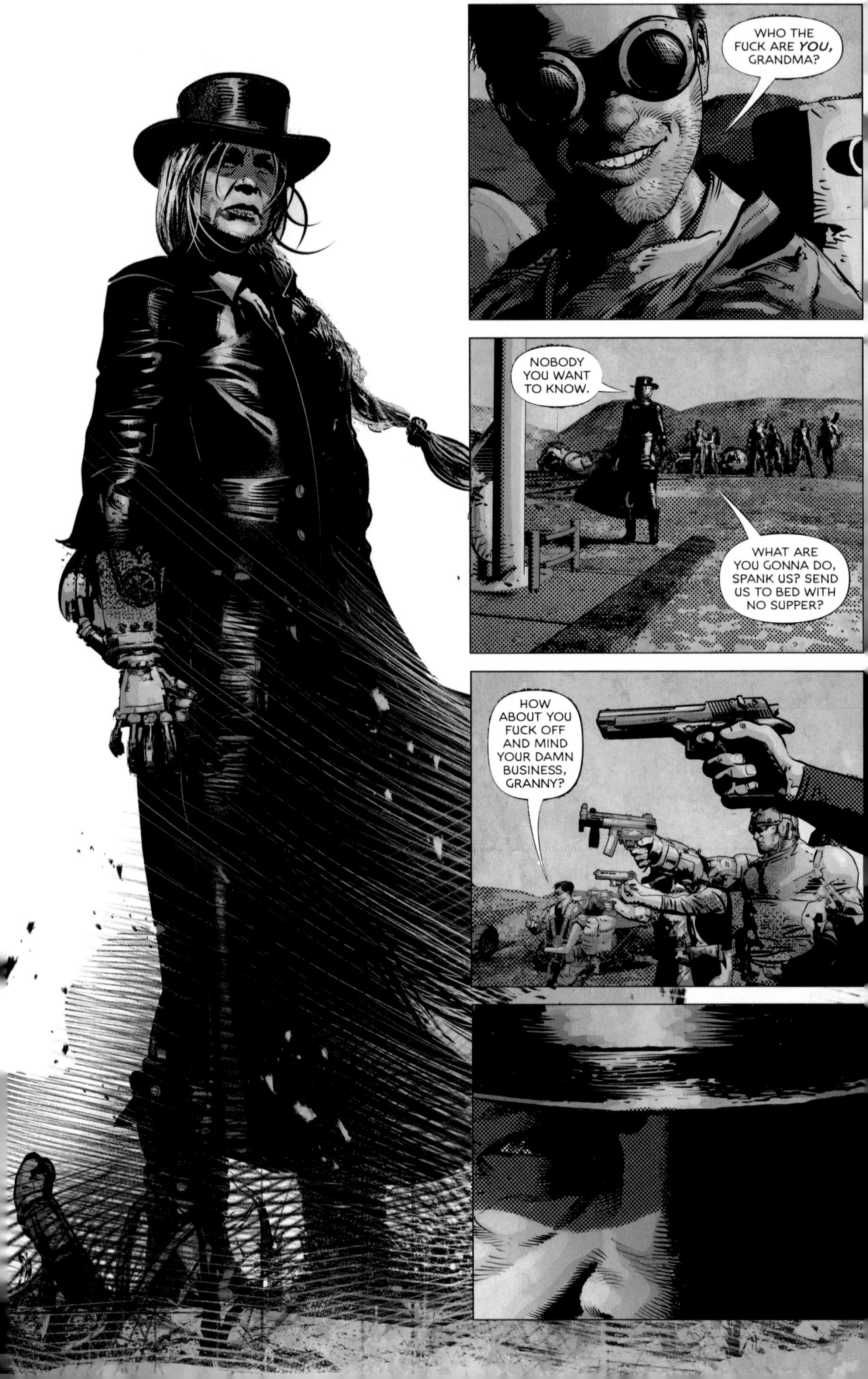
WHO THE FUCK ARE *YOU,* GRANDMA?
NOBODY YOU WANT TO KNOW.
WHAT ARE YOU GONNA DO, SPANK US? SEND US TO BED WITH NO SUPPER?
HOW ABOUT YOU FUCK OFF AND MIND YOUR DAMN BUSINESS, GRANNY?

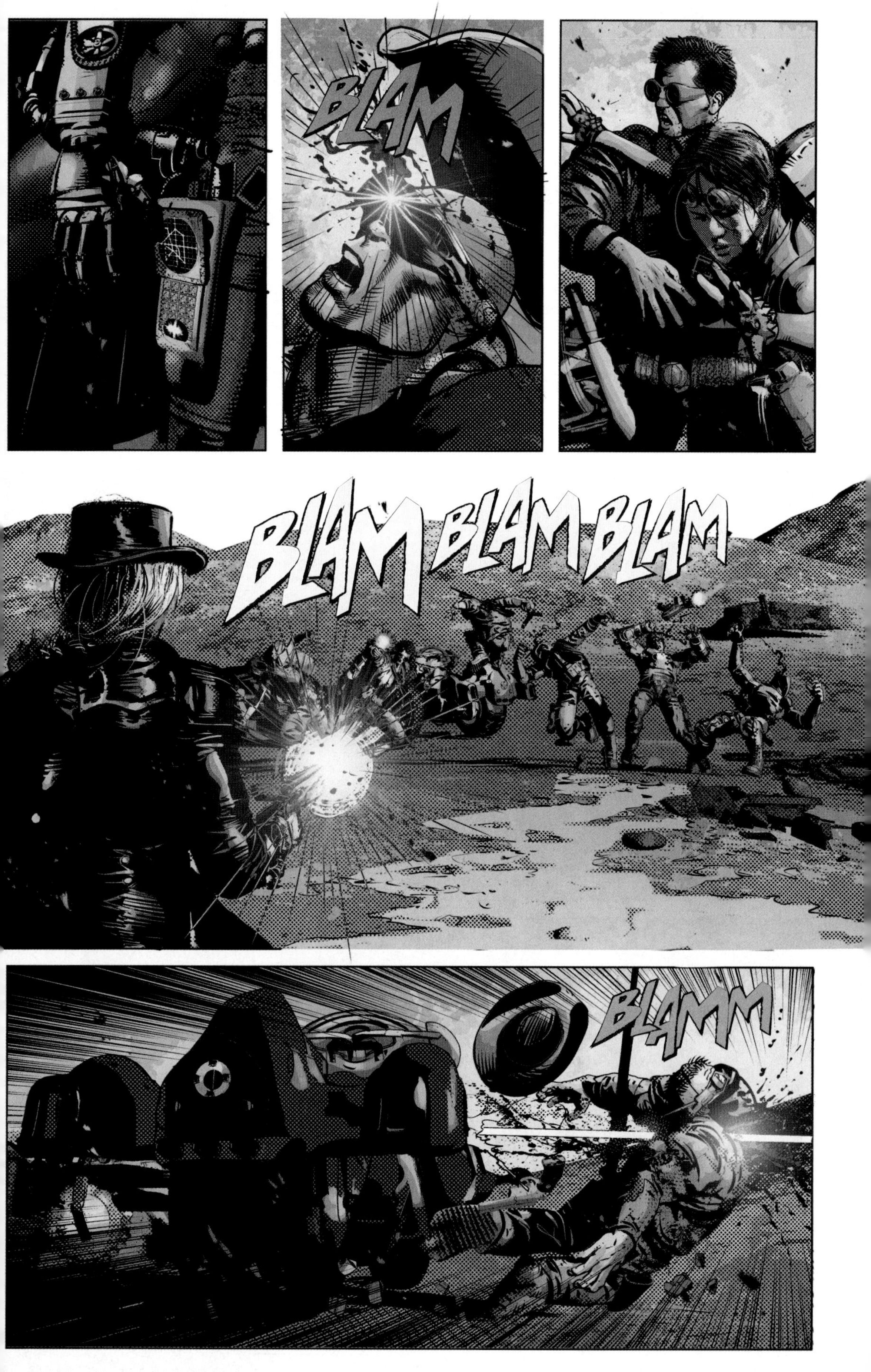
BLAM
BLAM BLAM BLAM
BLAMM

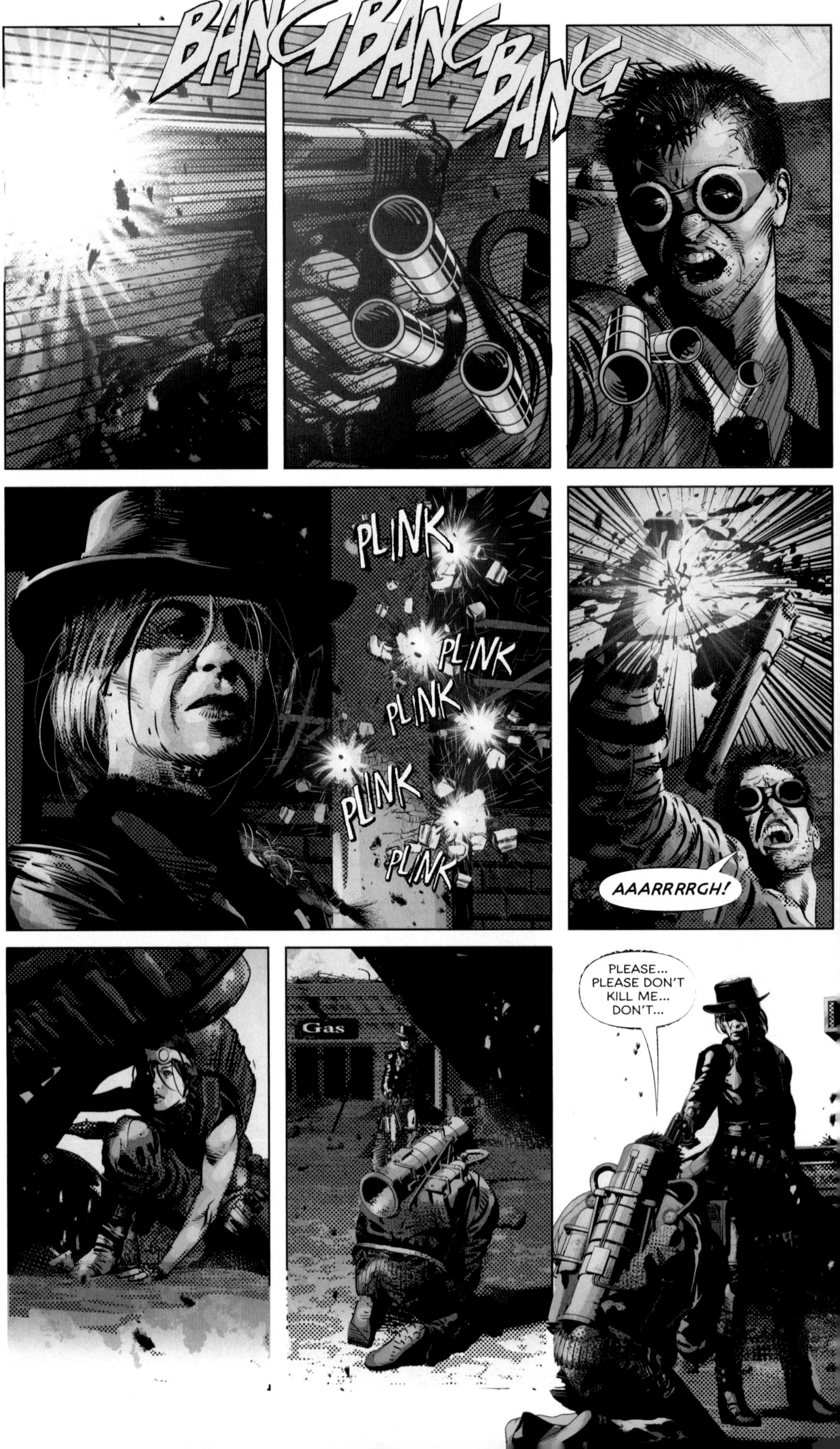
BANG BANG BANG
PLINK
PLINK
PLINK
PLINK
PLINK
AAARRRRGH!
Gas
PLEASE... PLEASE DON'T KILL ME... DON'T...

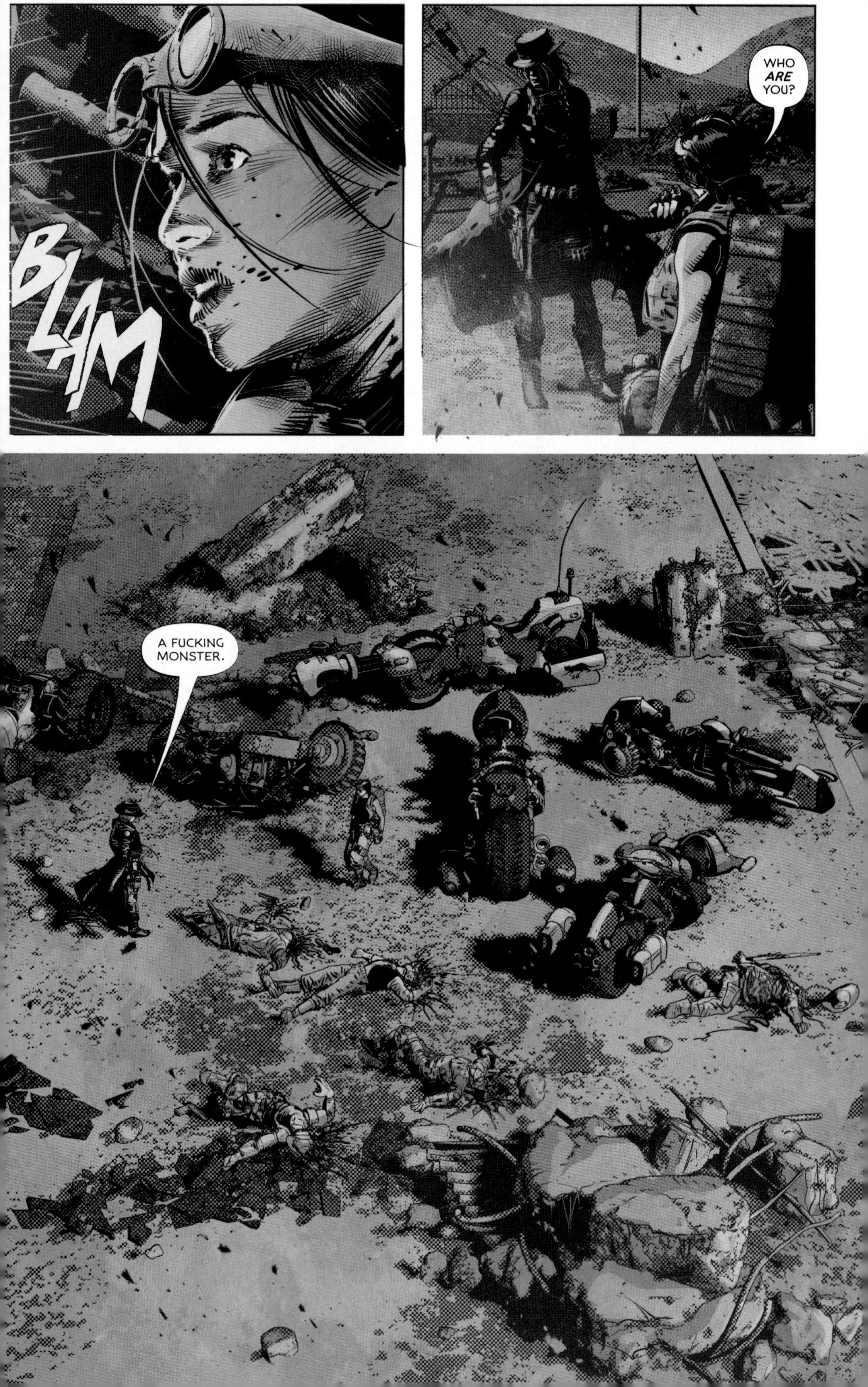
BLAM
WHO ARE YOU?
A FUCKING MONSTER.

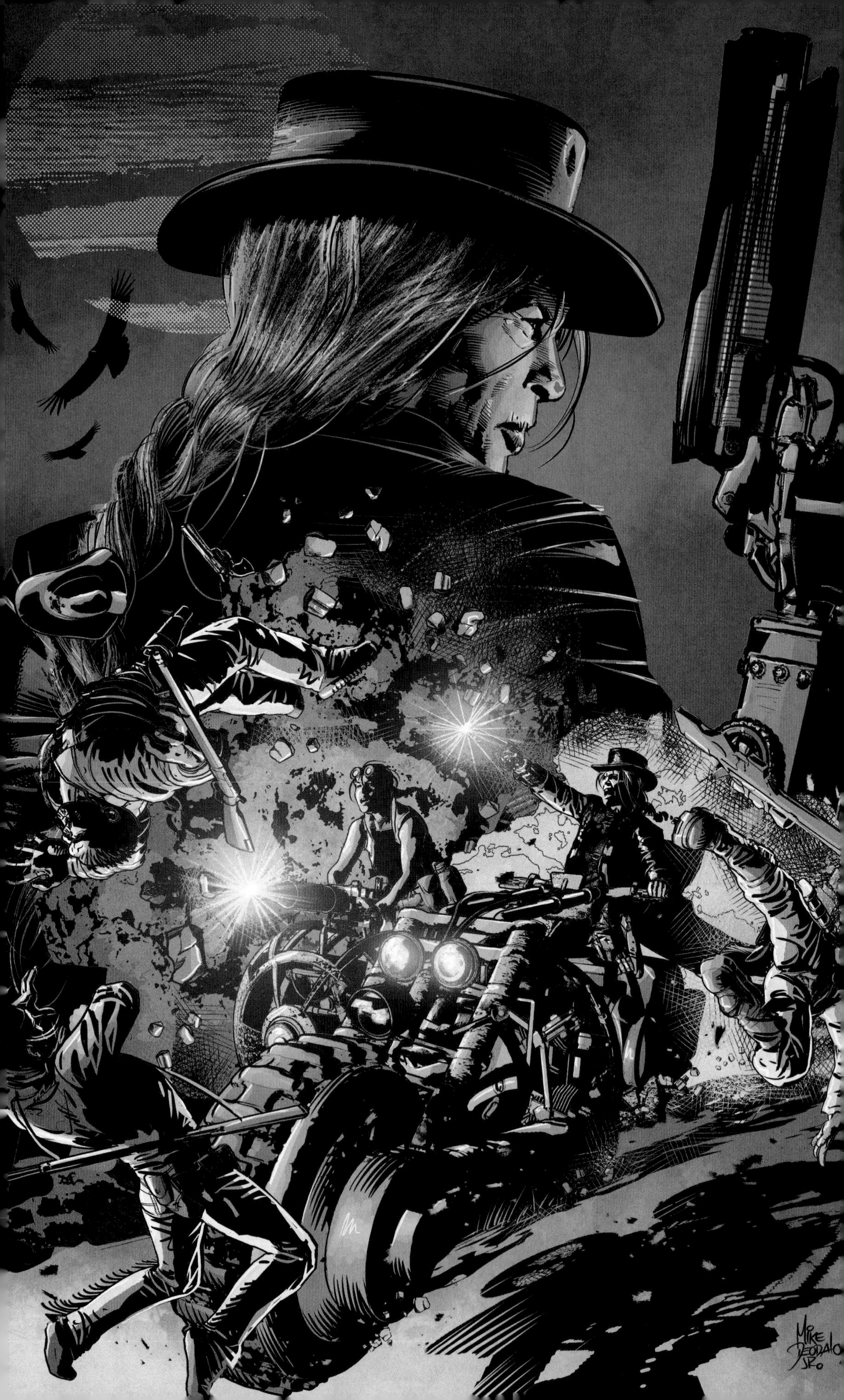
MIKE DEODATO JR.

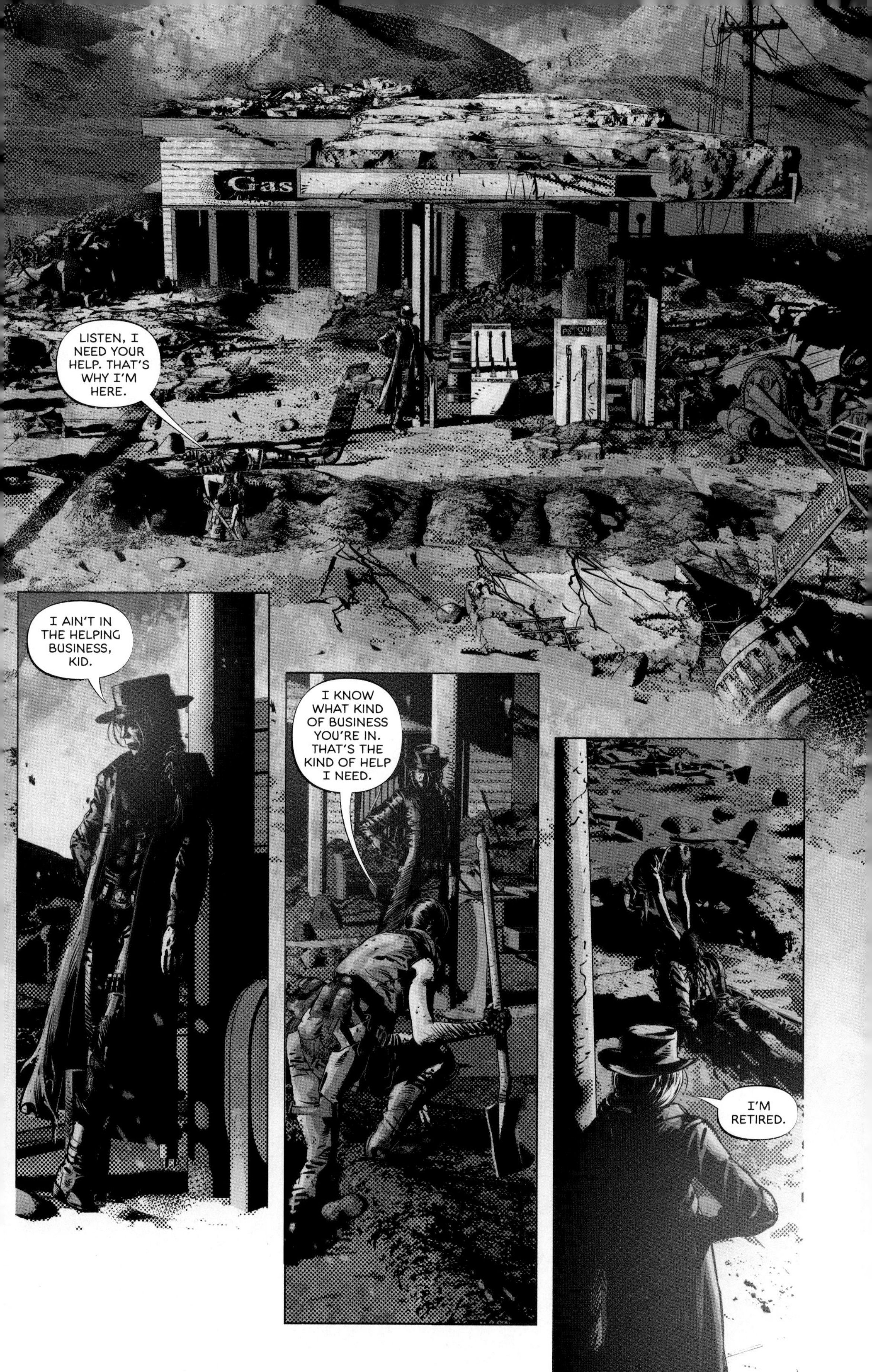
Gas
LISTEN, I NEED YOUR HELP. THAT'S WHY I'M HERE.
I AIN'T IN THE HELPING BUSINESS, KID.
I KNOW WHAT KIND OF BUSINESS YOU'RE IN. THAT'S THE KIND OF HELP I NEED.
I'M RETIRED.

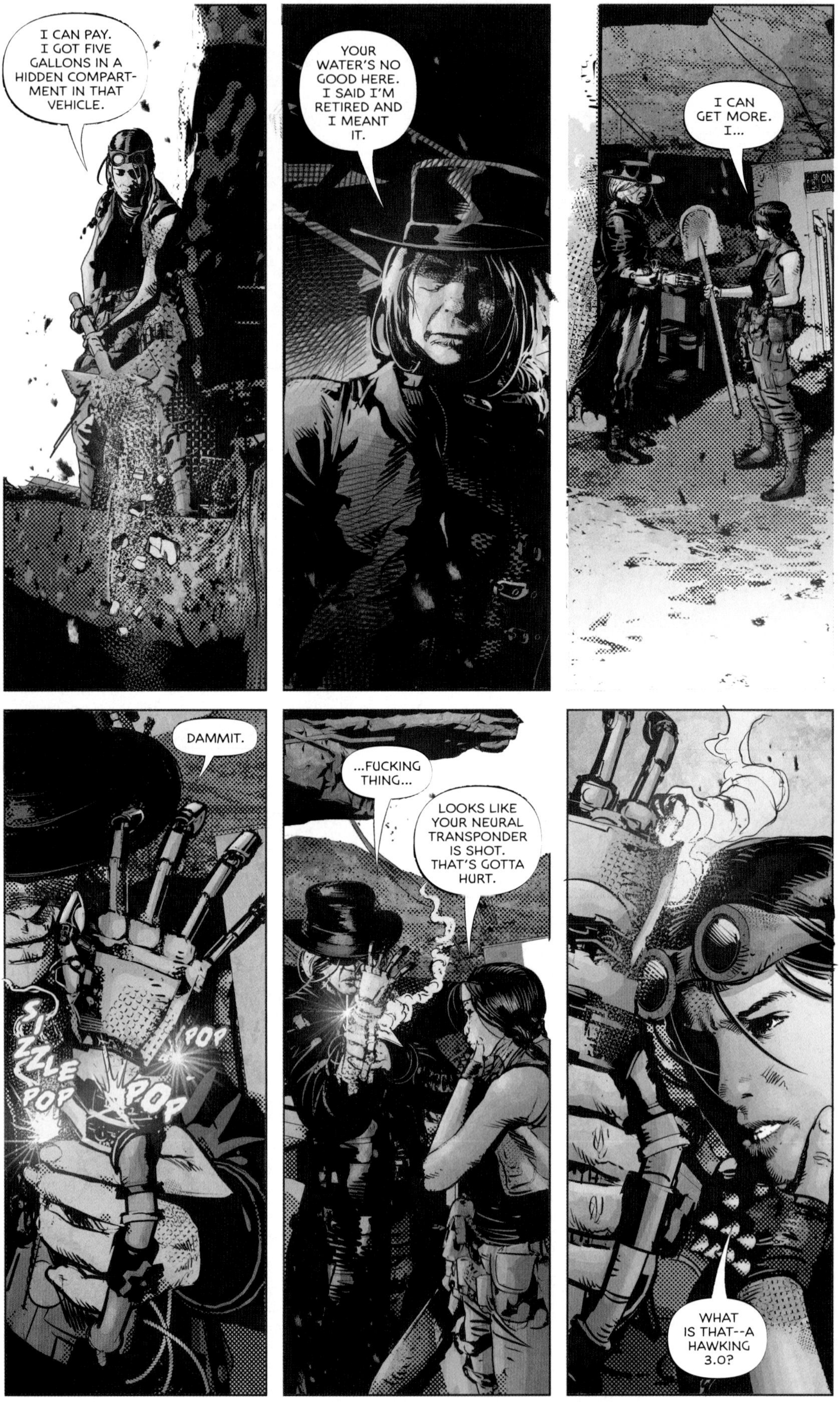
I CAN PAY. I GOT FIVE GALLONS IN A HIDDEN COMPART-MENT IN THAT VEHICLE.
YOUR WATER'S NO GOOD HERE. I SAID I'M RETIRED AND I MEANT IT.
I CAN GET MORE. I...
ON
DAMMIT.
SIZZLE
POP
POP
POP
...FUCKING THING...
LOOKS LIKE YOUR NEURAL TRANSPONDER IS SHOT. THAT'S GOTTA HURT.
WHAT IS THAT--A HAWKING 3.0?

LOOK, IT'S GETTING DARK. YOU'D BEST BE ON YOUR WAY BEFORE THE CANNIBALS GET A WHIFF OF ALL THIS BLOOD.

I CAN FIX THAT HAND FOR YOU, NO PROBLEM.

NO THANKS. I DON'T LIKE NOBODY MESSING WITH MY SHIT. ESPECIALLY NOT SHIT THAT'S ATTACHED.

I'M NOT JUST SOME SCAVENGER MECHANIC, YOU KNOW. I'VE STUDIED ANATOMY, NEURO-HACKING AND BASIC SURGERY, TOO.

MY MOM'S A DOCTOR. HER NAME'S INEZ.

MAYBE YOU KNOW HER?

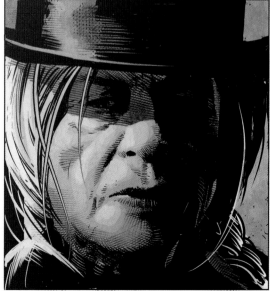

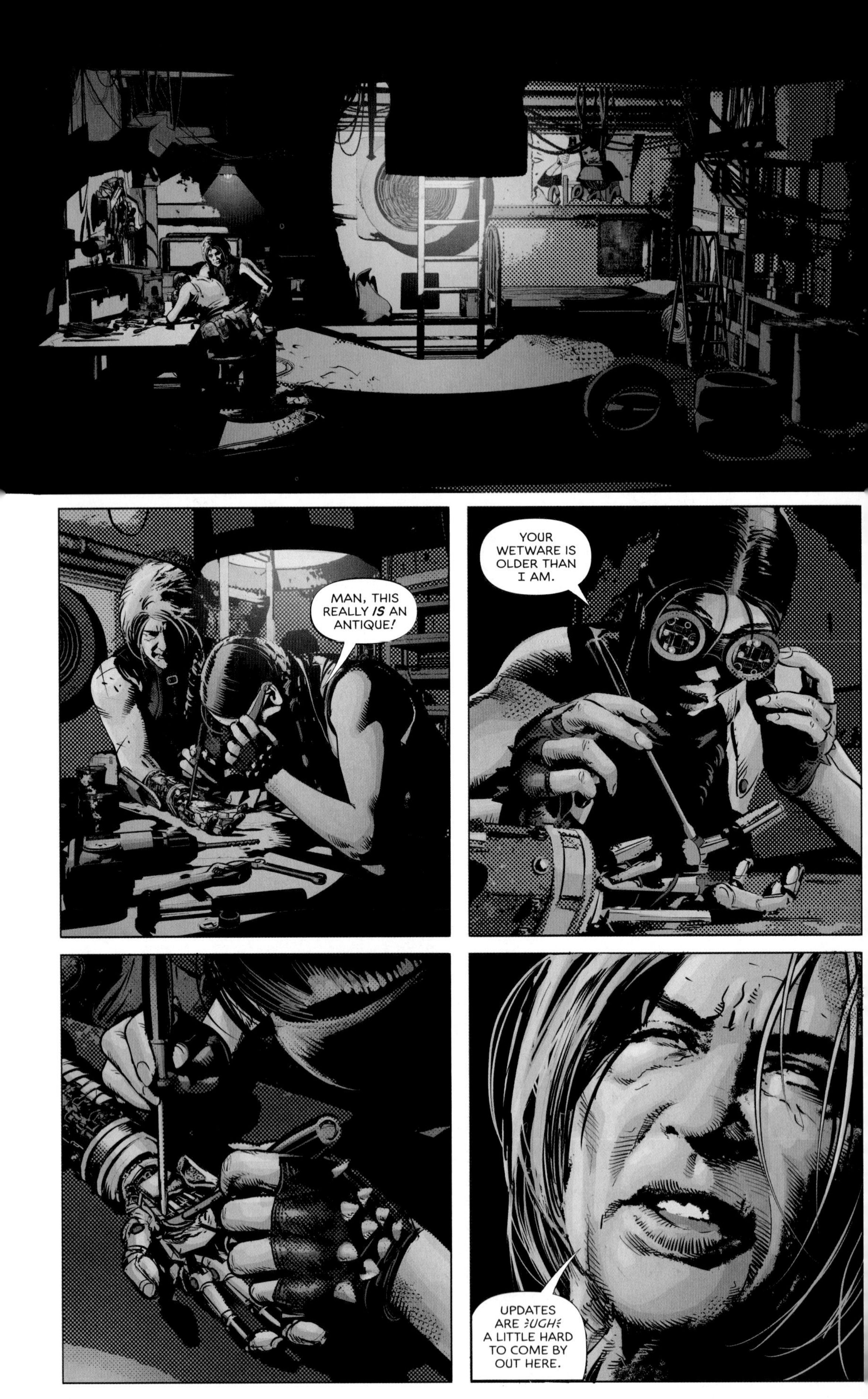
MAN, THIS REALLY *IS* AN ANTIQUE!
YOUR WETWARE IS OLDER THAN I AM.
UPDATES ARE *UGH* A LITTLE HARD TO COME BY OUT HERE.

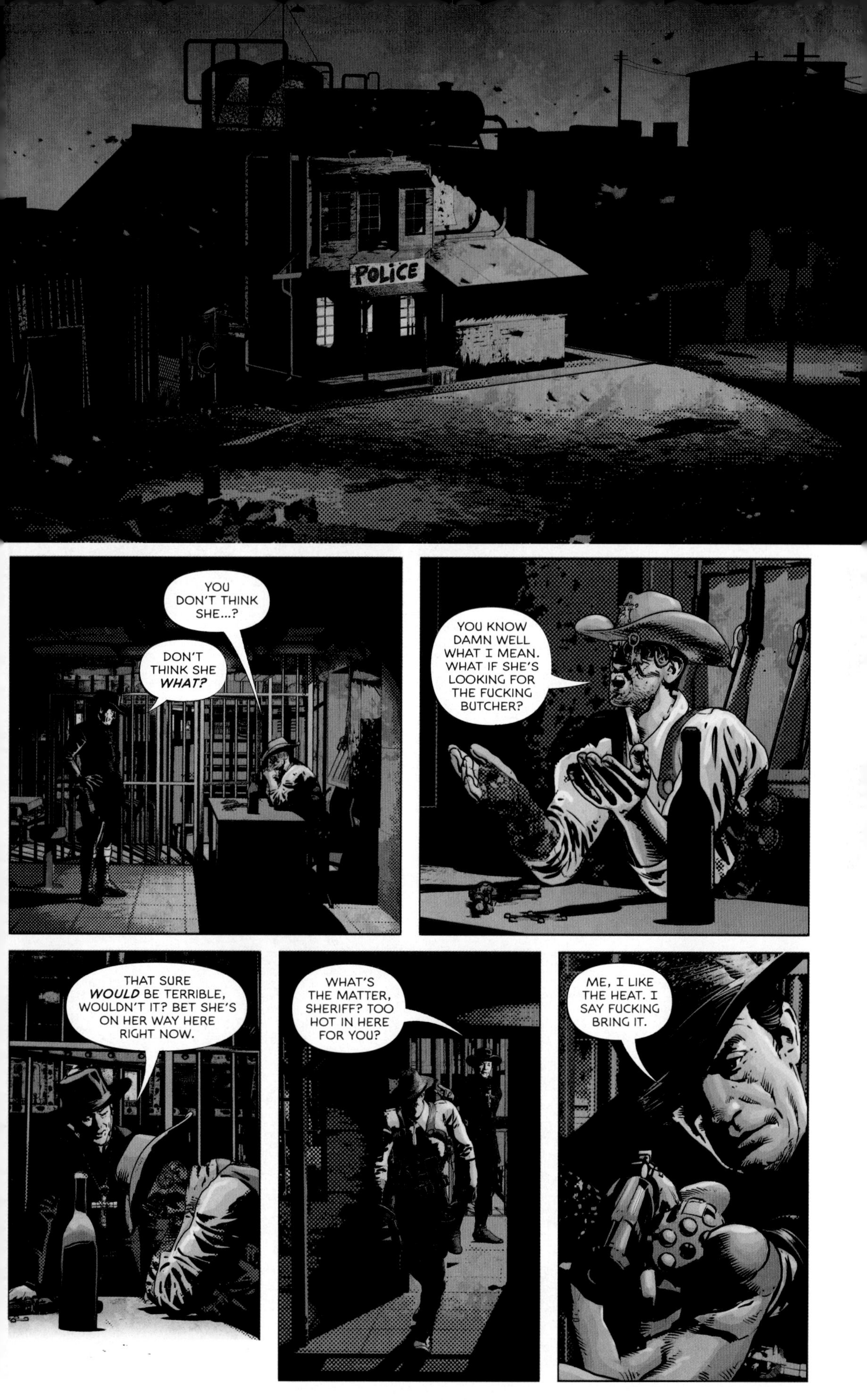
POLICE
YOU DON'T THINK SHE...?
DON'T THINK SHE *WHAT?*
YOU KNOW DAMN WELL WHAT I MEAN. WHAT IF SHE'S LOOKING FOR THE FUCKING BUTCHER?
THAT SURE *WOULD* BE TERRIBLE, WOULDN'T IT? BET SHE'S ON HER WAY HERE RIGHT NOW.
WHAT'S THE MATTER, SHERIFF? TOO HOT IN HERE FOR YOU?
ME, I LIKE THE HEAT. I SAY FUCKING BRING IT.

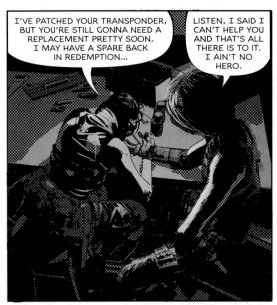

I'VE PATCHED YOUR TRANSPONDER, BUT YOU'RE STILL GONNA NEED A REPLACEMENT PRETTY SOON. I MAY HAVE A SPARE BACK IN REDEMPTION...

LISTEN, I SAID I CAN'T HELP YOU AND THAT'S ALL THERE IS TO IT. I AIN'T NO HERO.

BUT I JUST FIXED YOUR HAND FOR FREE!

AND I JUST SAVED YOUR LIFE, KID. I'D SAY THAT MAKES US EVEN.

OKAY, FINE. IF YOU WON'T TAKE THE JOB, CAN'T YOU RECOMMEND SOMEONE ELSE THAT WILL?

YOU DON'T LET UP, DO YOU?

IS THAT A YES?

FINE. YES.

WHATEVER IT TAKES TO MAKE YOU SOMEBODY ELSE'S PROBLEM.

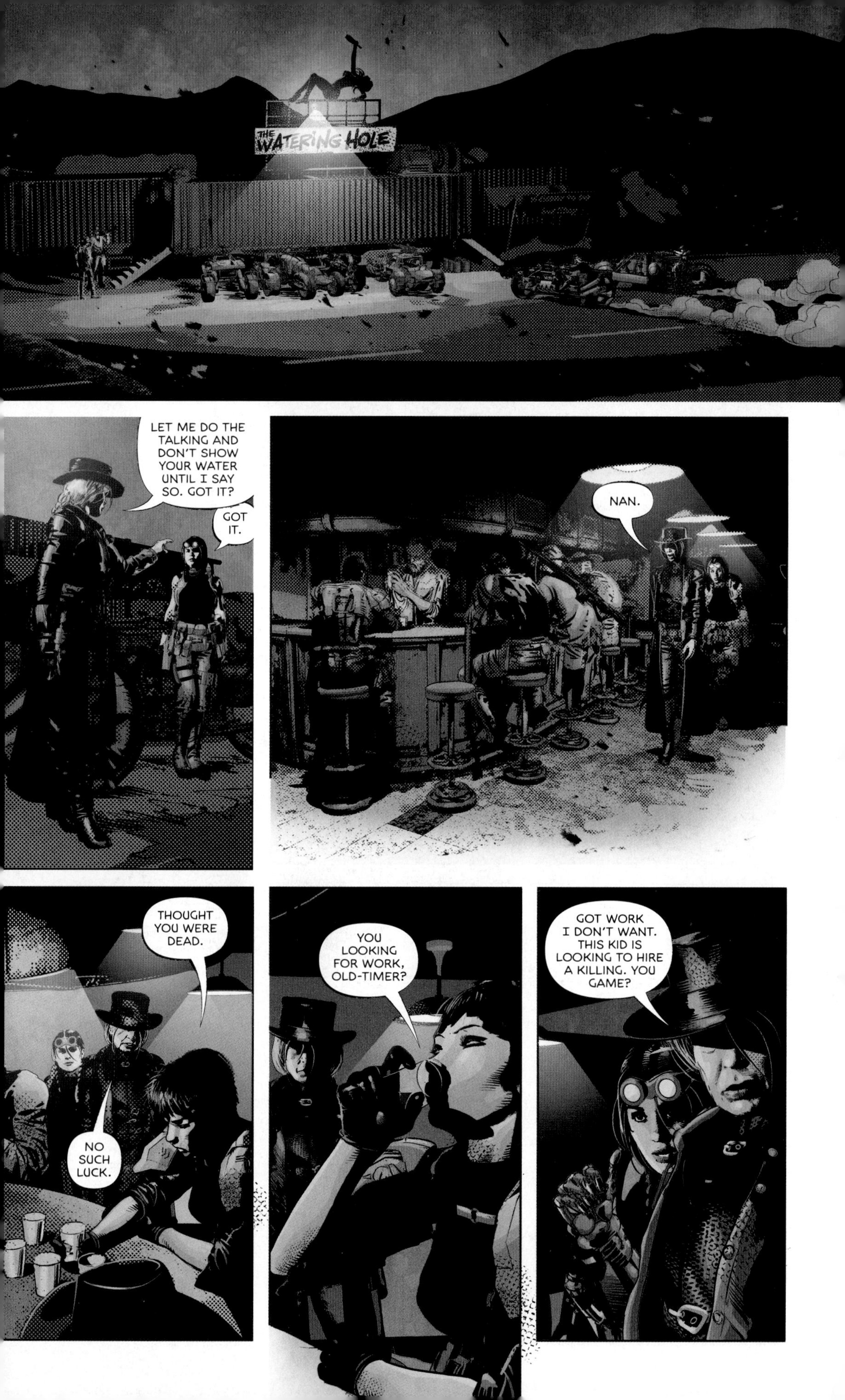
THE WATERING HOLE
LET ME DO THE TALKING AND DON'T SHOW YOUR WATER UNTIL I SAY SO. GOT IT?
GOT IT.
NAN.
THOUGHT YOU WERE DEAD.
NO SUCH LUCK.
YOU LOOKING FOR WORK, OLD-TIMER?
GOT WORK I DON'T WANT. THIS KID IS LOOKING TO HIRE A KILLING. YOU GAME?

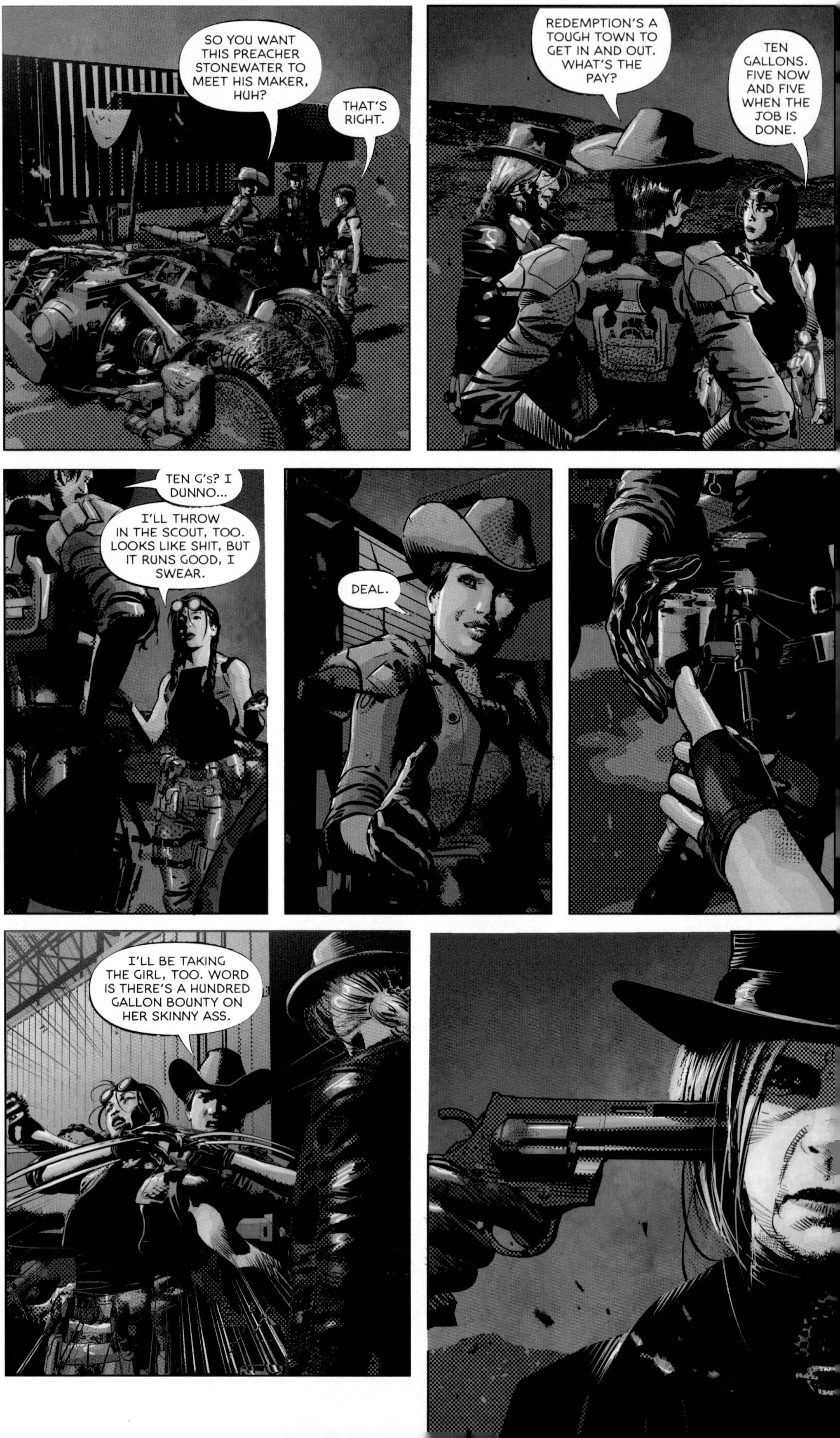
SO YOU WANT THIS PREACHER STONEWATER TO MEET HIS MAKER, HUH?
THAT'S RIGHT.
REDEMPTION'S A TOUGH TOWN TO GET IN AND OUT. WHAT'S THE PAY?
TEN GALLONS. FIVE NOW AND FIVE WHEN THE JOB IS DONE.
TEN G's? I DUNNO...
I'LL THROW IN THE SCOUT, TOO. LOOKS LIKE SHIT, BUT IT RUNS GOOD, I SWEAR.
DEAL.
I'LL BE TAKING THE GIRL, TOO. WORD IS THERE'S A HUNDRED GALLON BOUNTY ON HER SKINNY ASS.

GET ON, SWEETHEART.

YOU'RE GONNA REGRET THIS.

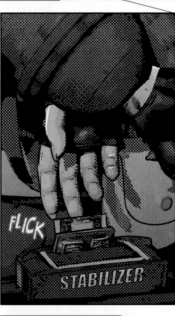

FLICK

STABILIZER

STABILIZER

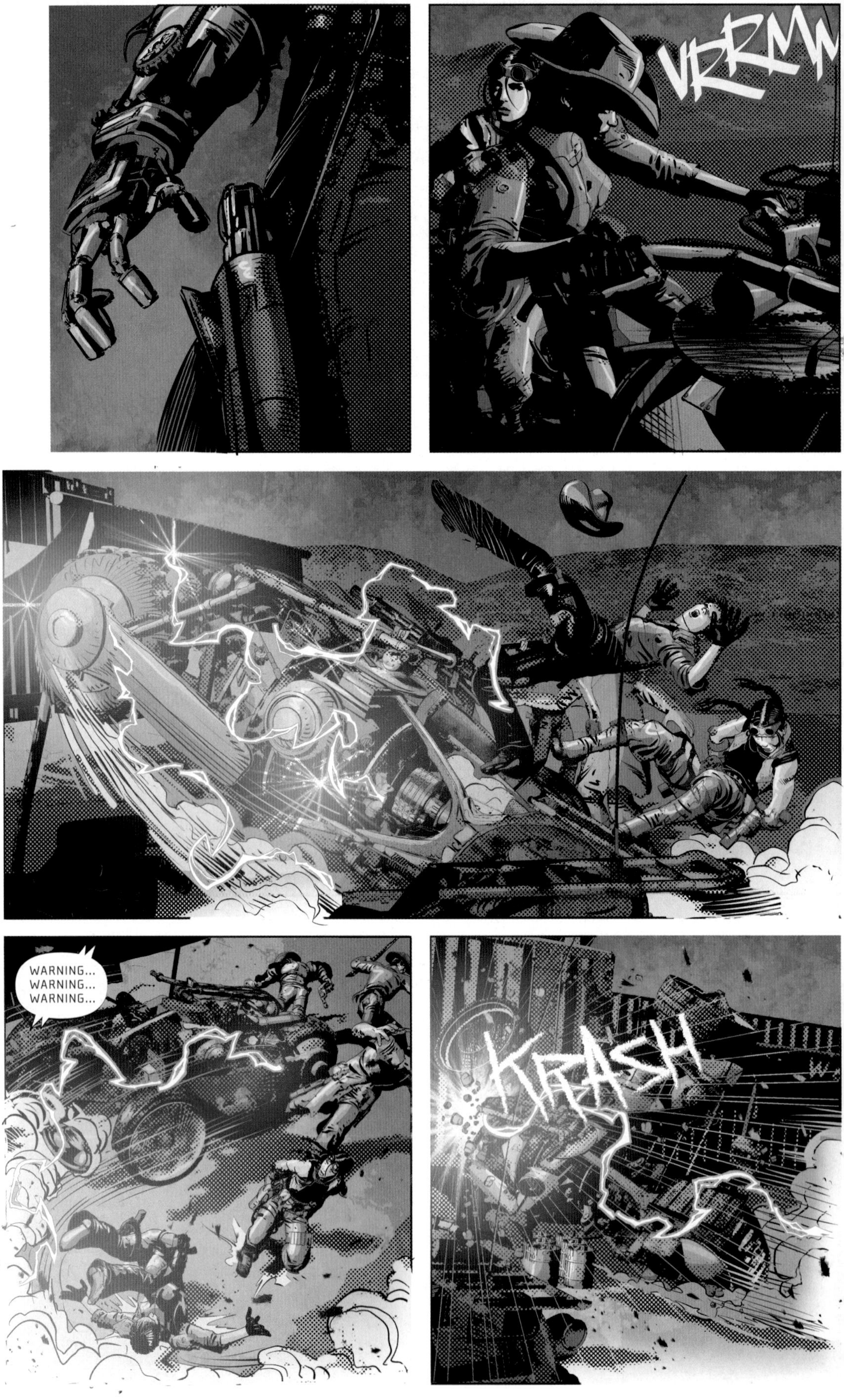
VRRMM
WARNING...
WARNING...
WARNING...
KRASH

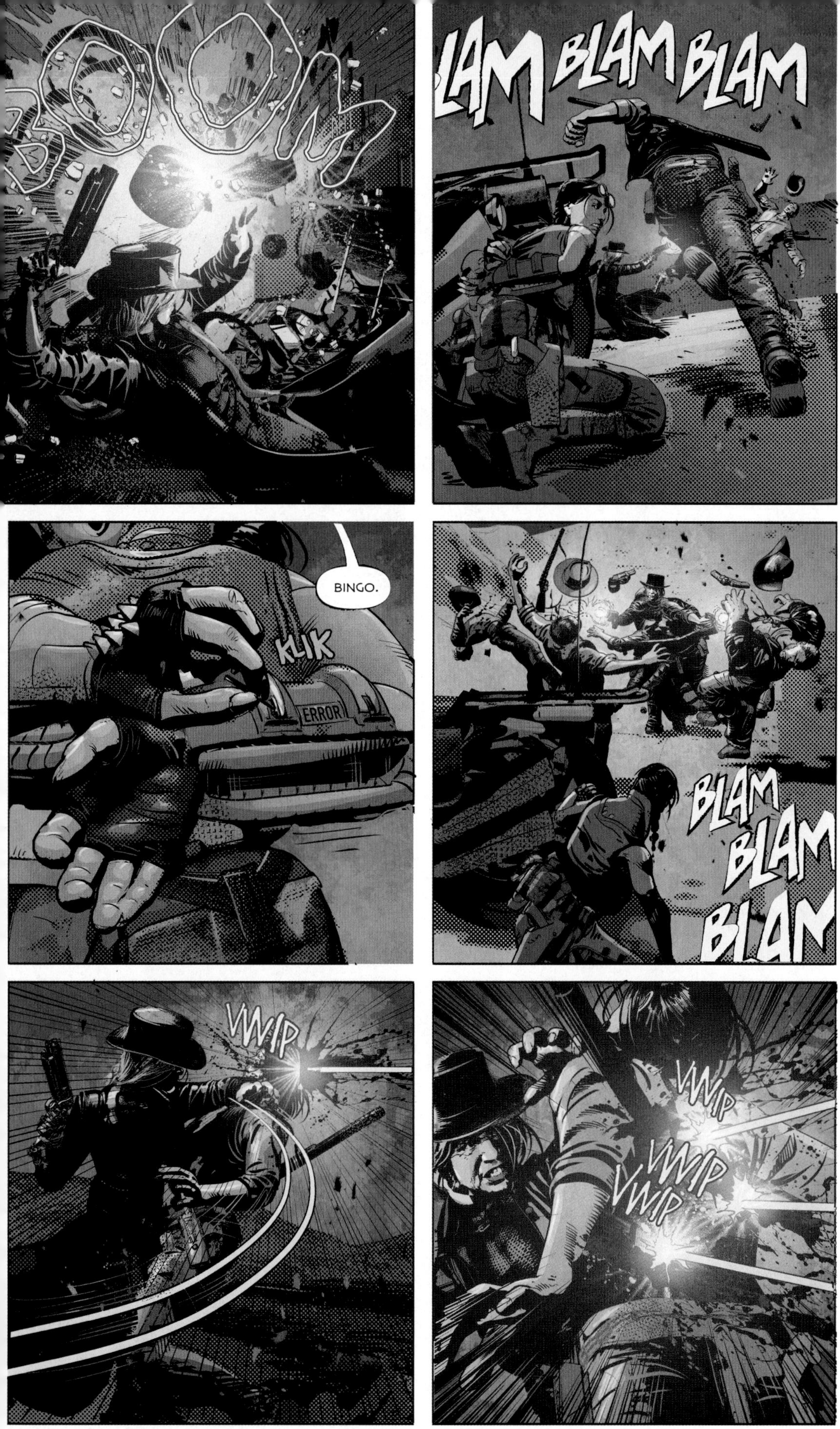
BOOM
BLAM BLAM BLAM
KLIK
ERROR
BINGO.
BLAM
BLAM
BLAM
VWIP
VWIP
VWIP
VWIP

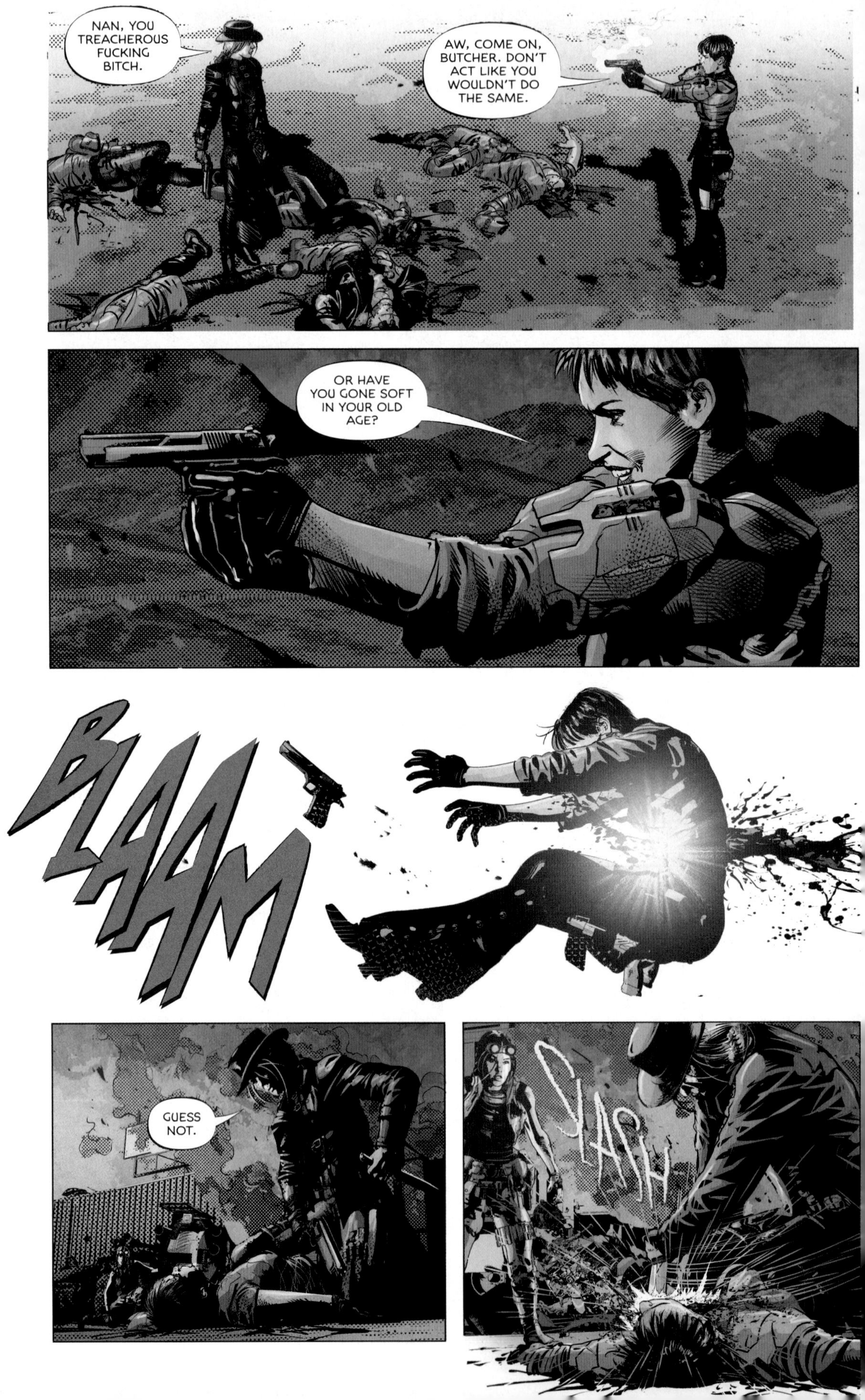
NAN, YOU TREACHEROUS FUCKING BITCH.
AW, COME ON, BUTCHER. DON'T ACT LIKE YOU WOULDN'T DO THE SAME.
OR HAVE YOU GONE SOFT IN YOUR OLD AGE?
BLAAM
GUESS NOT.
SLASH

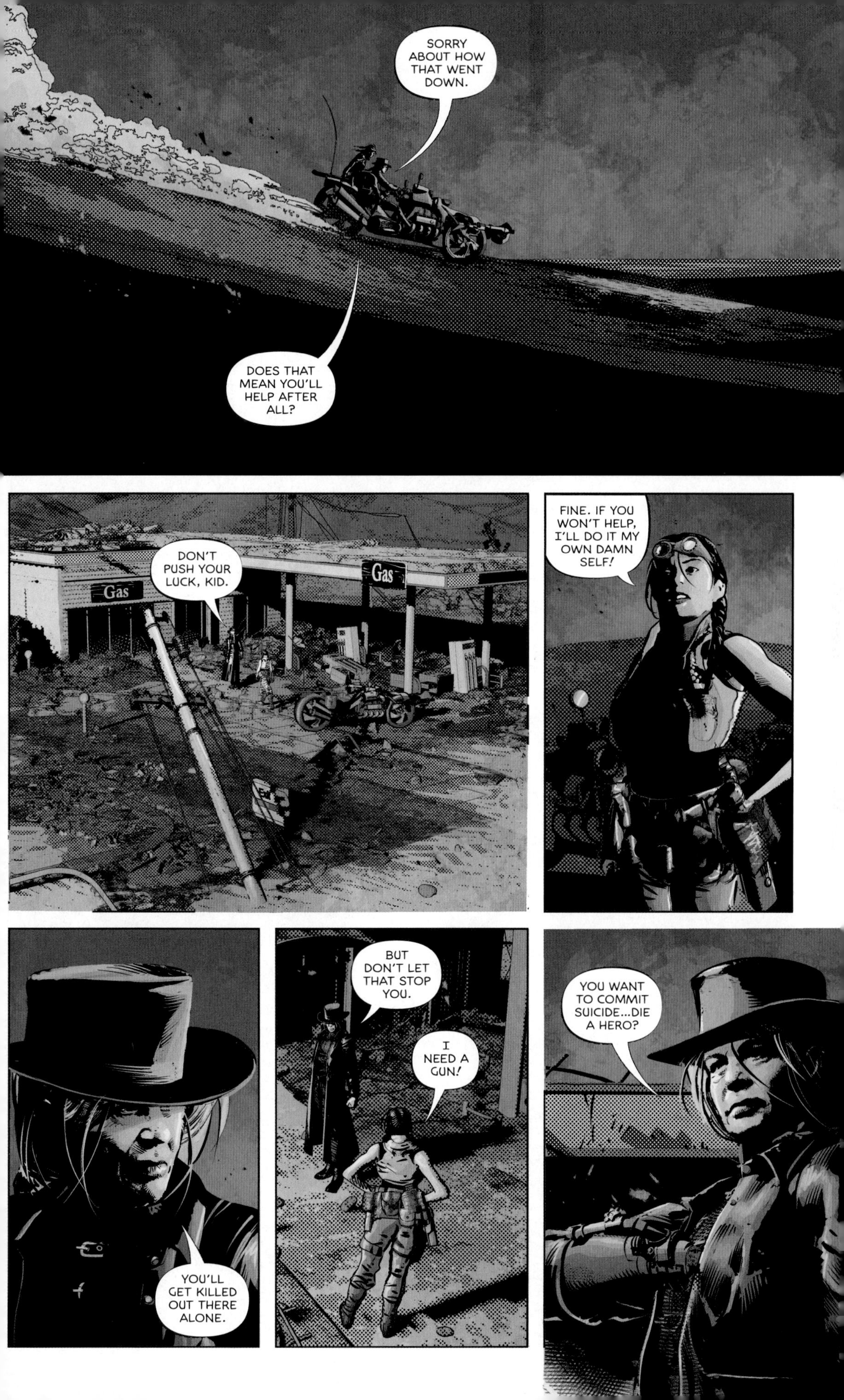
SORRY ABOUT HOW THAT WENT DOWN.
DOES THAT MEAN YOU'LL HELP AFTER ALL?
DON'T PUSH YOUR LUCK, KID.
Gas
Gas
FINE. IF YOU WON'T HELP, I'LL DO IT MY OWN DAMN SELF!
YOU'LL GET KILLED OUT THERE ALONE.
BUT DON'T LET THAT STOP YOU.
I NEED A GUN!
YOU WANT TO COMMIT SUICIDE...DIE A HERO?

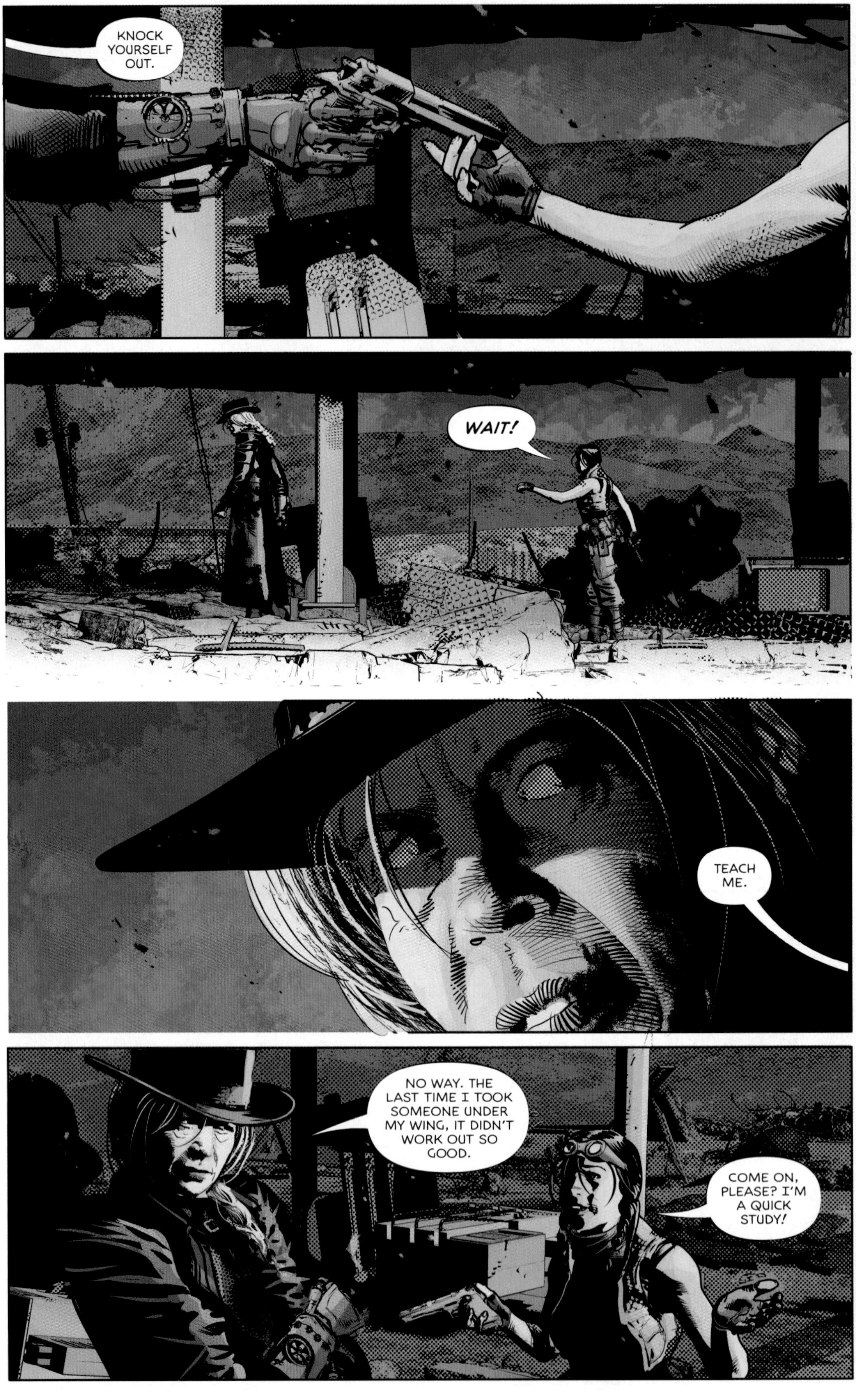
KNOCK YOURSELF OUT.
WAIT!
TEACH ME.
NO WAY. THE LAST TIME I TOOK SOMEONE UNDER MY WING, IT DIDN'T WORK OUT SO GOOD.
COME ON, PLEASE? I'M A QUICK STUDY!

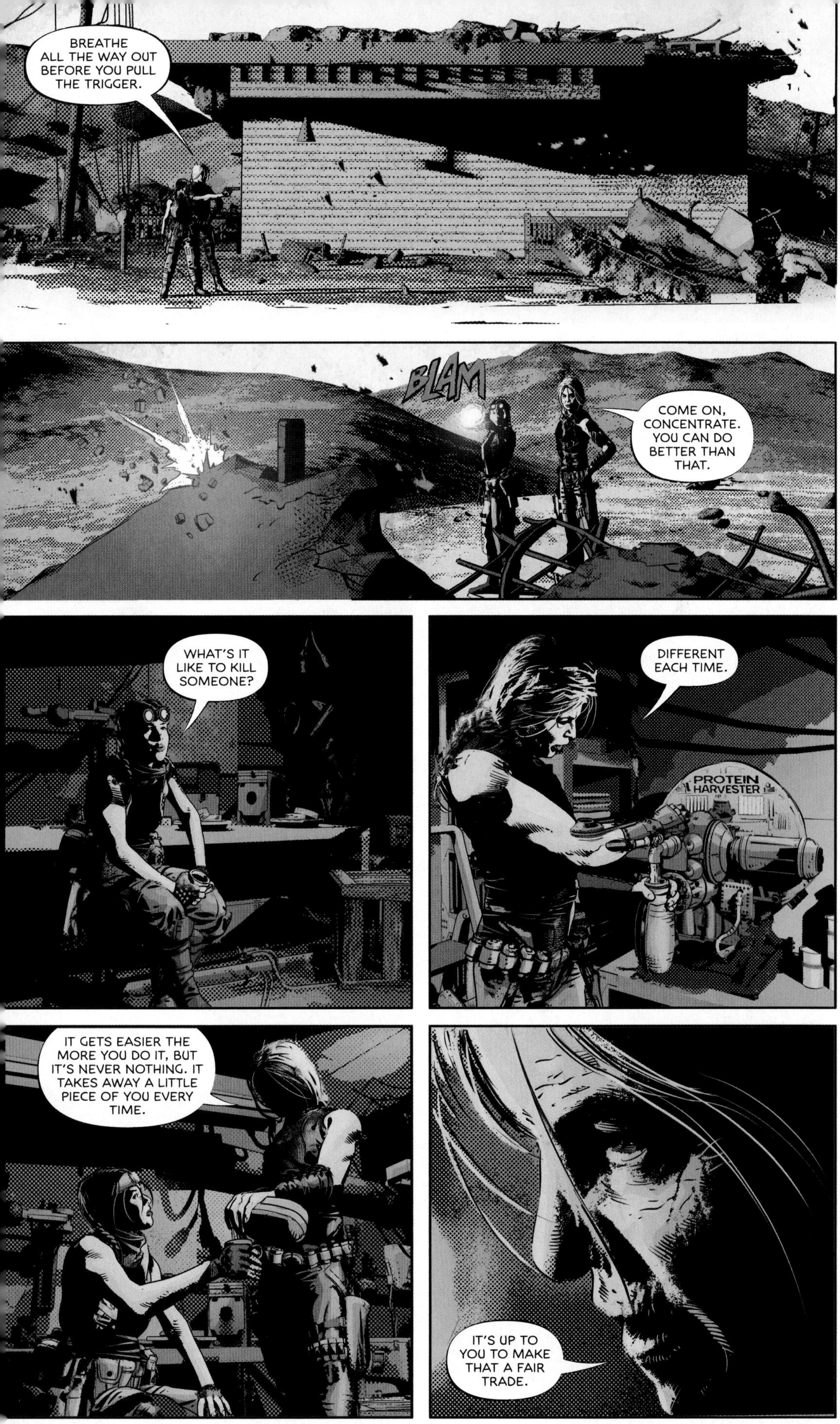
BREATHE ALL THE WAY OUT BEFORE YOU PULL THE TRIGGER.
BLAM
COME ON, CONCENTRATE. YOU CAN DO BETTER THAN THAT.
WHAT'S IT LIKE TO KILL SOMEONE?
DIFFERENT EACH TIME.
PROTEIN HARVESTER
IT GETS EASIER THE MORE YOU DO IT, BUT IT'S NEVER NOTHING. IT TAKES AWAY A LITTLE PIECE OF YOU EVERY TIME.
IT'S UP TO YOU TO MAKE THAT A FAIR TRADE.

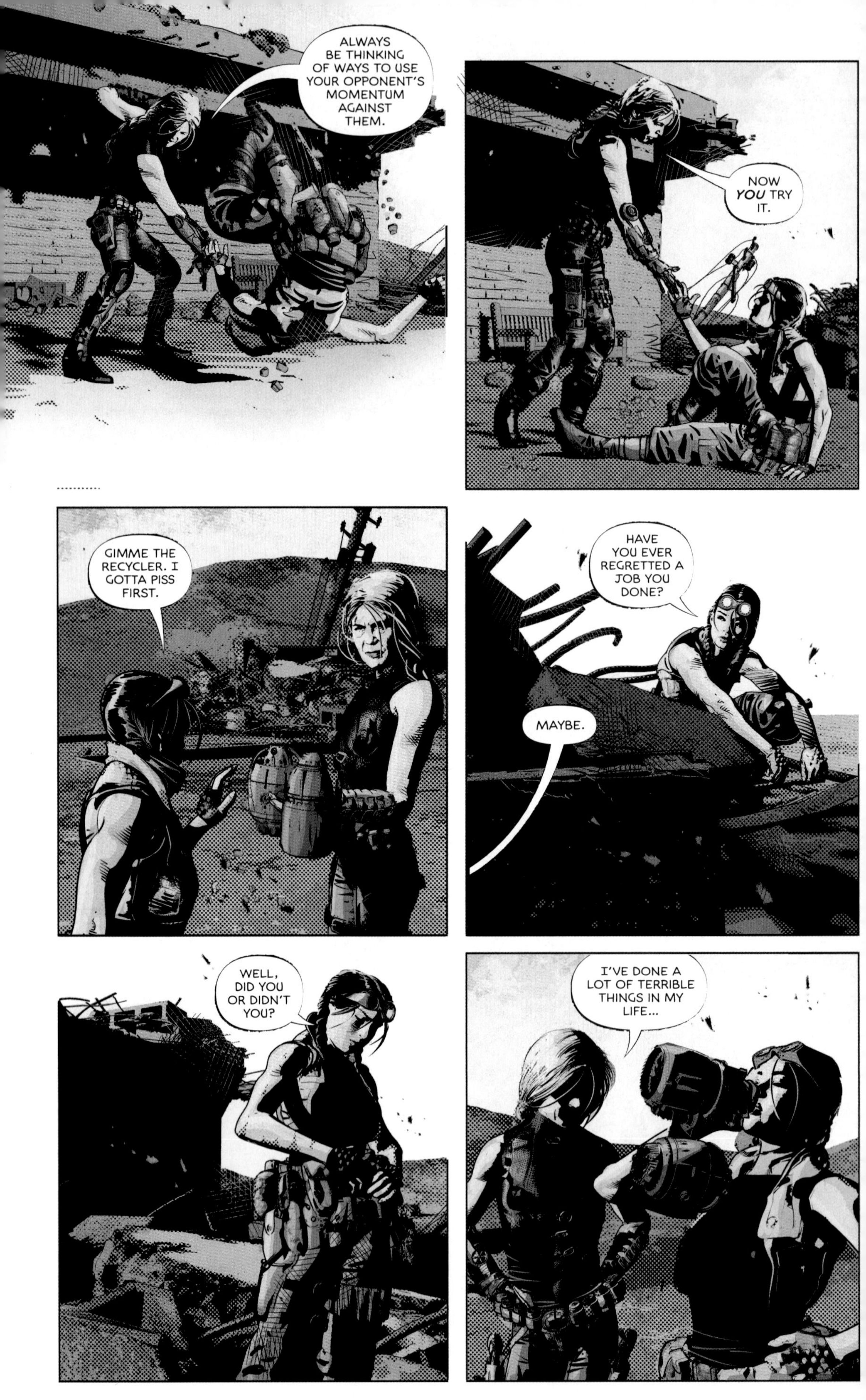
ALWAYS BE THINKING OF WAYS TO USE YOUR OPPONENT'S MOMENTUM AGAINST THEM.
NOW *YOU* TRY IT.
GIMME THE RECYCLER. I GOTTA PISS FIRST.
HAVE YOU EVER REGRETTED A JOB YOU DONE?
MAYBE.
WELL, DID YOU OR DIDN'T YOU?
I'VE DONE A LOT OF TERRIBLE THINGS IN MY LIFE...

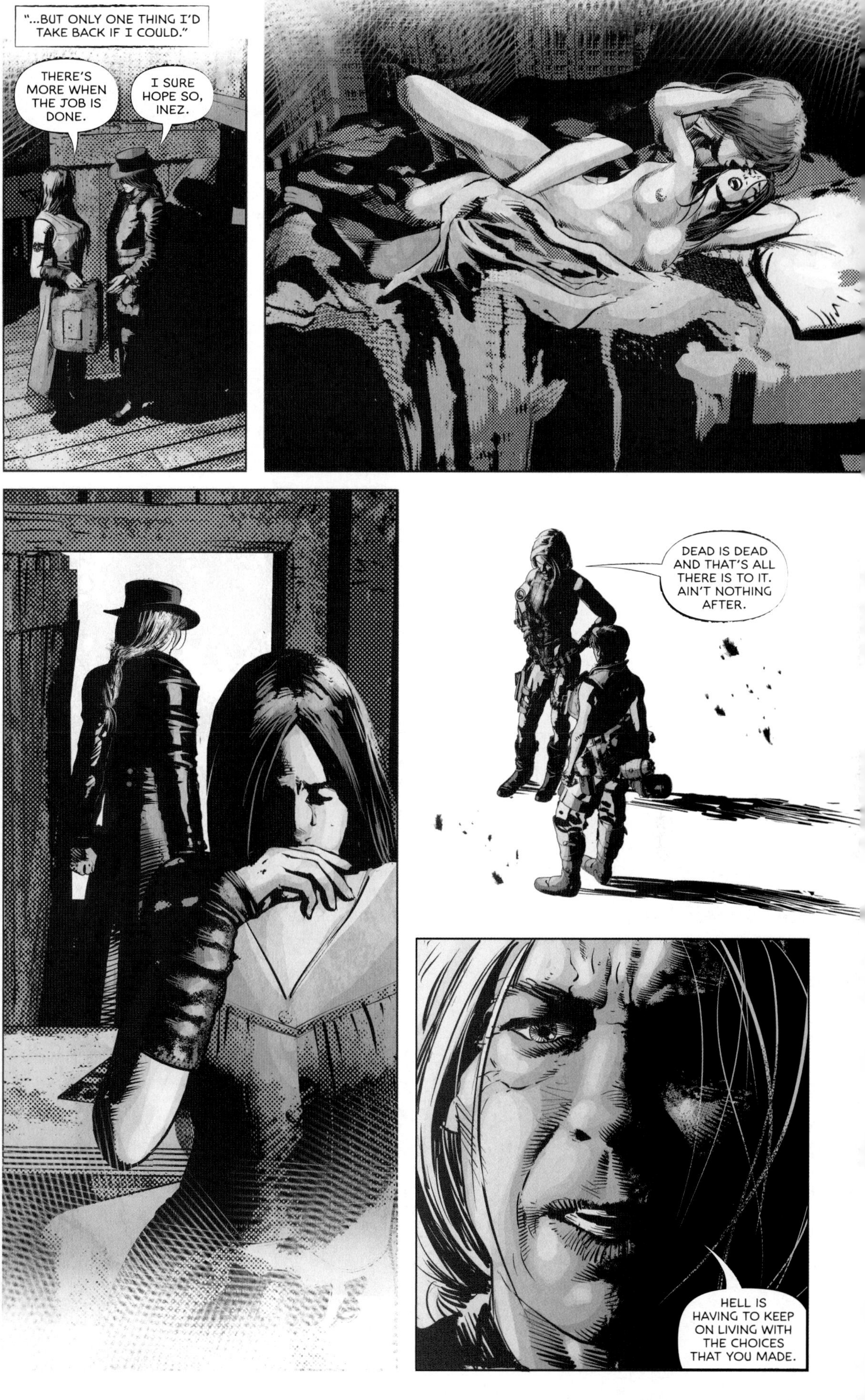

"...BUT ONLY ONE THING I'D TAKE BACK IF I COULD."
THERE'S MORE WHEN THE JOB IS DONE.
I SURE HOPE SO, INEZ.
DEAD IS DEAD AND THAT'S ALL THERE IS TO IT. AIN'T NOTHING AFTER.
HELL IS HAVING TO KEEP ON LIVING WITH THE CHOICES THAT YOU MADE.

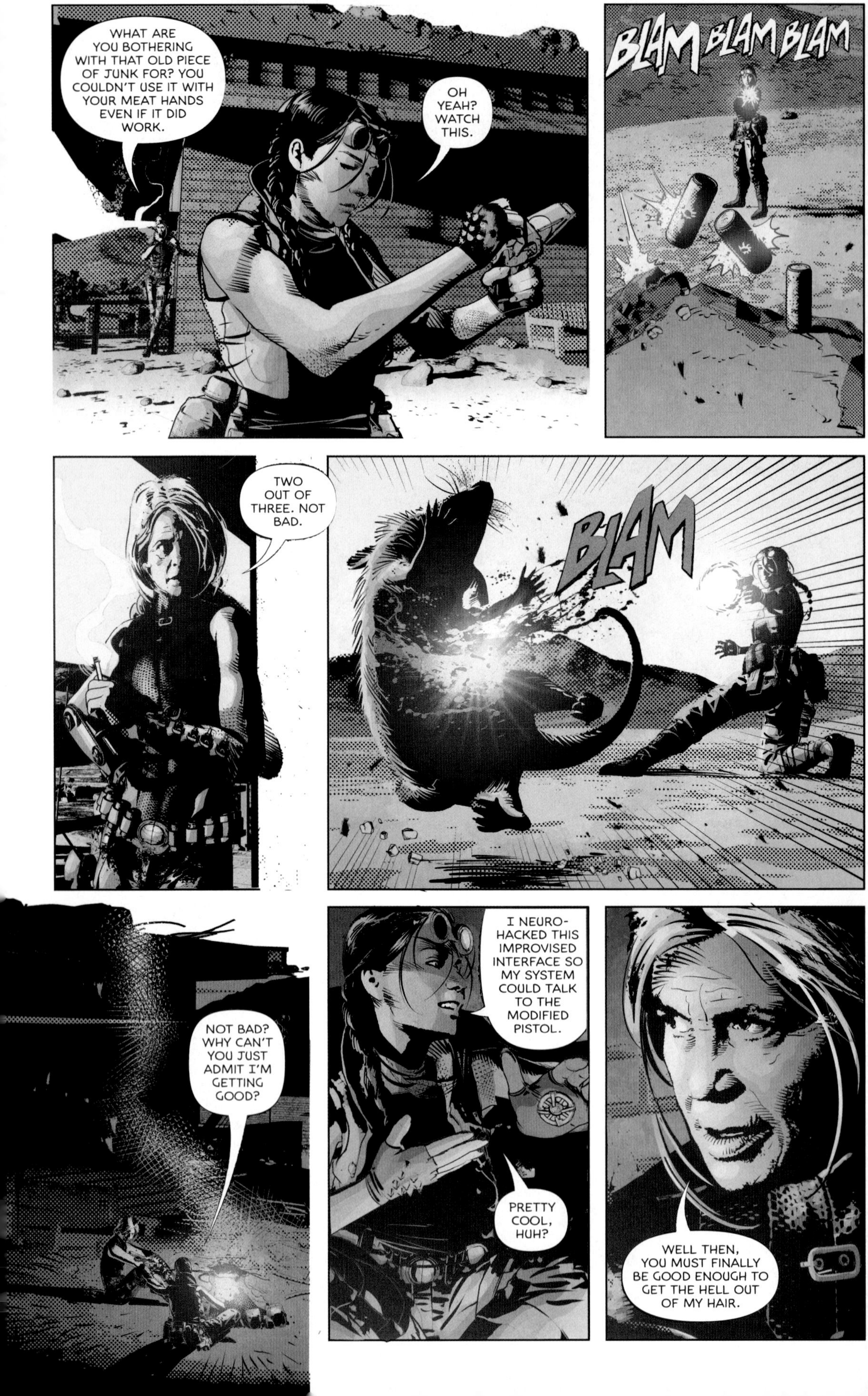

WHAT ARE YOU BOTHERING WITH THAT OLD PIECE OF JUNK FOR? YOU COULDN'T USE IT WITH YOUR MEAT HANDS EVEN IF IT DID WORK.
OH YEAH? WATCH THIS.
BLAM BLAM BLAM
TWO OUT OF THREE. NOT BAD.
BLAM
NOT BAD? WHY CAN'T YOU JUST ADMIT I'M GETTING GOOD?
I NEURO-HACKED THIS IMPROVISED INTERFACE SO MY SYSTEM COULD TALK TO THE MODIFIED PISTOL.
PRETTY COOL, HUH?
WELL THEN, YOU MUST FINALLY BE GOOD ENOUGH TO GET THE HELL OUT OF MY HAIR.

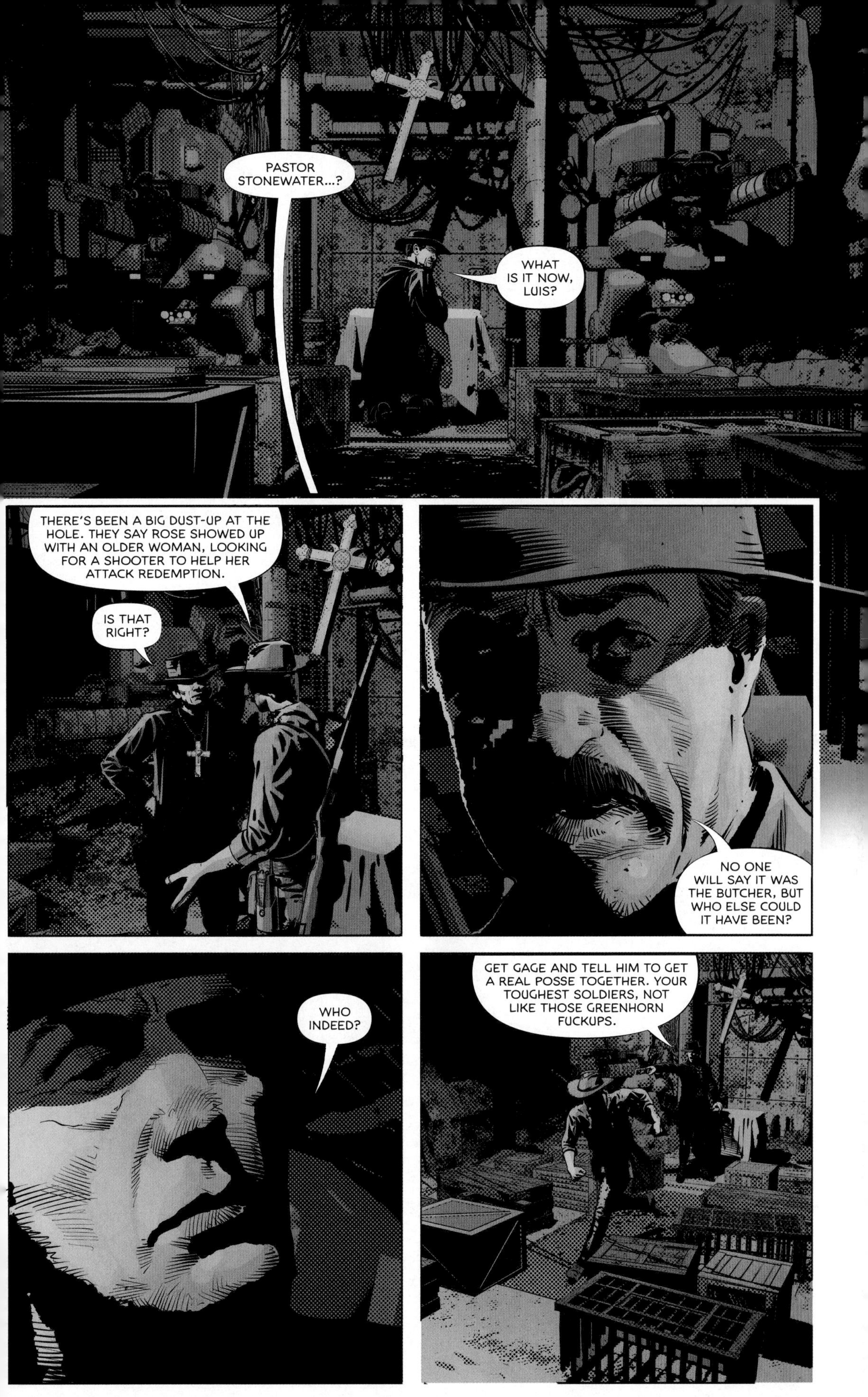
PASTOR STONEWATER...?
WHAT IS IT NOW, LUIS?
THERE'S BEEN A BIG DUST-UP AT THE HOLE. THEY SAY ROSE SHOWED UP WITH AN OLDER WOMAN, LOOKING FOR A SHOOTER TO HELP HER ATTACK REDEMPTION.
IS THAT RIGHT?
NO ONE WILL SAY IT WAS THE BUTCHER, BUT WHO ELSE COULD IT HAVE BEEN?
WHO INDEED?
GET GAGE AND TELL HIM TO GET A REAL POSSE TOGETHER. YOUR TOUGHEST SOLDIERS, NOT LIKE THOSE GREENHORN FUCKUPS.

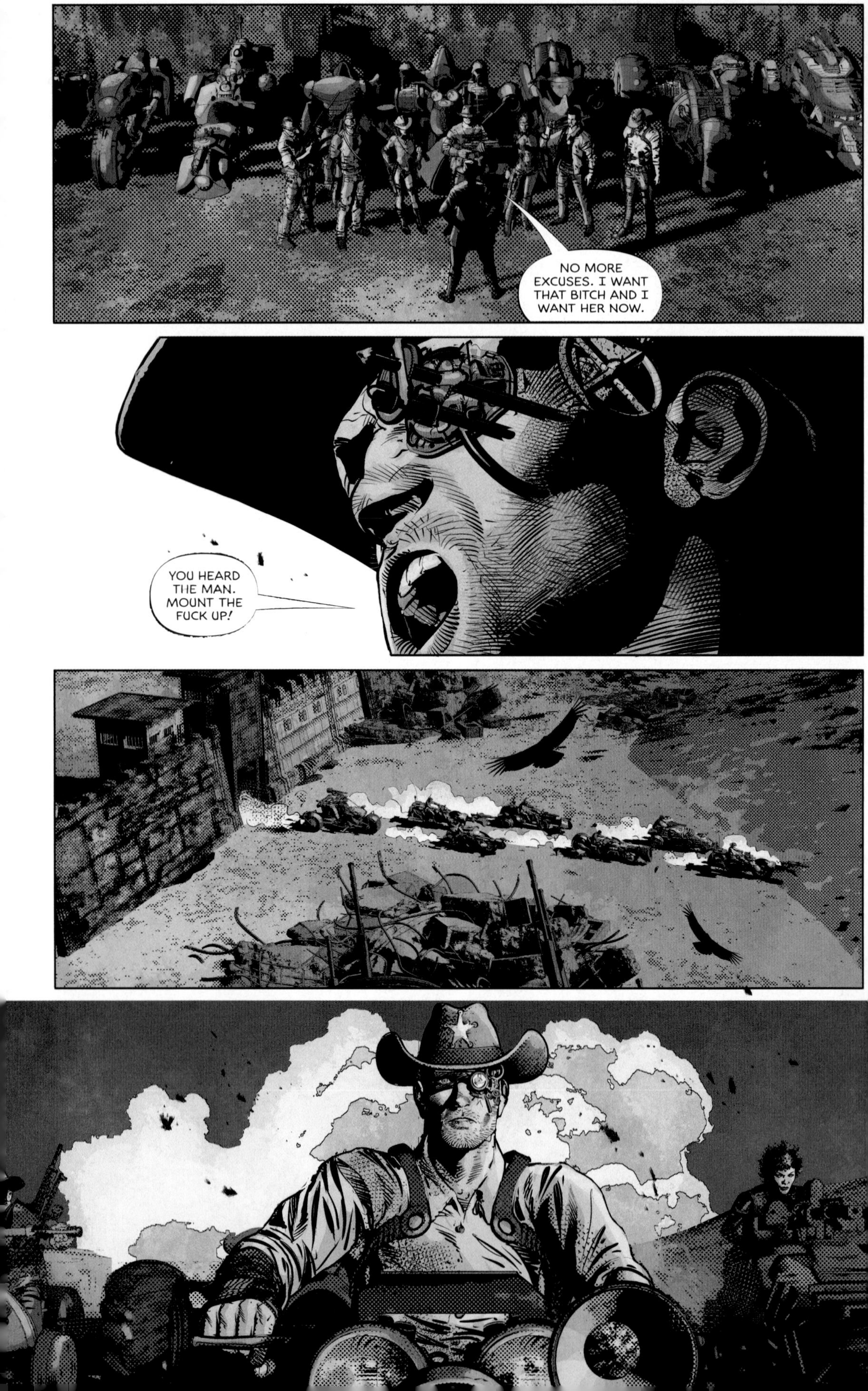
NO MORE EXCUSES. I WANT THAT BITCH AND I WANT HER NOW.
YOU HEARD THE MAN. MOUNT THE FUCK UP!

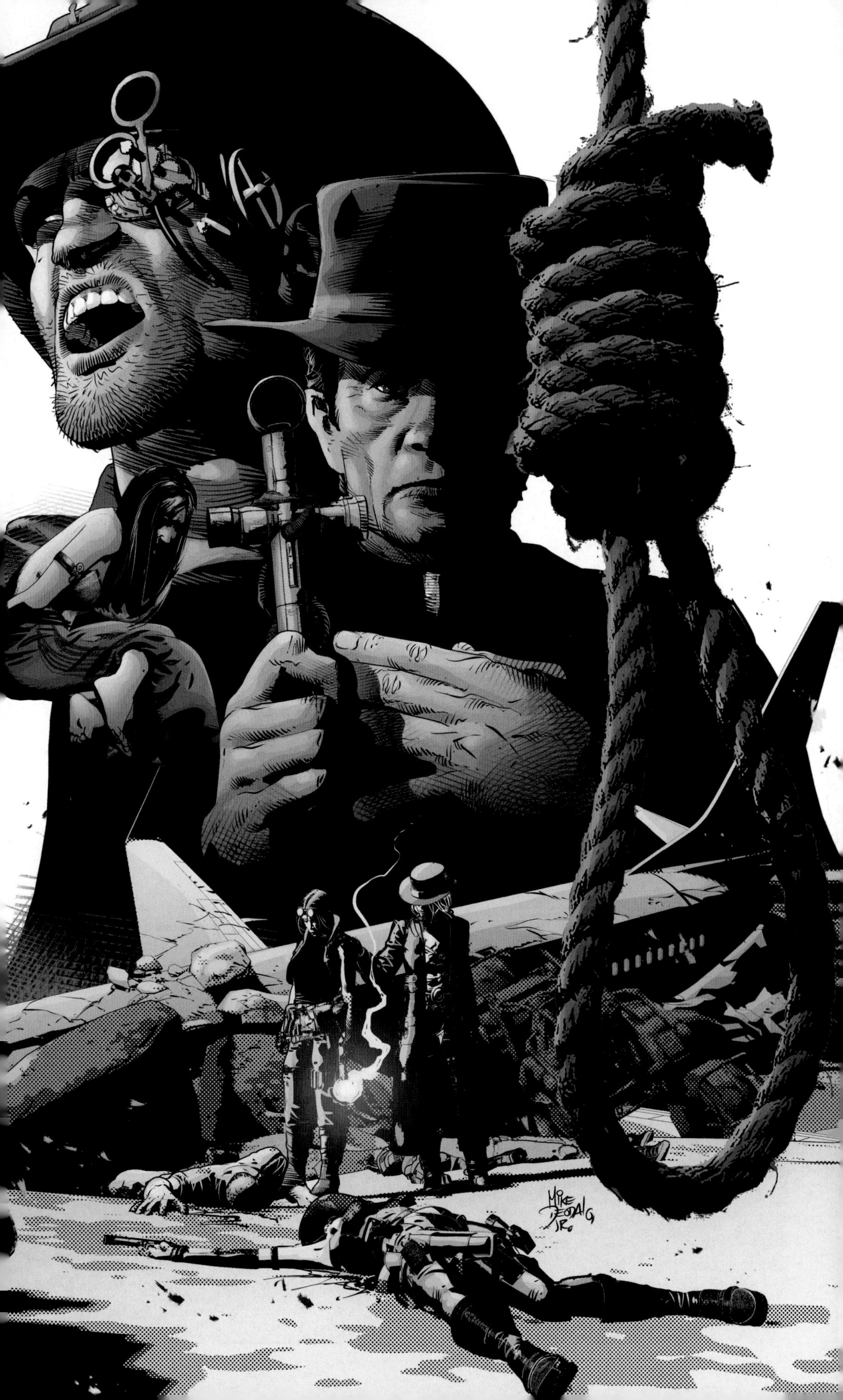

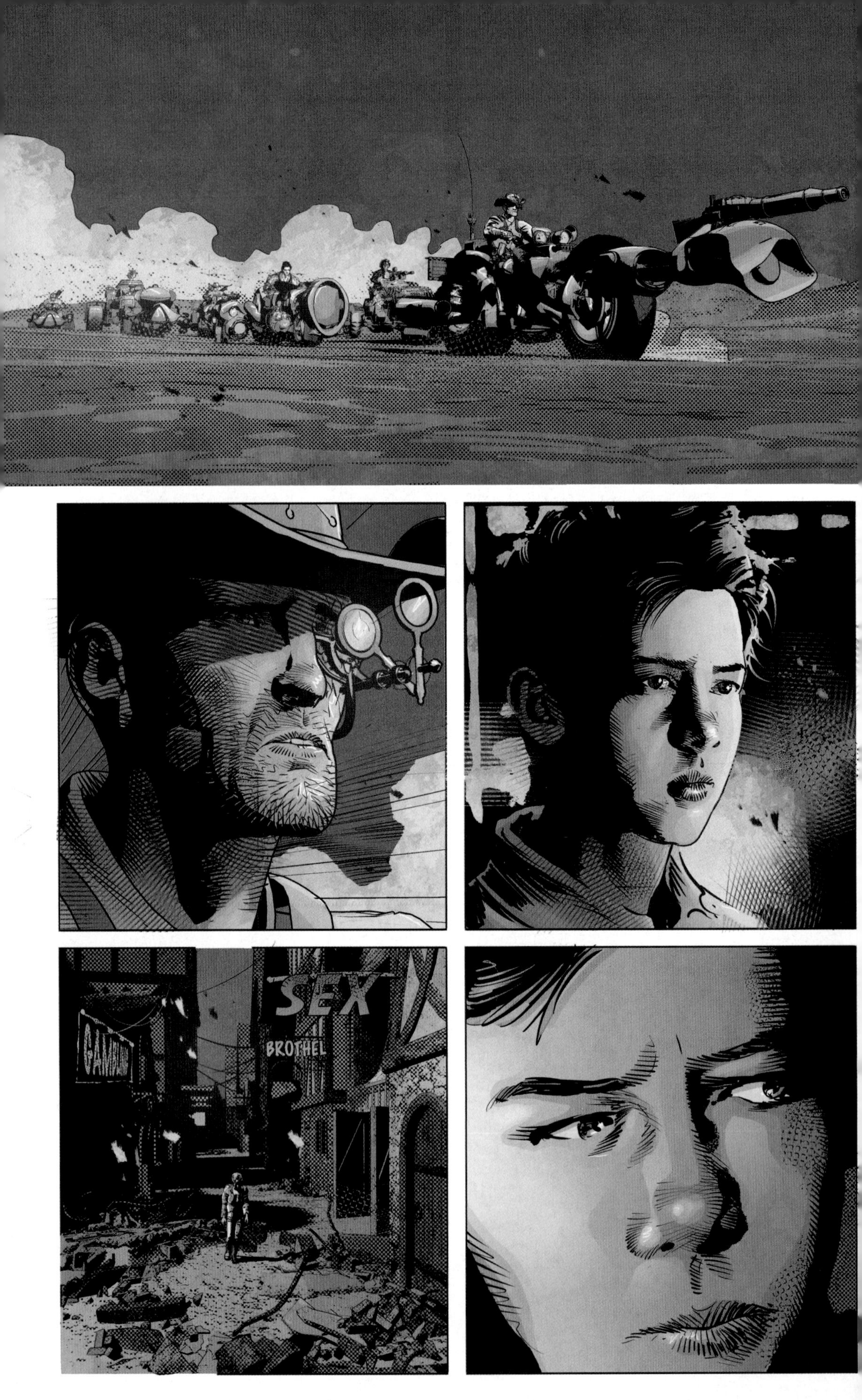
SEX
BROTHEL

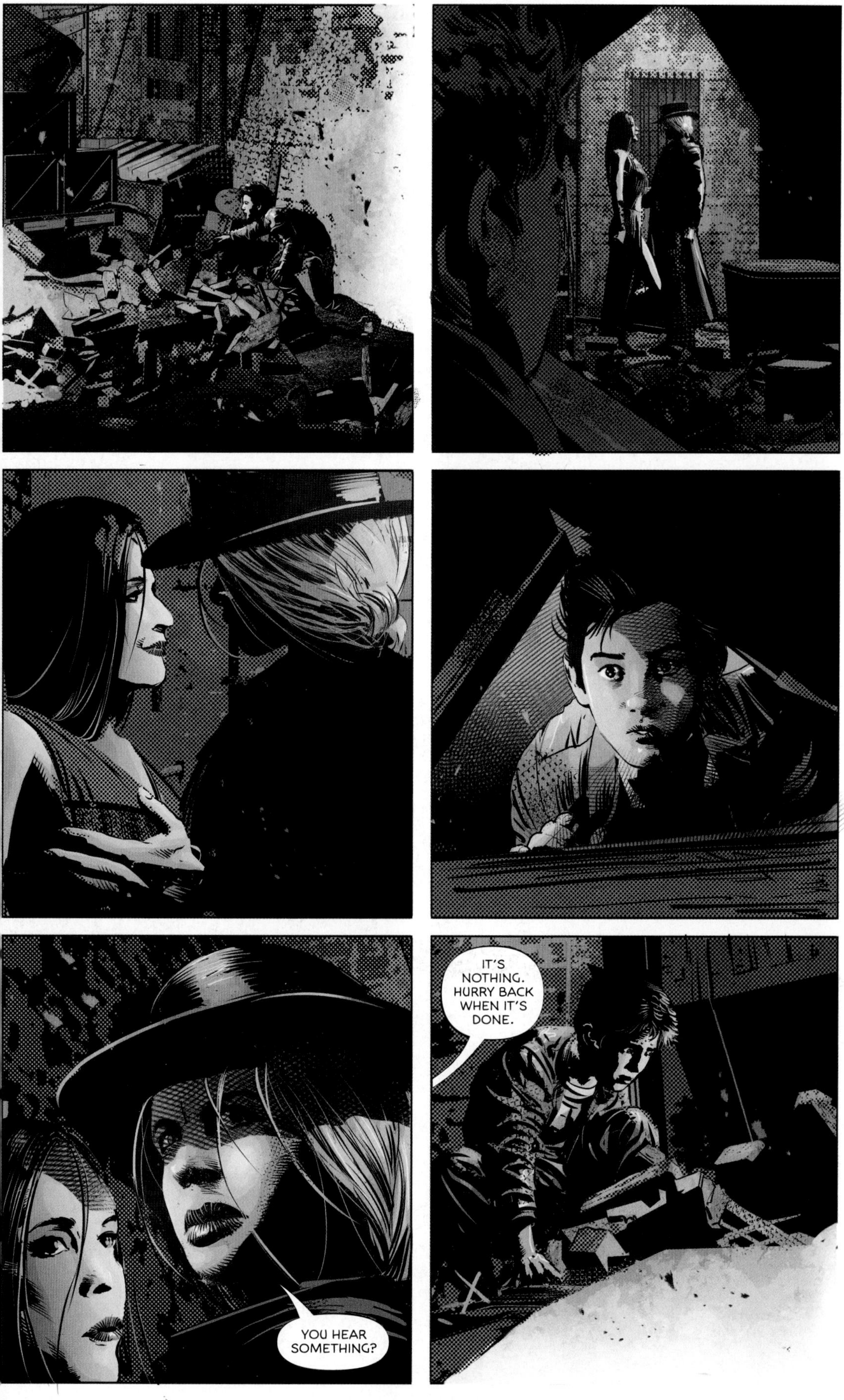
YOU HEAR SOMETHING?
IT'S NOTHING. HURRY BACK WHEN IT'S DONE.

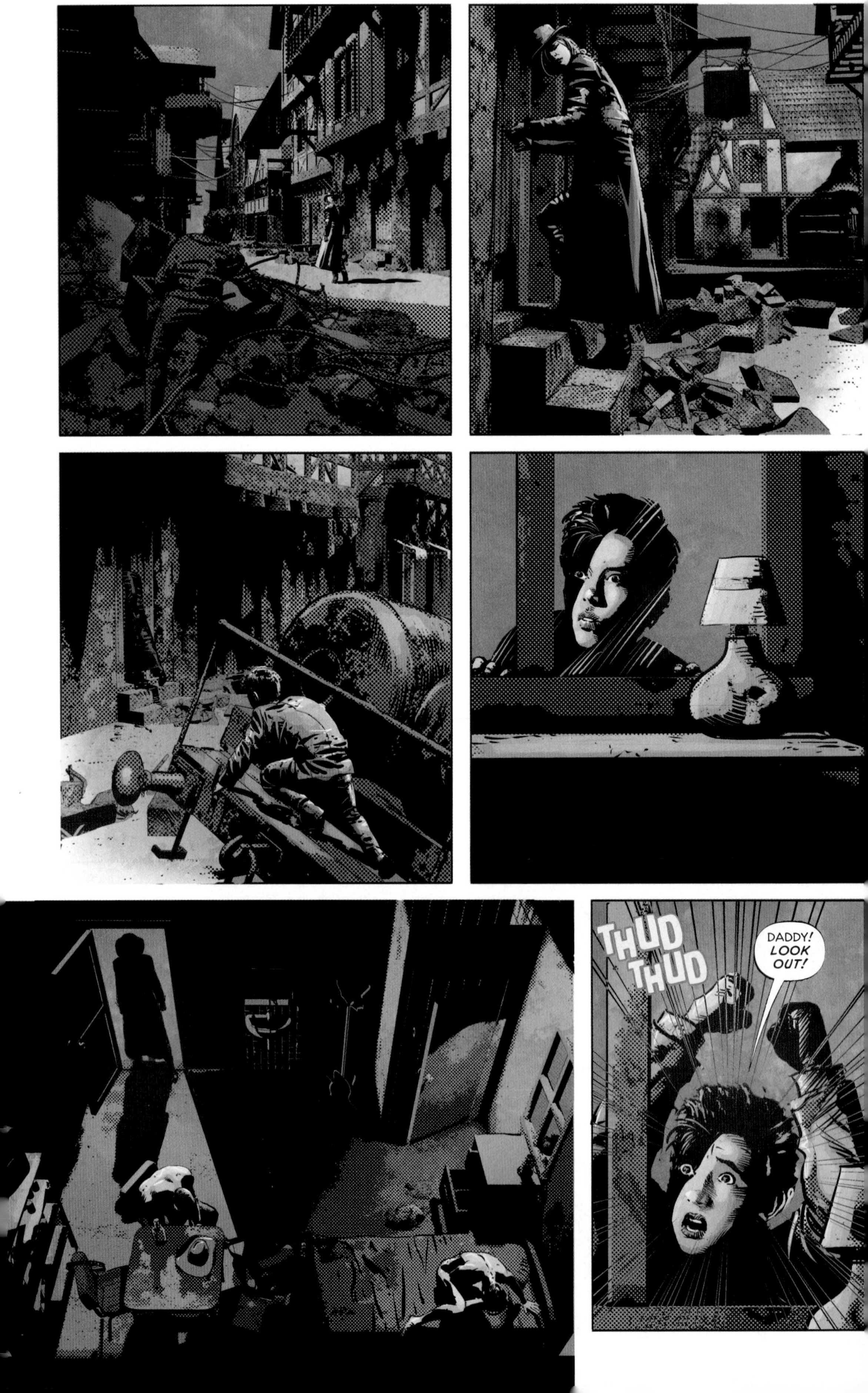
THUD
THUD
DADDY! LOOK OUT!

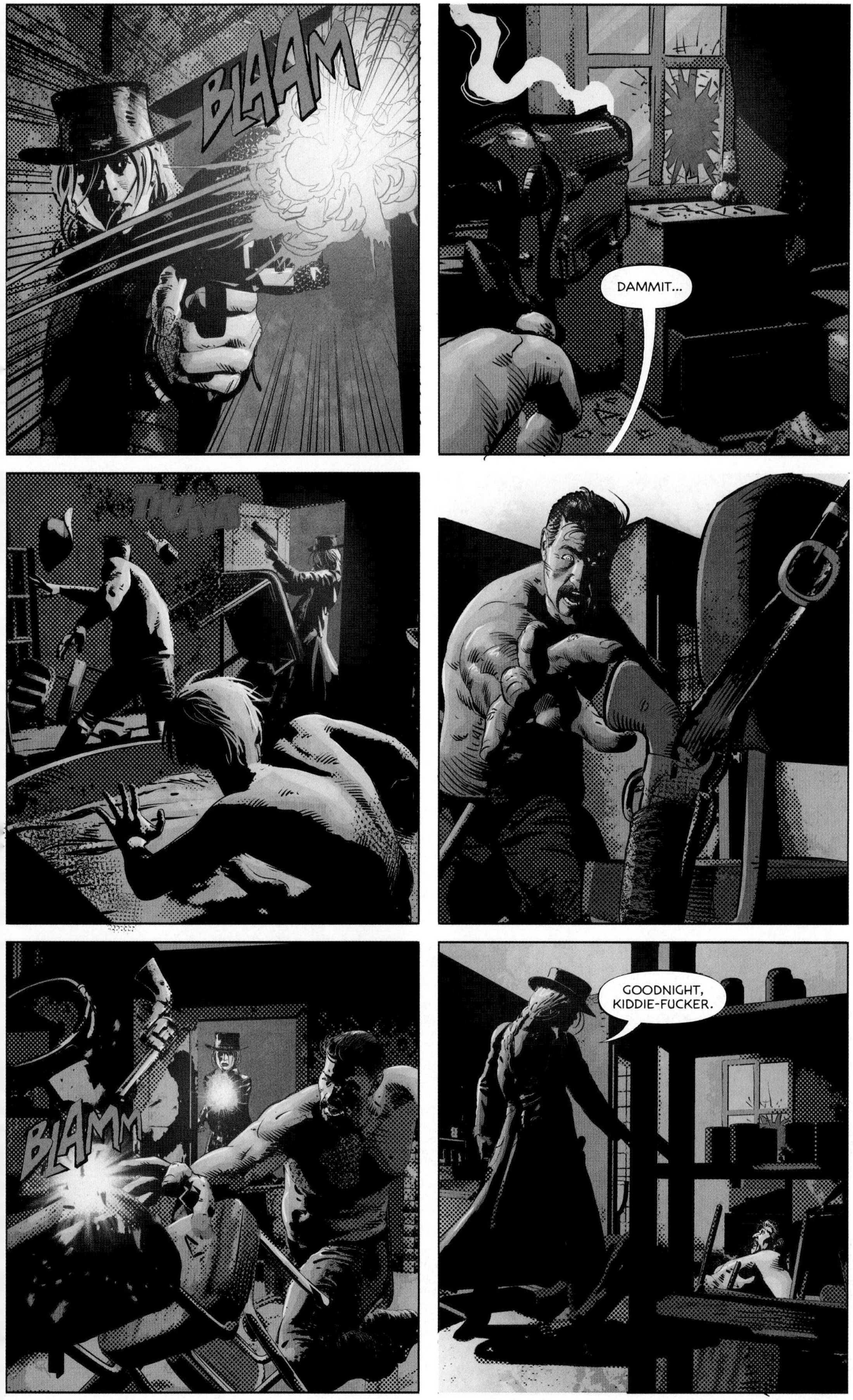
BLAAM
DAMMIT...
BLAMM
GOODNIGHT, KIDDIE-FUCKER.

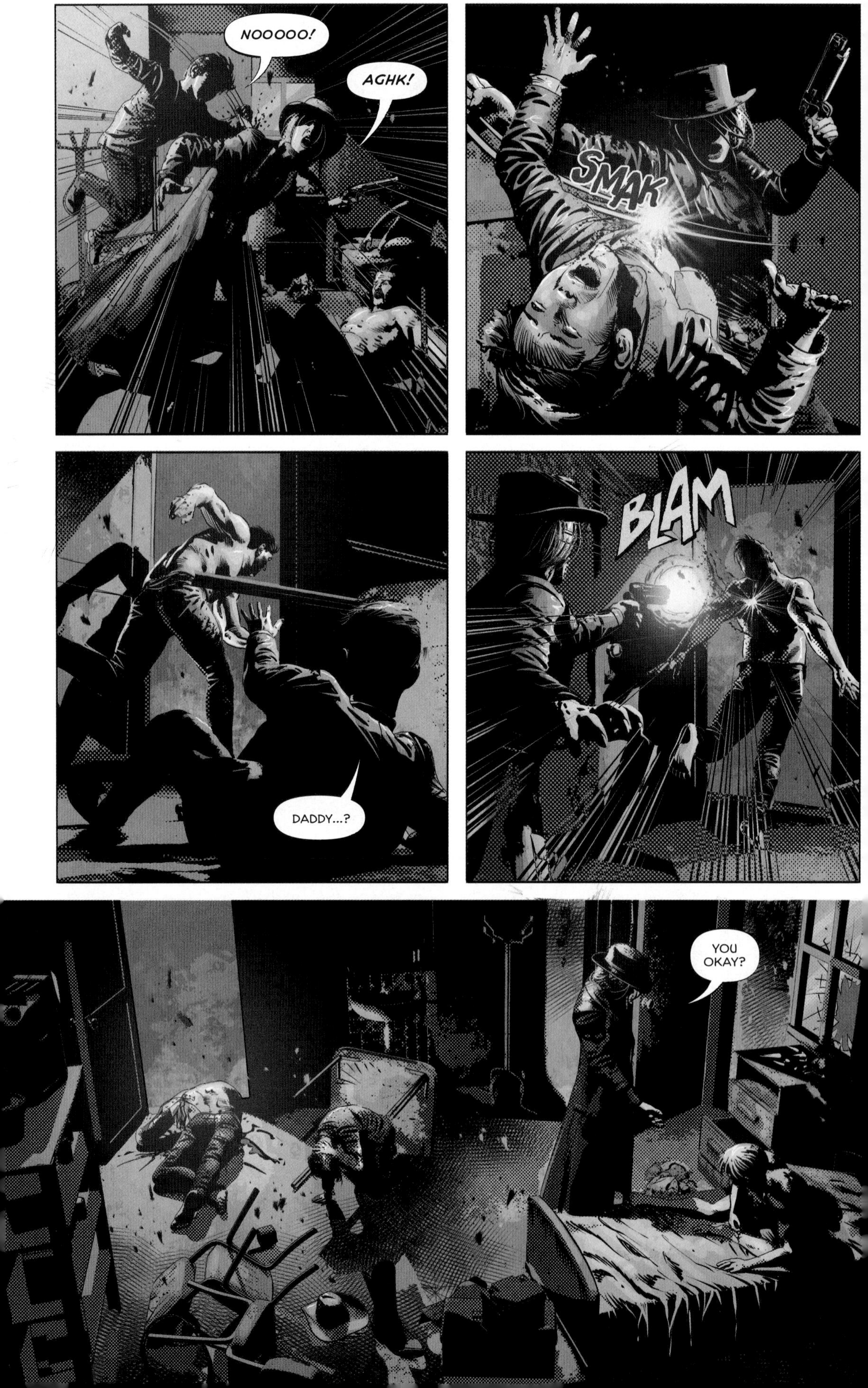
NOOOOO!
AGHK!
SMAK
DADDY...?
BLAM
YOU OKAY?

I'LL KILL YOU!

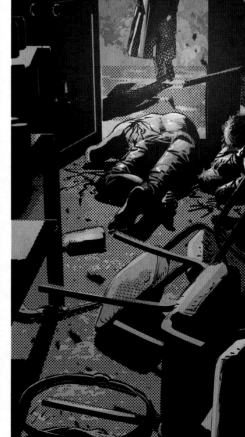

NOBODY LIKES A PEEPING TOM.

SHUNK

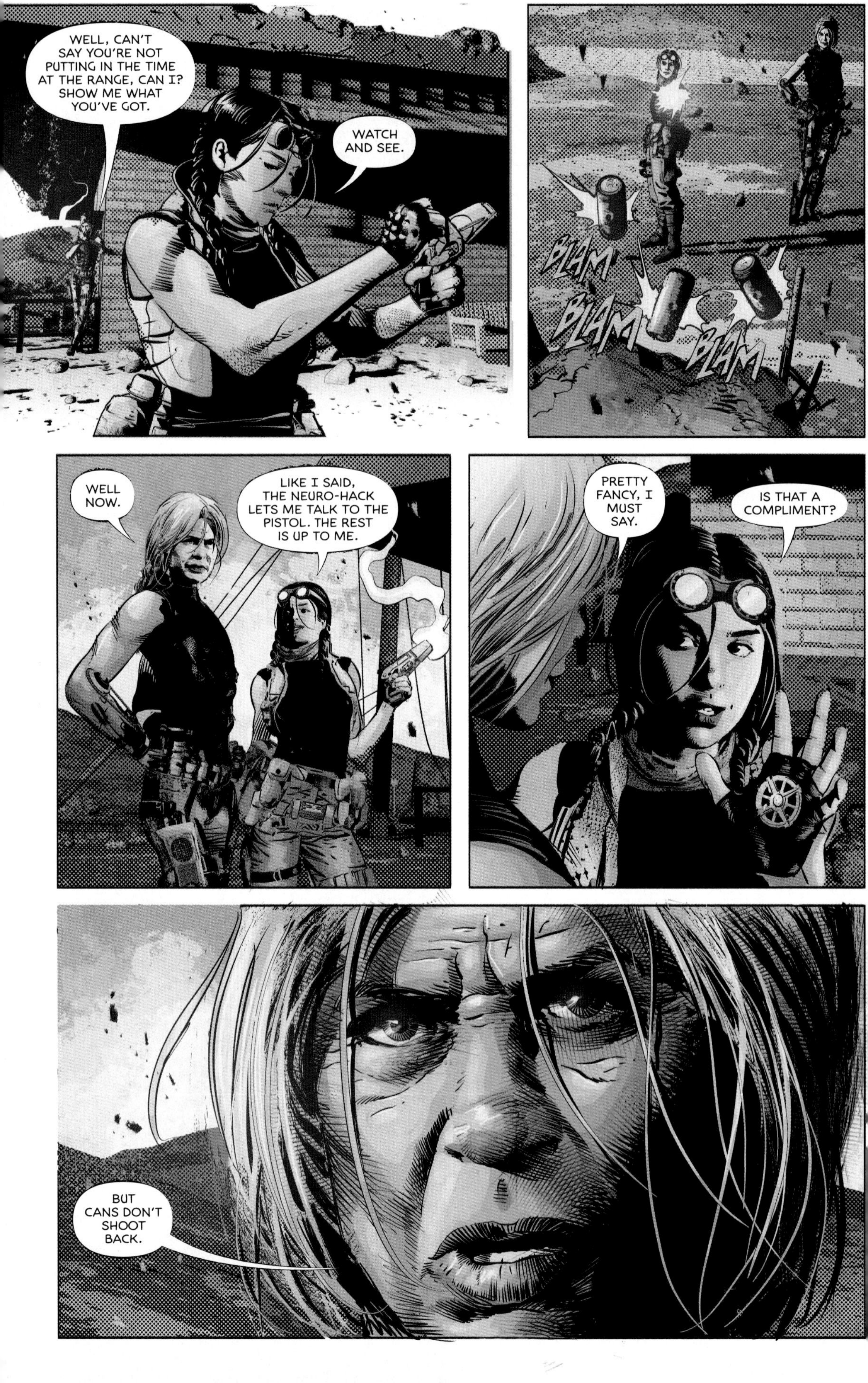
WELL, CAN'T SAY YOU'RE NOT PUTTING IN THE TIME AT THE RANGE, CAN I? SHOW ME WHAT YOU'VE GOT.
WATCH AND SEE.
BLAM
BLAM
BLAM
BLAM
WELL NOW.
LIKE I SAID, THE NEURO-HACK LETS ME TALK TO THE PISTOL. THE REST IS UP TO ME.
PRETTY FANCY, I MUST SAY.
IS THAT A COMPLIMENT?
BUT CANS DON'T SHOOT BACK.

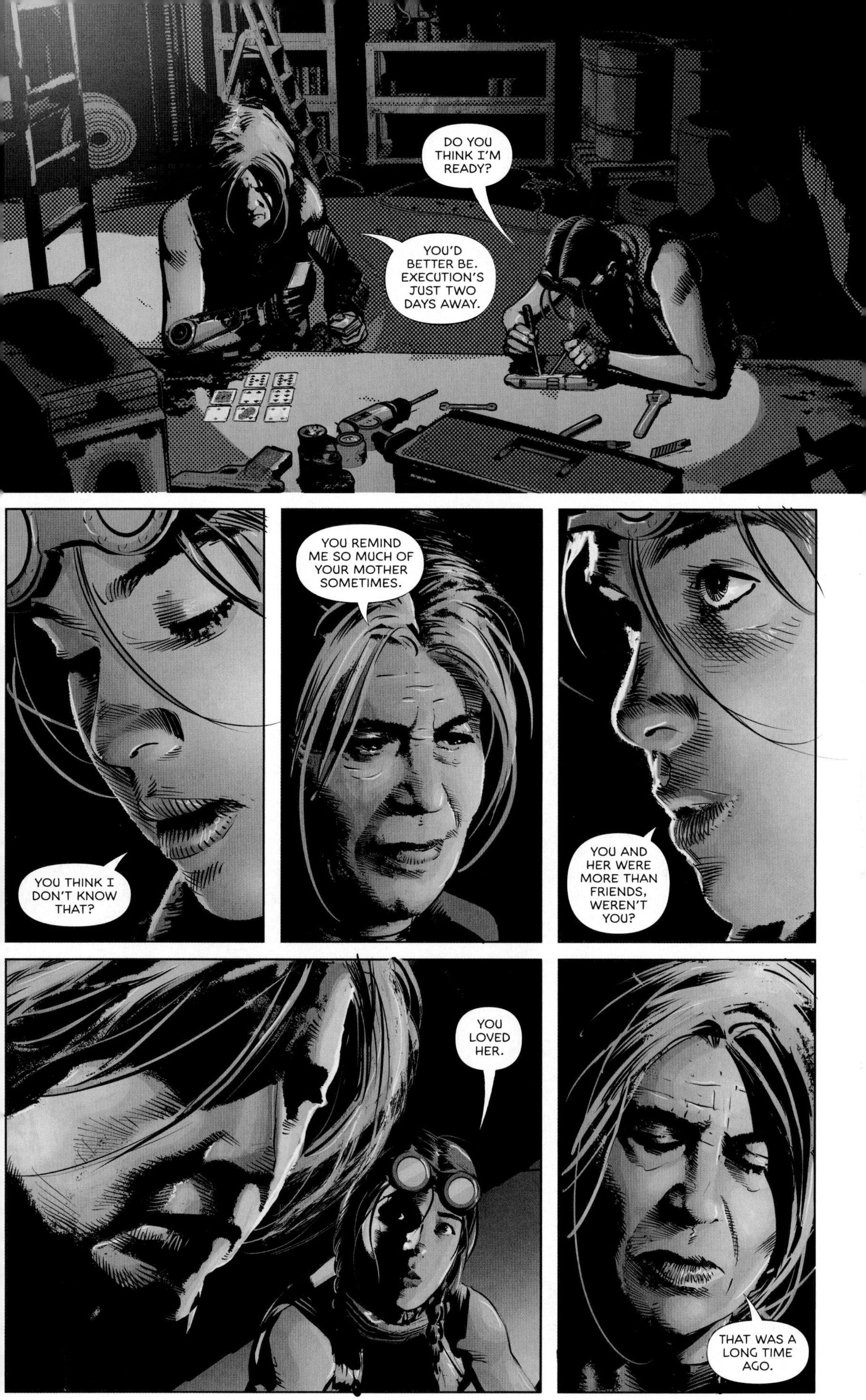
DO YOU THINK I'M READY?
YOU'D BETTER BE. EXECUTION'S JUST TWO DAYS AWAY.
YOU THINK I DON'T KNOW THAT?
YOU REMIND ME SO MUCH OF YOUR MOTHER SOMETIMES.
YOU AND HER WERE MORE THAN FRIENDS, WEREN'T YOU?
YOU LOVED HER.
THAT WAS A LONG TIME AGO.

THEN WHY WON'T YOU GO WITH ME? HELP ME SAVE HER?

I'M A KILLER, KID. NOT A SAVIOR.

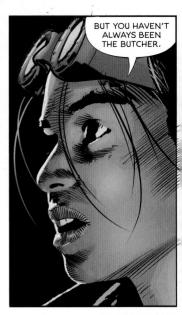

BUT YOU HAVEN'T ALWAYS BEEN THE BUTCHER.

YOU DIDN'T KILL ALL THOSE MINERS UNTIL AFTER WHATEVER WENT DOWN BETWEEN YOU AND MY MOTHER, RIGHT?

YOU SHOULDN'T BELIEVE EVERY TALL TALE YOU HEAR.

ANYWAY, IT DON'T MAKE NO DIFFERENCE NOW. THIS IS YOUR PROBLEM, NOT MINE.

YOU DON'T GIVE A SHIT ABOUT...

...ANYONE BUT YOURSELF!

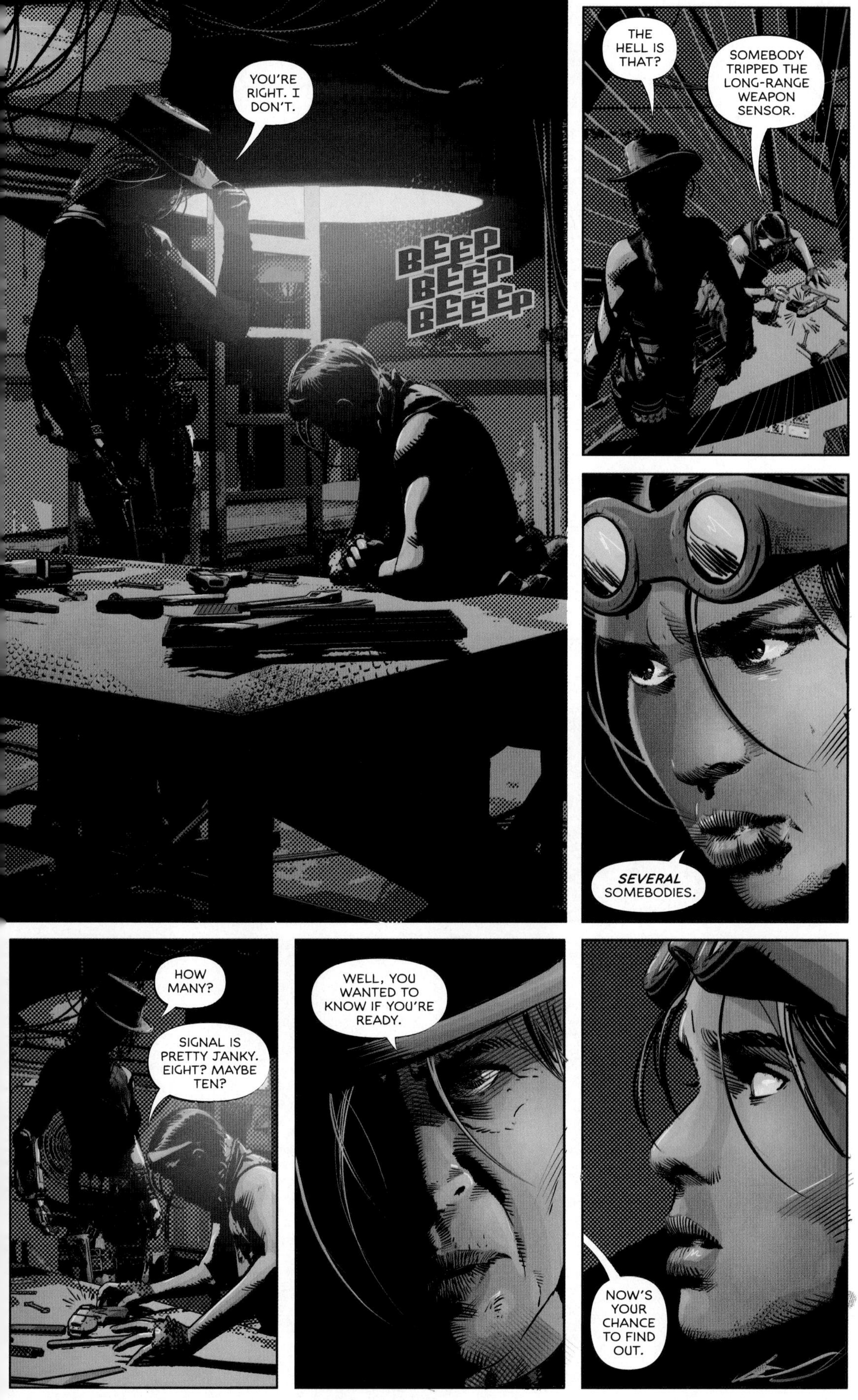
YOU'RE RIGHT. I DON'T.
BEEEP BEEEP BEEEP
THE HELL IS THAT?
SOMEBODY TRIPPED THE LONG-RANGE WEAPON SENSOR.
SEVERAL SOMEBODIES.
HOW MANY?
SIGNAL IS PRETTY JANKY. EIGHT? MAYBE TEN?
WELL, YOU WANTED TO KNOW IF YOU'RE READY.
NOW'S YOUR CHANCE TO FIND OUT.

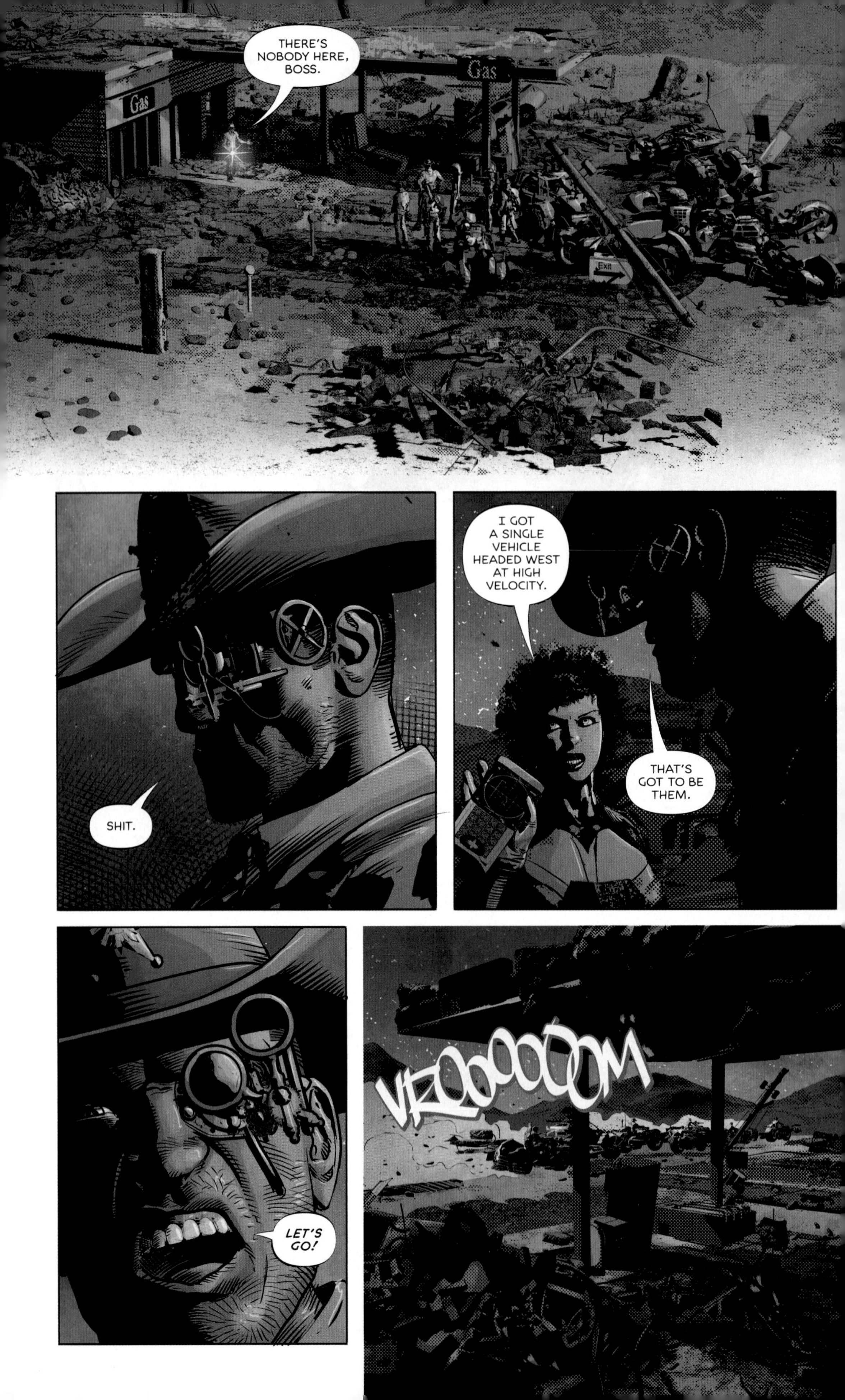
THERE'S NOBODY HERE, BOSS.
Gas
Gas
Exit
SHIT.
I GOT A SINGLE VEHICLE HEADED WEST AT HIGH VELOCITY.
THAT'S GOT TO BE THEM.
LET'S GO!
VROOOOOOM

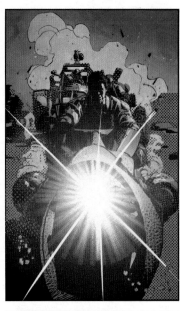

NO RIDER, SIR.

IT'S A *TRAP!* FALL BACK!

NOW!

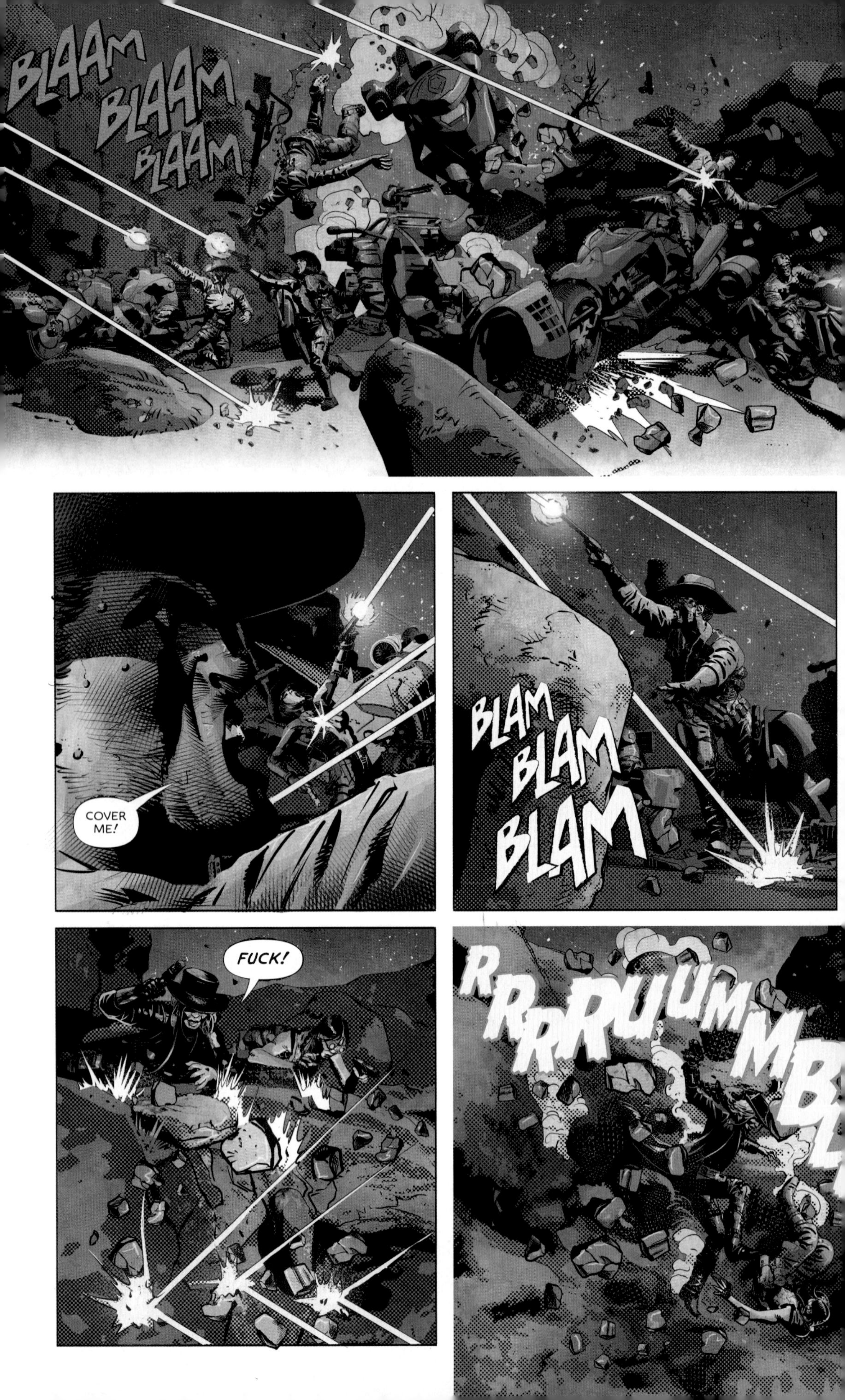
BLAAM
BLAAM
BLAAM
COVER ME!
BLAM
BLAM
BLAM
FUCK!
RRRRUUMMBL

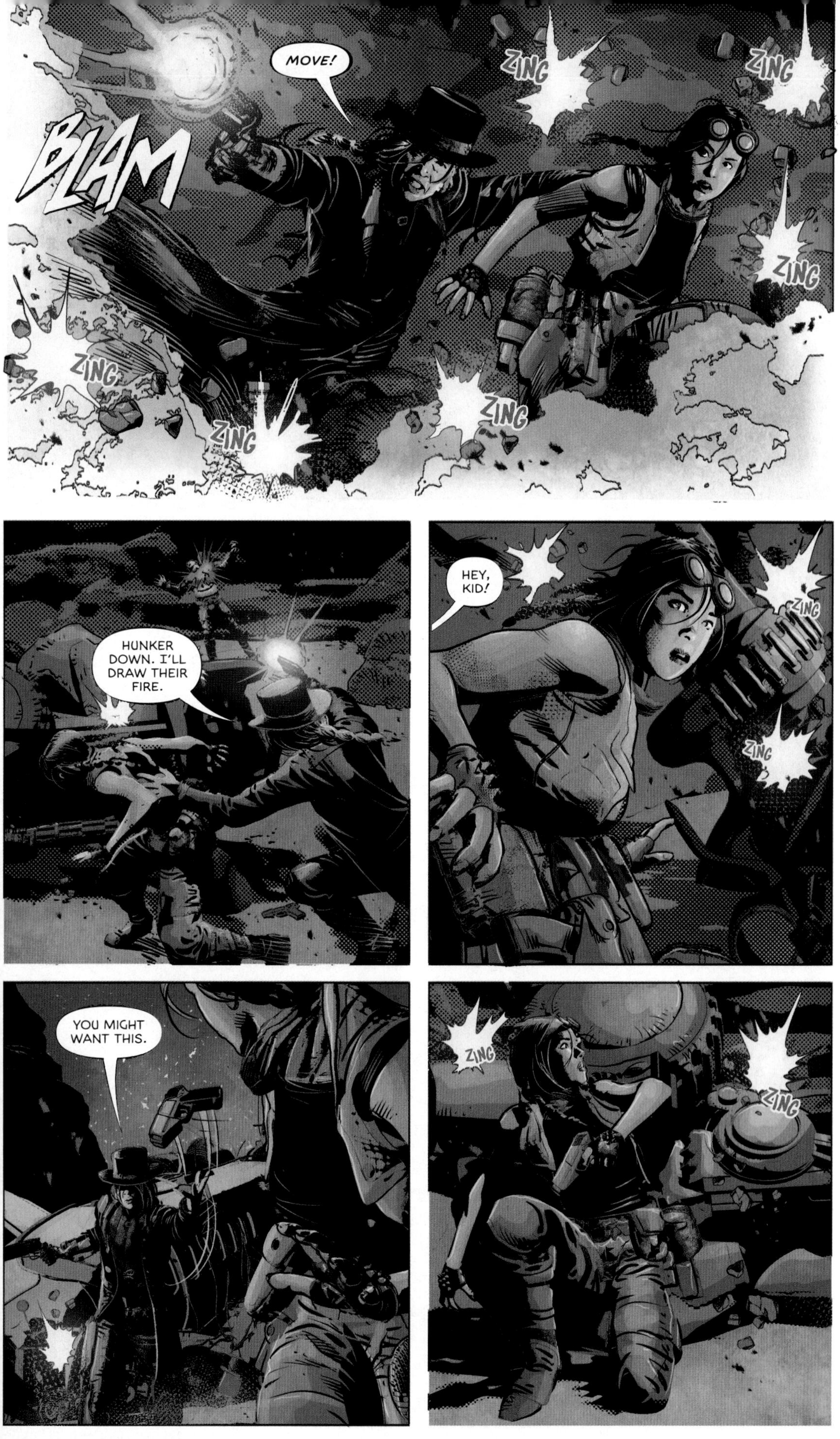
BLAM
MOVE!
ZING
ZING
ZING
ZING
ZING
ZING
HUNKER DOWN. I'LL DRAW THEIR FIRE.
HEY, KID!
ZING
ZING
YOU MIGHT WANT THIS.
ZING
ZING

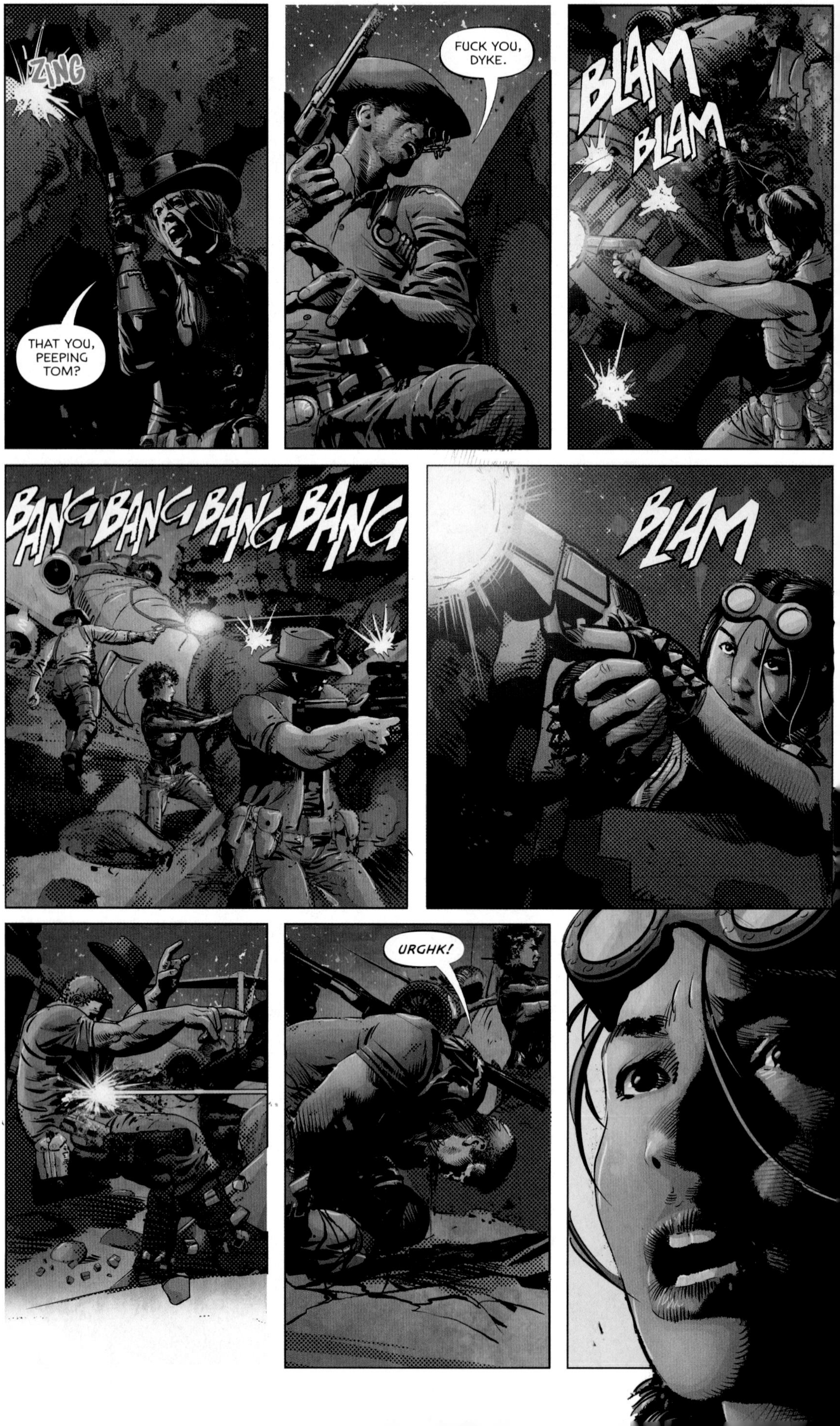
ZING
THAT YOU, PEEPING TOM?
FUCK YOU, DYKE.
BLAM
BLAM
BANG BANG BANG BANG
BLAM
URGHK!

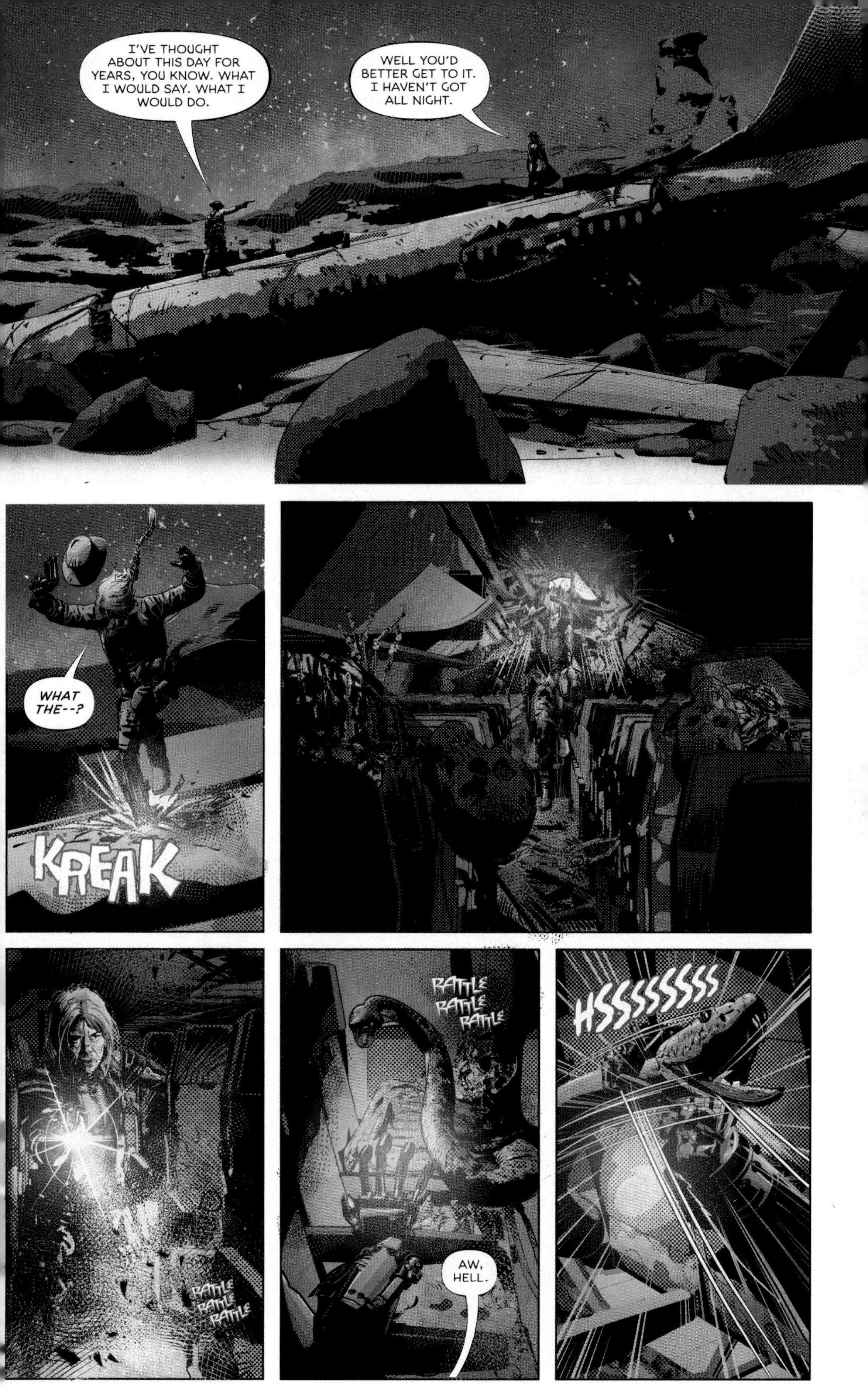
I'VE THOUGHT ABOUT THIS DAY FOR YEARS, YOU KNOW. WHAT I WOULD SAY. WHAT I WOULD DO.
WELL YOU'D BETTER GET TO IT. I HAVEN'T GOT ALL NIGHT.
WHAT THE--?
KREAK
RATTLE RATTLE RATTLE
RATTLE RATTLE RATTLE
AW, HELL.
HSSSSSSSS

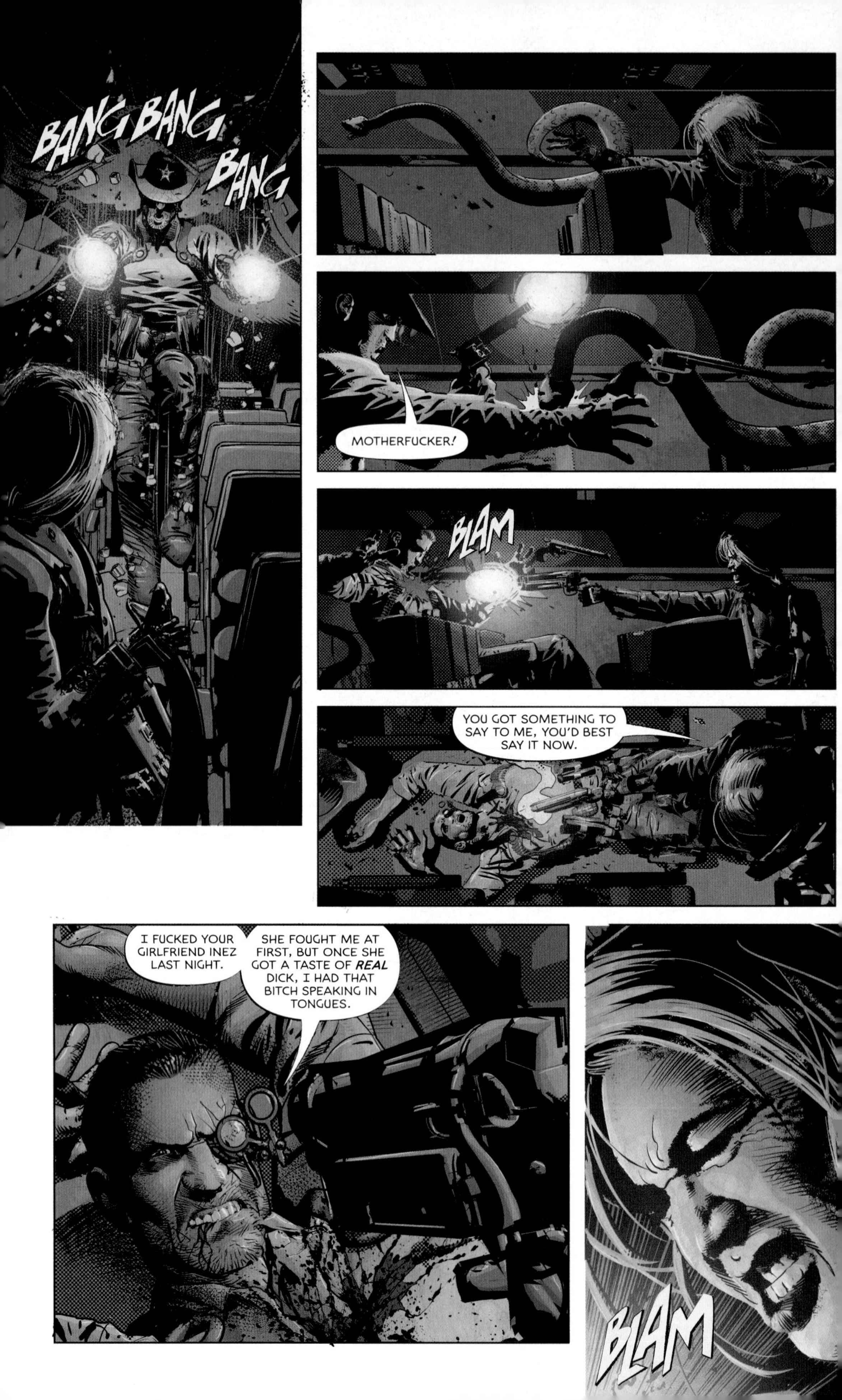
BANG BANG BANG
MOTHERFUCKER!
BLAM
YOU GOT SOMETHING TO SAY TO ME, YOU'D BEST SAY IT NOW.
I FUCKED YOUR GIRLFRIEND INEZ LAST NIGHT.
SHE FOUGHT ME AT FIRST, BUT ONCE SHE GOT A TASTE OF *REAL* DICK, I HAD THAT BITCH SPEAKING IN TONGUES.
BLAM

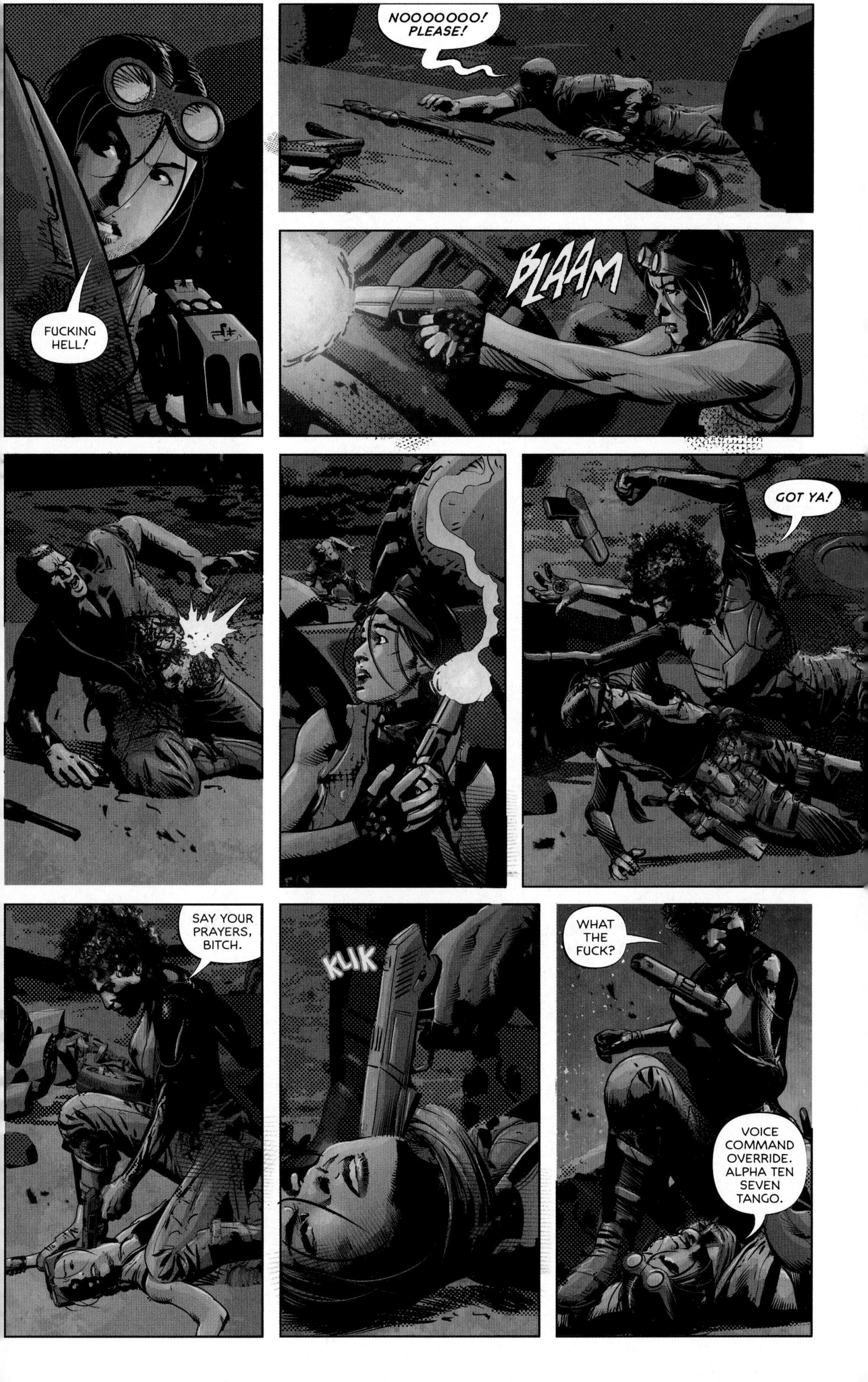
FUCKING HELL!
NOOOOOOO! PLEASE!
BLAAM
GOT YA!
SAY YOUR PRAYERS, BITCH.
KLIK
WHAT THE FUCK?
VOICE COMMAND OVERRIDE. ALPHA TEN SEVEN TANGO.

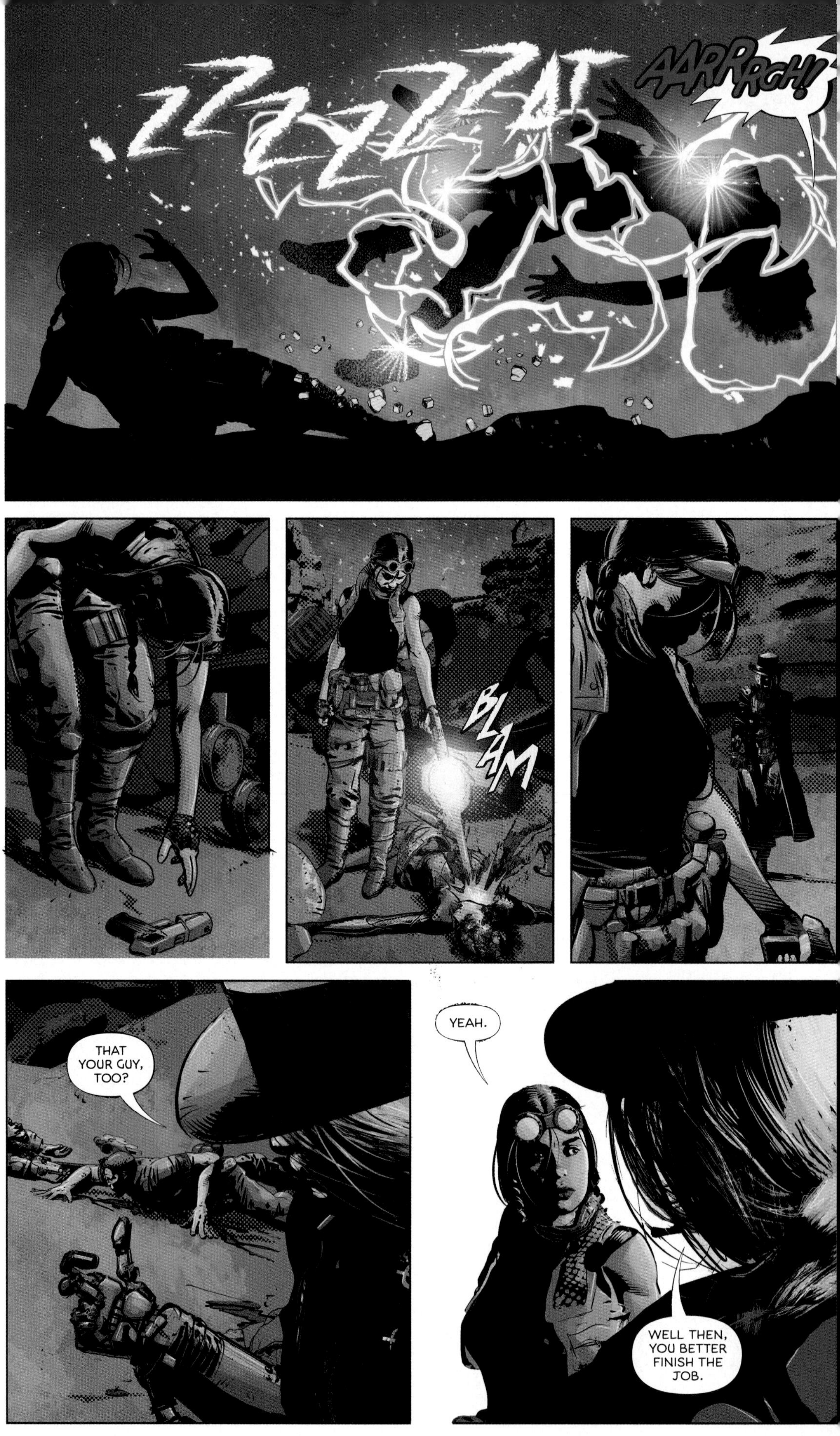
ZZZZZAT
AARRRGH!
BLAM
THAT YOUR GUY, TOO?
YEAH.
WELL THEN, YOU BETTER FINISH THE JOB.

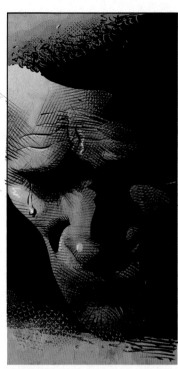

GOOD JOB, KID.

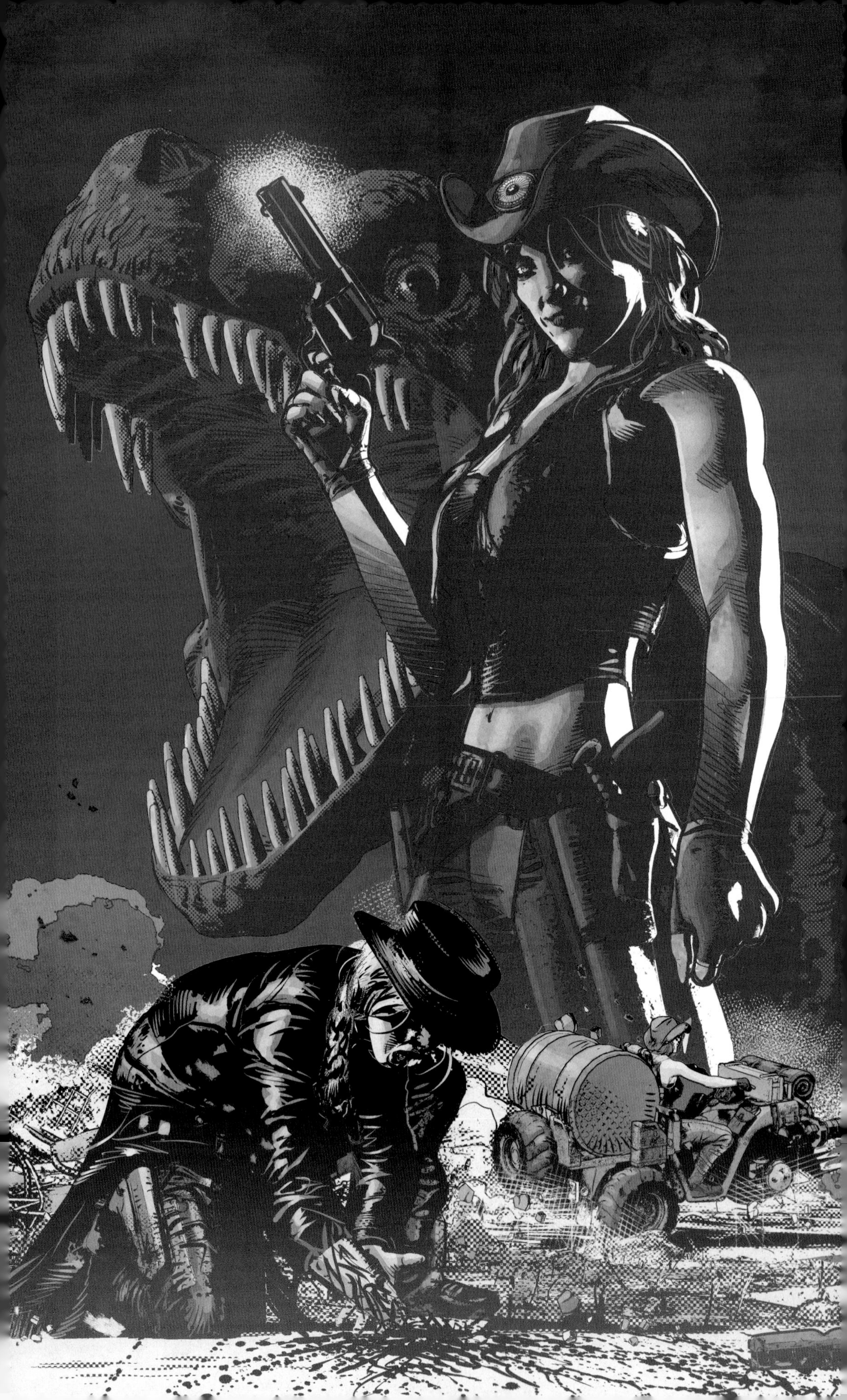

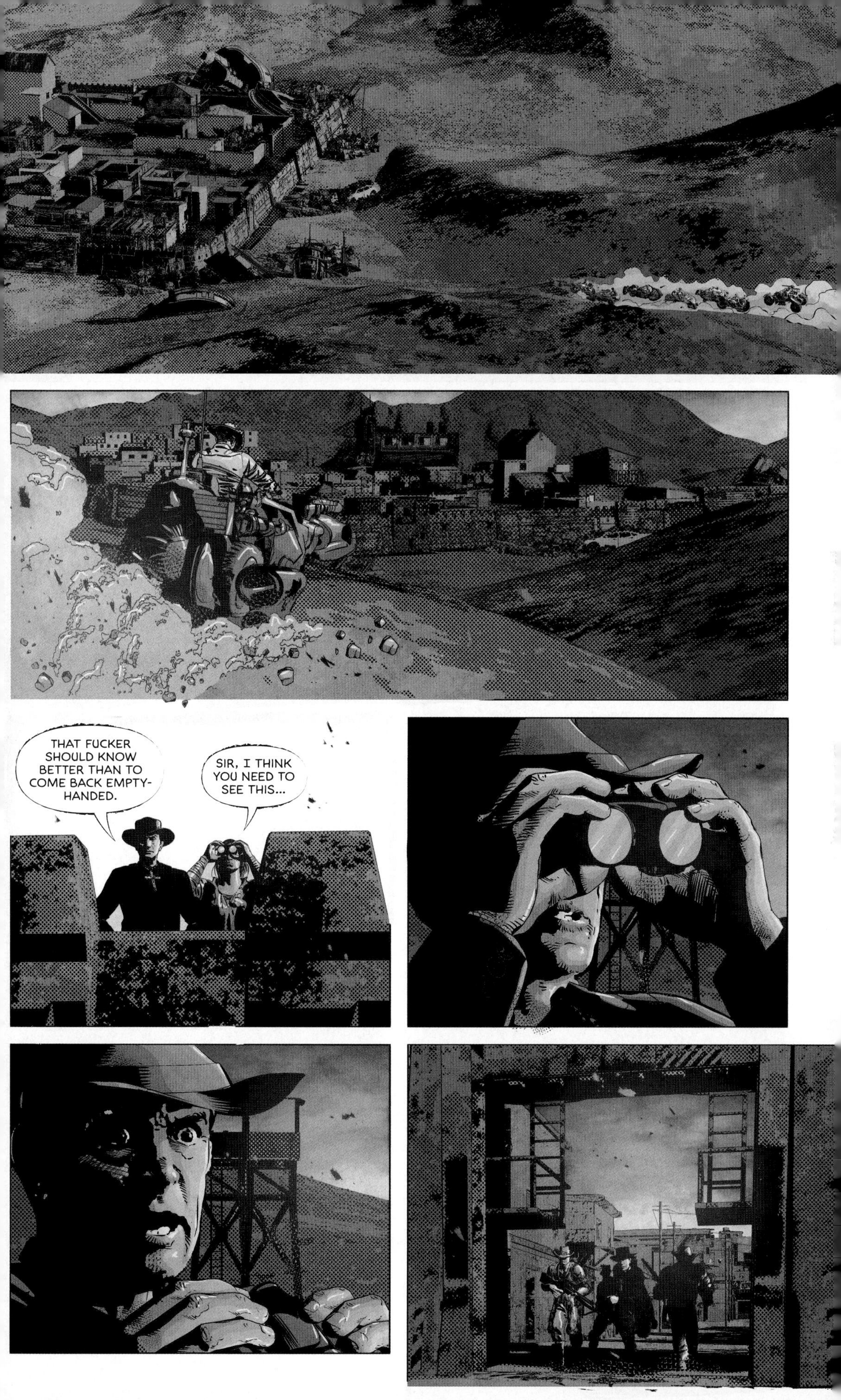
THAT FUCKER SHOULD KNOW BETTER THAN TO COME BACK EMPTY-HANDED.
SIR, I THINK YOU NEED TO SEE THIS...

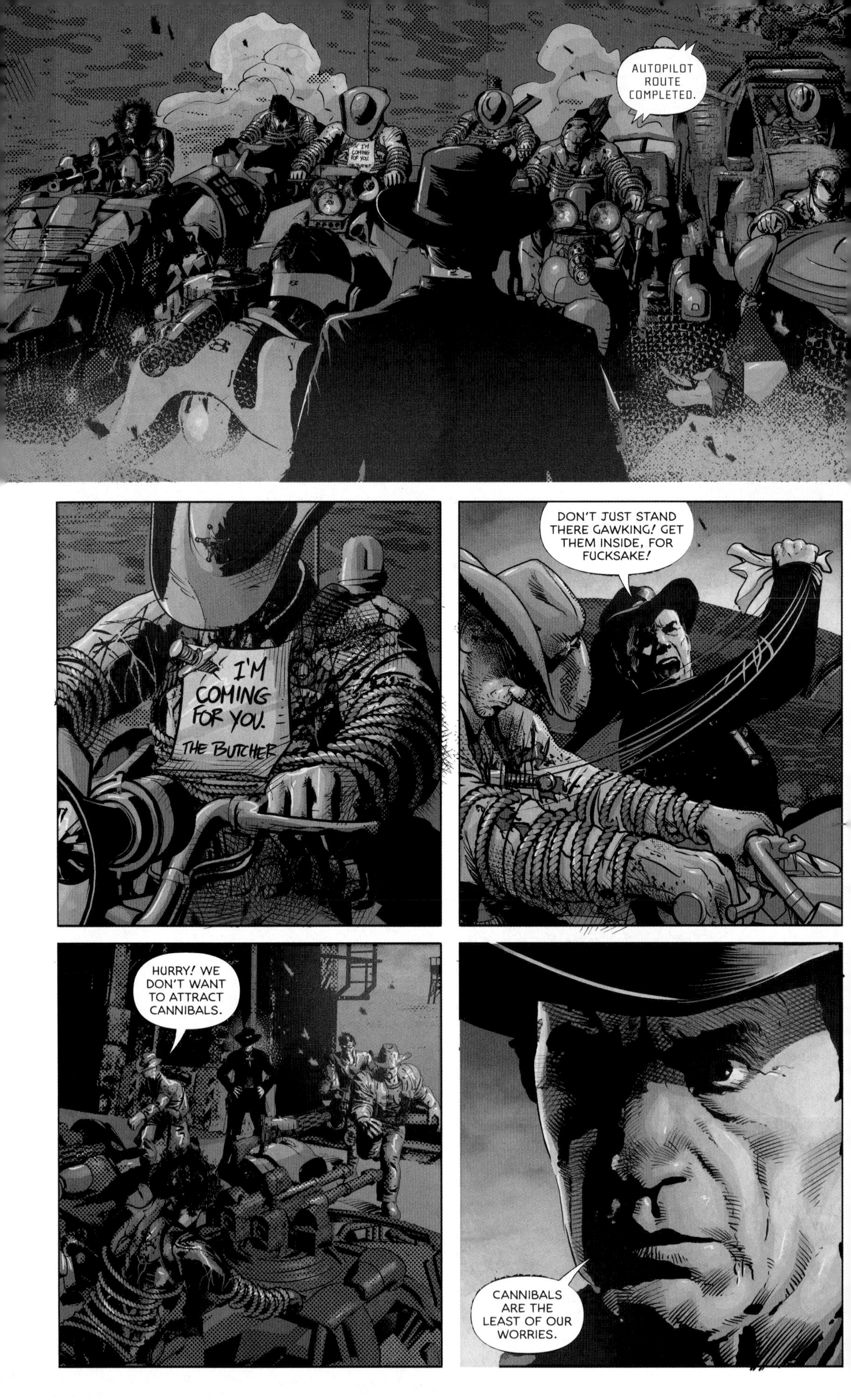
AUTOPILOT ROUTE COMPLETED.
I'M COMING FOR YOU. THE BUTCHER
DON'T JUST STAND THERE GAWKING! GET THEM INSIDE, FOR FUCKSAKE!
HURRY! WE DON'T WANT TO ATTRACT CANNIBALS.
CANNIBALS ARE THE LEAST OF OUR WORRIES.

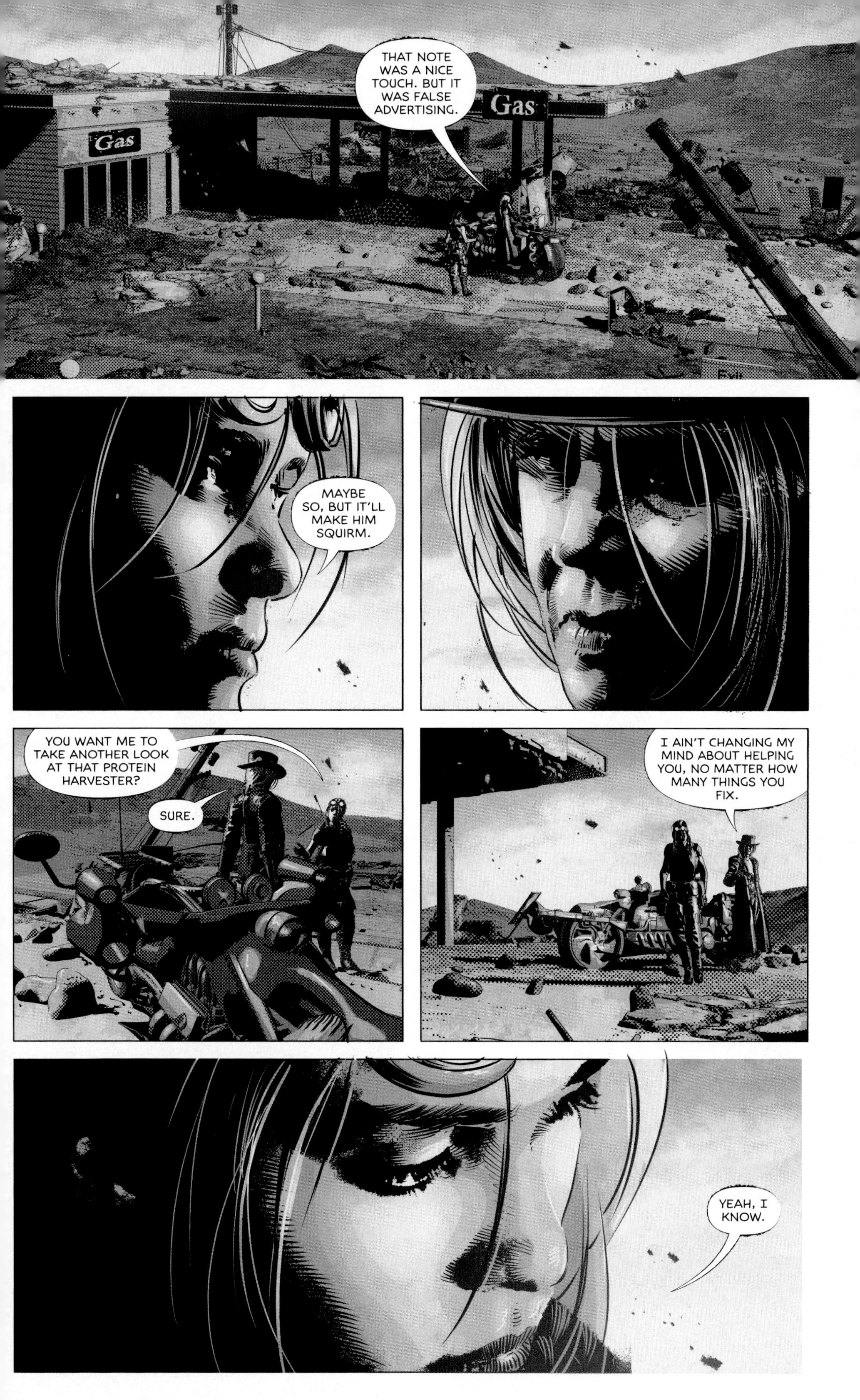

Gas
Gas
THAT NOTE WAS A NICE TOUCH. BUT IT WAS FALSE ADVERTISING.
MAYBE SO, BUT IT'LL MAKE HIM SQUIRM.
YOU WANT ME TO TAKE ANOTHER LOOK AT THAT PROTEIN HARVESTER?
SURE.
I AIN'T CHANGING MY MIND ABOUT HELPING YOU, NO MATTER HOW MANY THINGS YOU FIX.
YEAH, I KNOW.

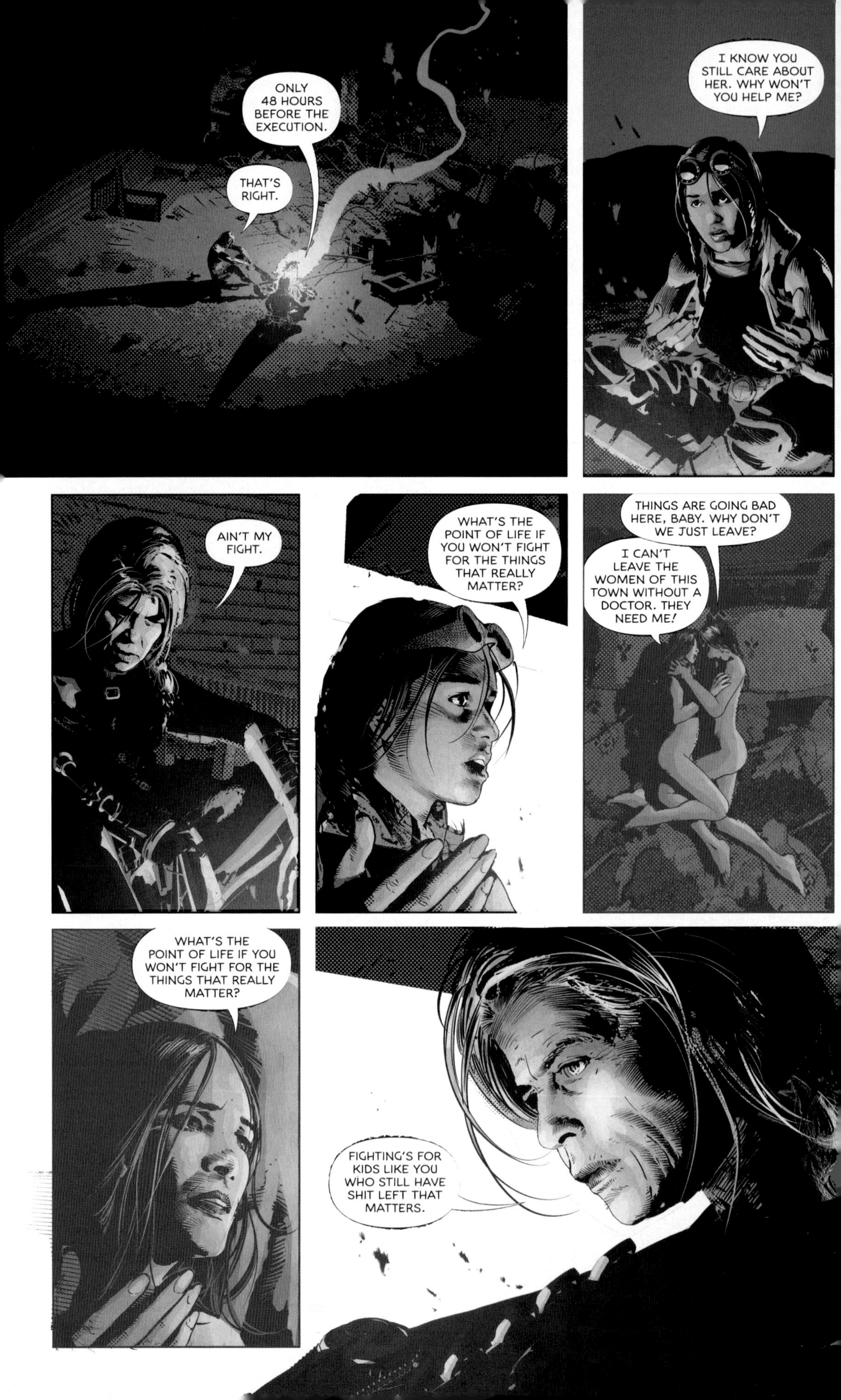
ONLY 48 HOURS BEFORE THE EXECUTION.
THAT'S RIGHT.
I KNOW YOU STILL CARE ABOUT HER. WHY WON'T YOU HELP ME?
AIN'T MY FIGHT.
WHAT'S THE POINT OF LIFE IF YOU WON'T FIGHT FOR THE THINGS THAT REALLY MATTER?
THINGS ARE GOING BAD HERE, BABY. WHY DON'T WE JUST LEAVE?
I CAN'T LEAVE THE WOMEN OF THIS TOWN WITHOUT A DOCTOR. THEY NEED ME!
WHAT'S THE POINT OF LIFE IF YOU WON'T FIGHT FOR THE THINGS THAT REALLY MATTER?
FIGHTING'S FOR KIDS LIKE YOU WHO STILL HAVE SHIT LEFT THAT MATTERS.

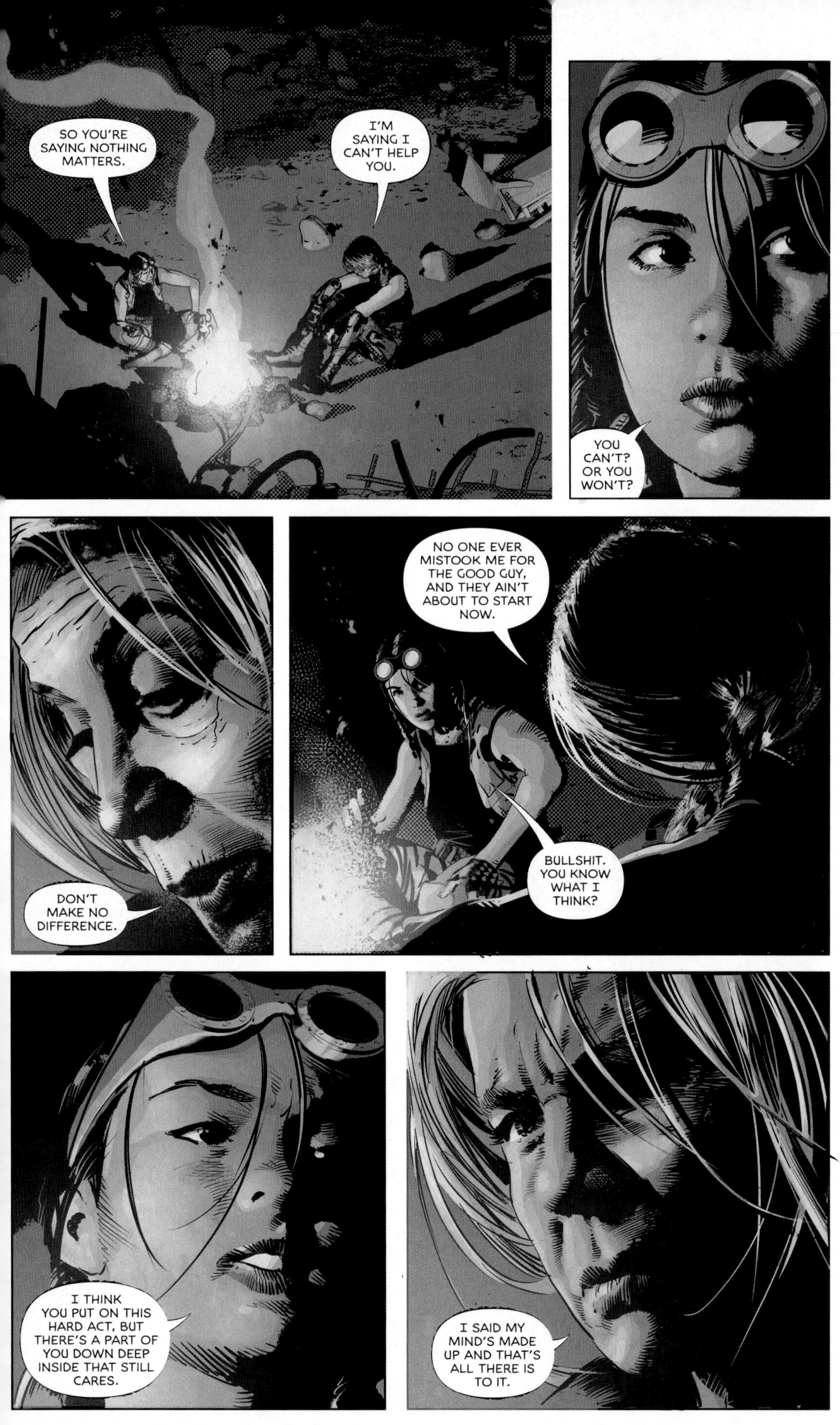
SO YOU'RE SAYING NOTHING MATTERS.
I'M SAYING I CAN'T HELP YOU.
YOU CAN'T? OR YOU WON'T?
DON'T MAKE NO DIFFERENCE.
NO ONE EVER MISTOOK ME FOR THE GOOD GUY, AND THEY AIN'T ABOUT TO START NOW.
BULLSHIT. YOU KNOW WHAT I THINK?
I THINK YOU PUT ON THIS HARD ACT, BUT THERE'S A PART OF YOU DOWN DEEP INSIDE THAT STILL CARES.
I SAID MY MIND'S MADE UP AND THAT'S ALL THERE IS TO IT.

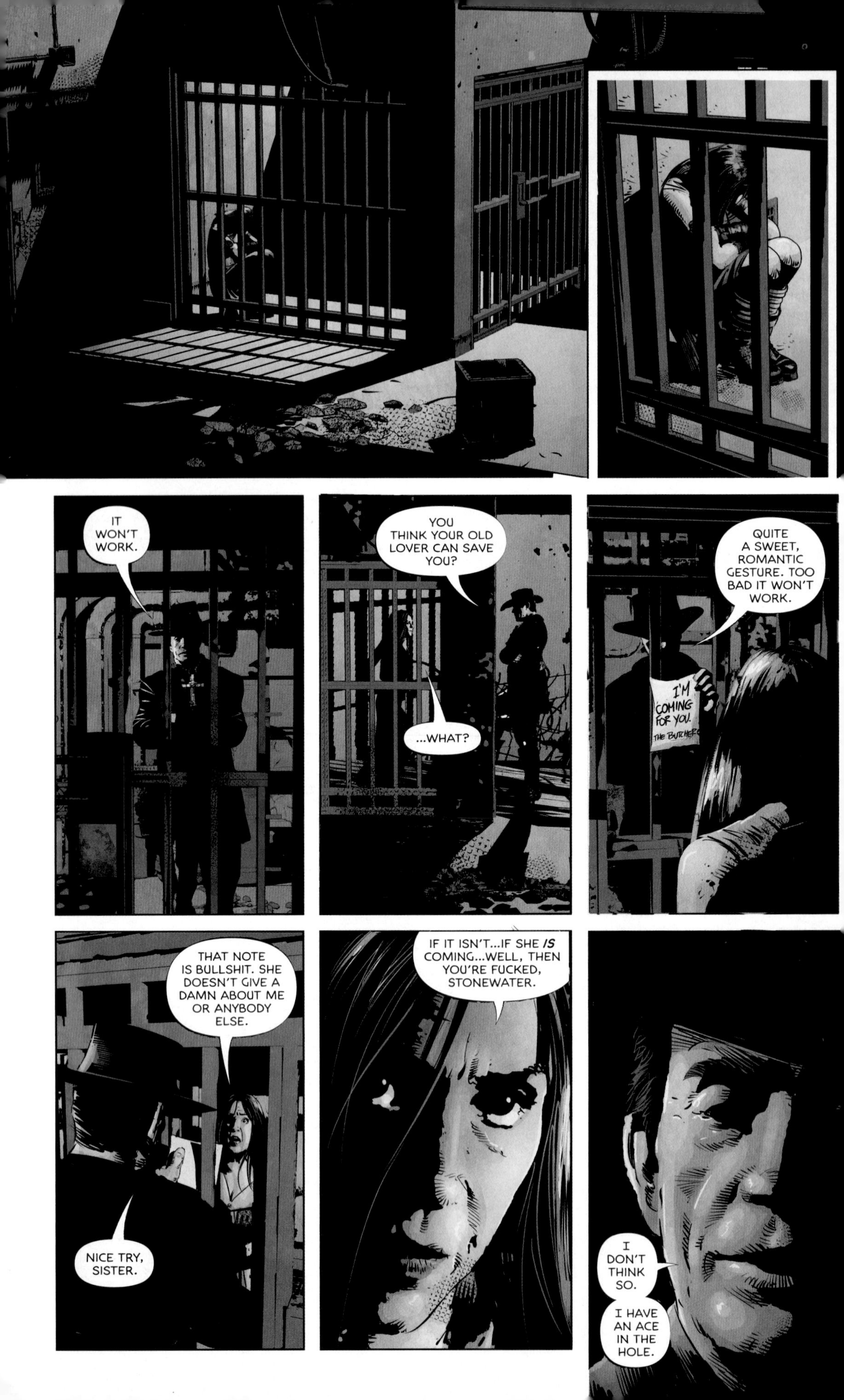
IT WON'T WORK.
YOU THINK YOUR OLD LOVER CAN SAVE YOU?
...WHAT?
QUITE A SWEET, ROMANTIC GESTURE. TOO BAD IT WON'T WORK.
I'M COMING FOR YOU. THE BUTCHER
THAT NOTE IS BULLSHIT. SHE DOESN'T GIVE A DAMN ABOUT ME OR ANYBODY ELSE.
NICE TRY, SISTER.
IF IT ISN'T...IF SHE *IS* COMING...WELL, THEN YOU'RE FUCKED, STONEWATER.
I DON'T THINK SO.
I HAVE AN ACE IN THE HOLE.

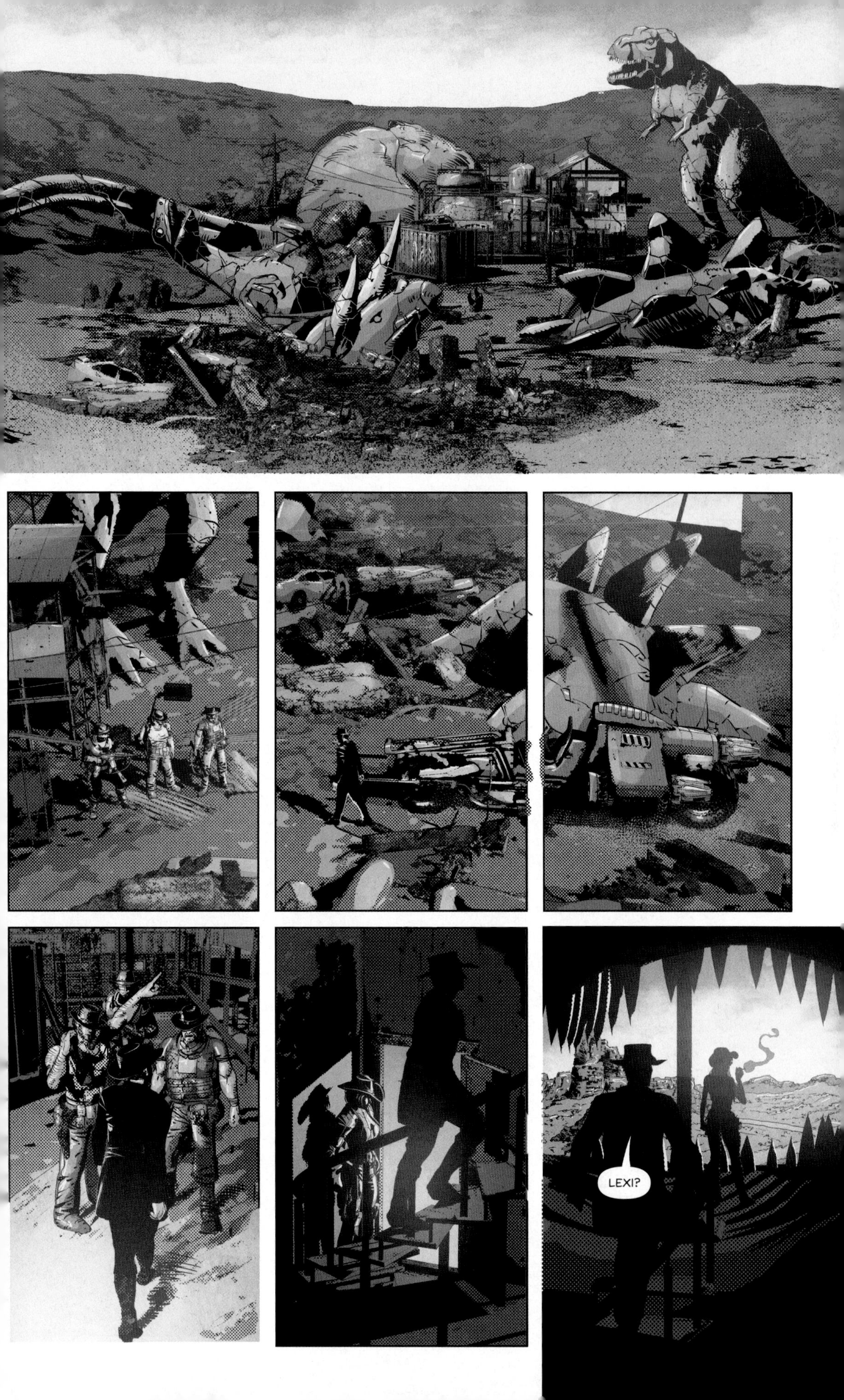
LEXI?

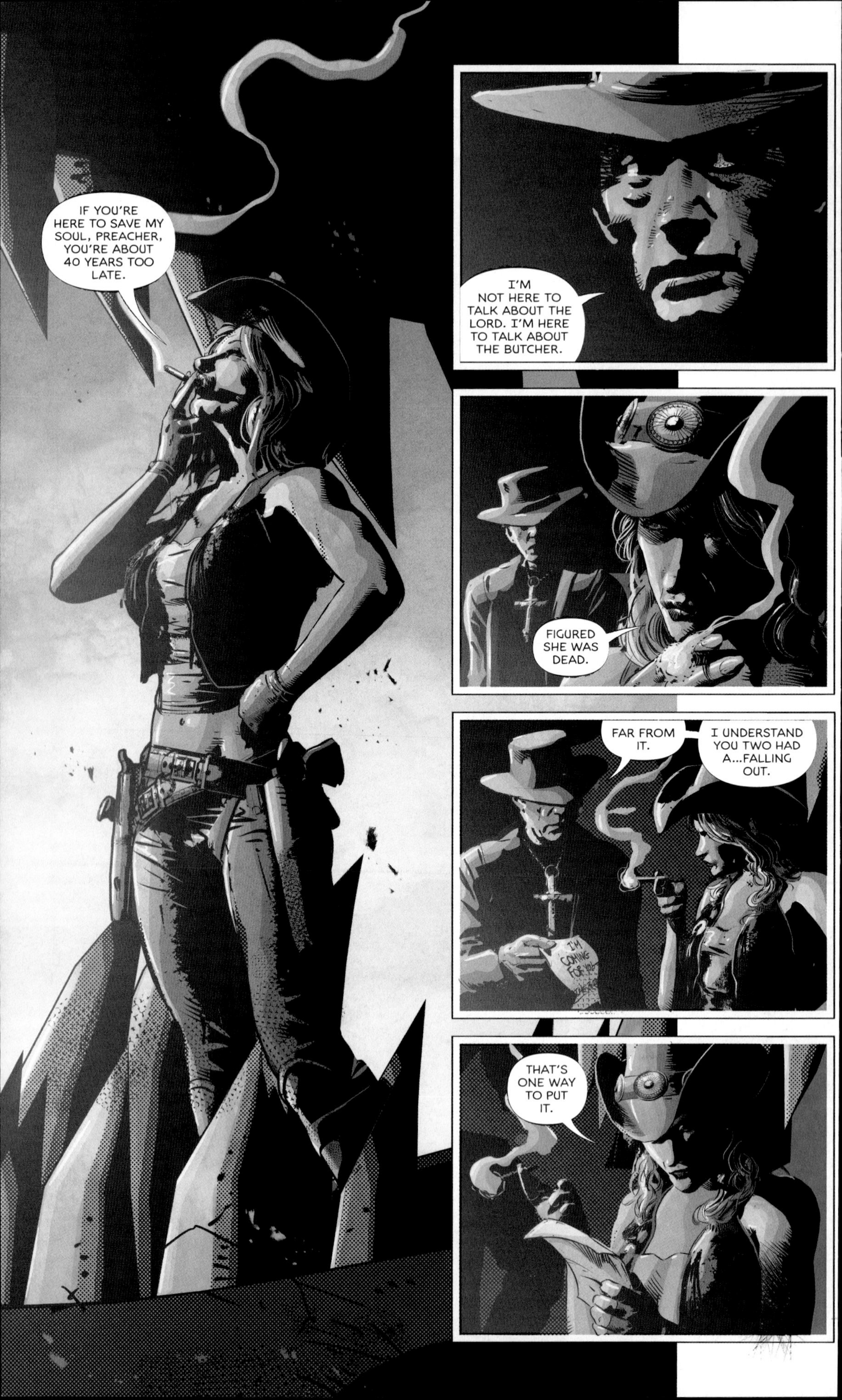
IF YOU'RE HERE TO SAVE MY SOUL, PREACHER, YOU'RE ABOUT 40 YEARS TOO LATE.
I'M NOT HERE TO TALK ABOUT THE LORD. I'M HERE TO TALK ABOUT THE BUTCHER.
FIGURED SHE WAS DEAD.
FAR FROM IT.
I UNDERSTAND YOU TWO HAD A...FALLING OUT.
I'M COMING FOR YOU
THAT'S ONE WAY TO PUT IT.

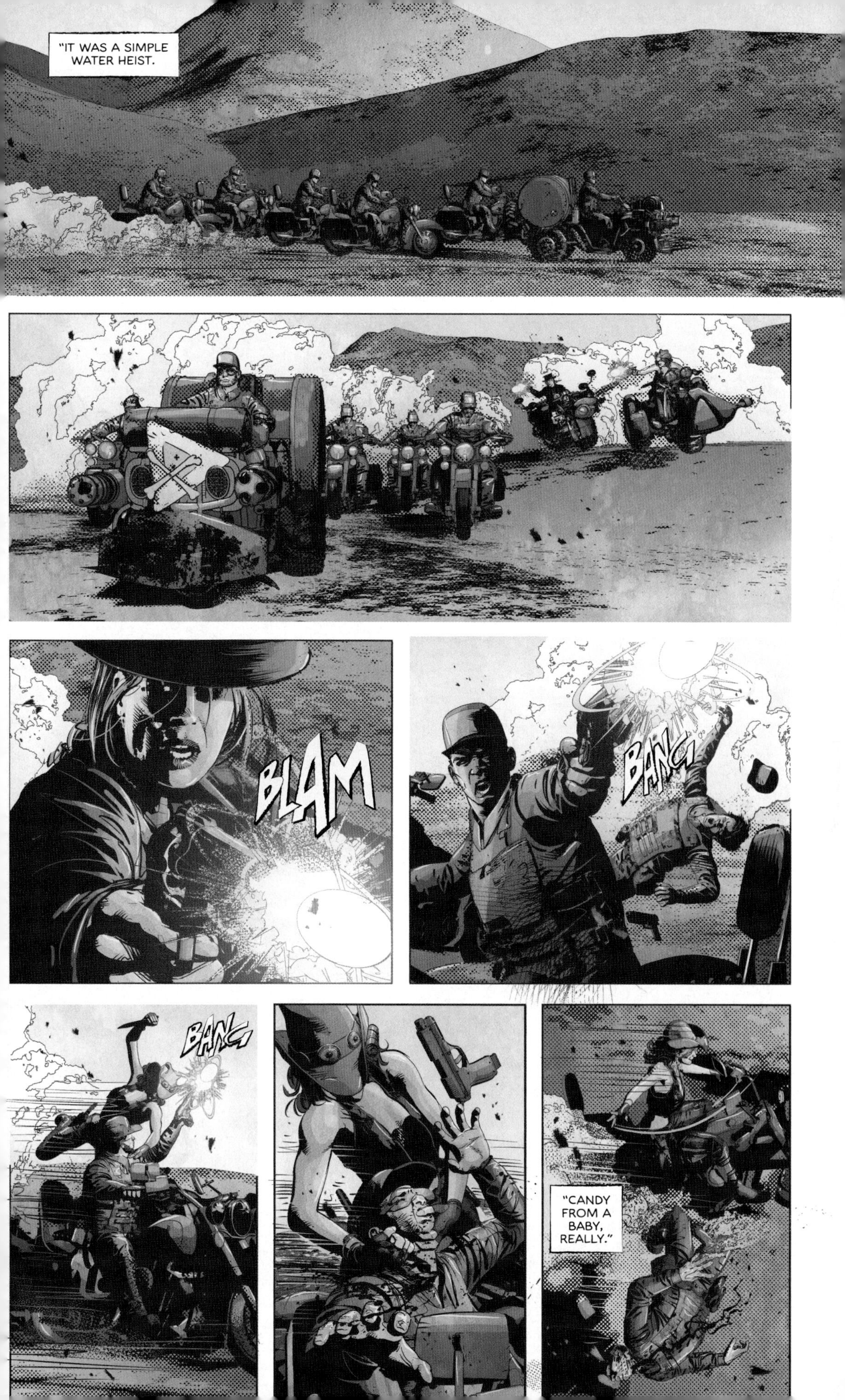
"IT WAS A SIMPLE WATER HEIST.
BLAM
BANG
BANG
"CANDY FROM A BABY, REALLY."

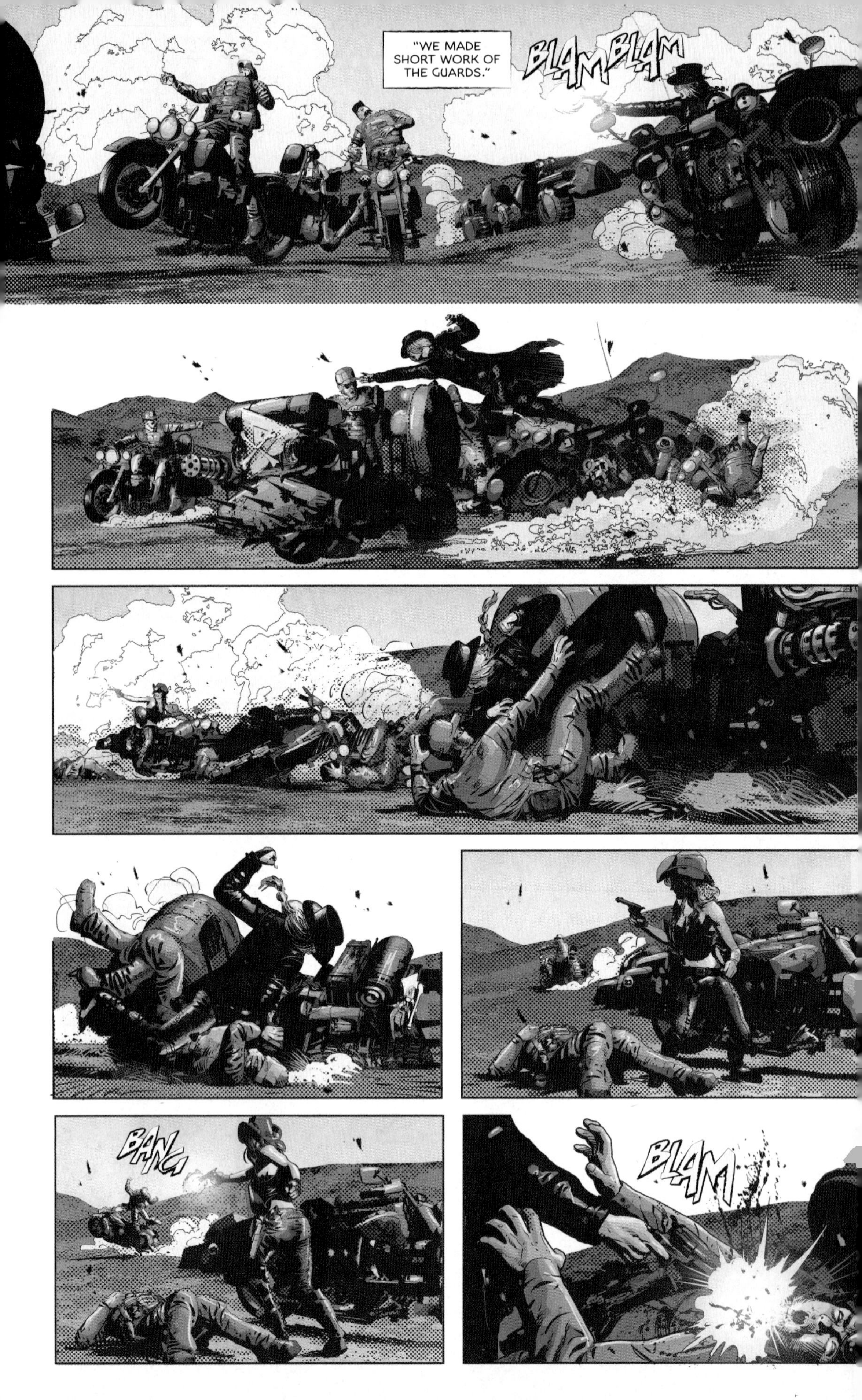
"WE MADE SHORT WORK OF THE GUARDS."
BLAM BLAM
BANG
BLAM

"IT WAS THE KIND OF JOB WE COULD HAVE PULLED IN OUR SLEEP.

"THAT'S WHAT MADE IT PERFECT.

MUST HAVE DROPPED MY SPEEDLOADER IN THE TUSSLE.

NO PROBLEM. I HAVE A SPARE.

"OF COURSE, SHE DIDN'T DROP IT.

"I USED TO BE A PICKPOCKET AND A CARD SHARP BEFORE I BECAME A KILLER, SO IT WAS NO PROBLEM FOR ME TO LIFT THAT SPEEDLOADER. PEOPLE WHO TRUST YOU ARE THE EASIEST TO STEAL FROM.

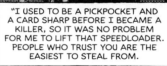

KLIK

"AND THE ONE I GAVE HER INSTEAD WAS LOADED WITH A LITTLE SURPRISE."

I'LL BE TAKING ALL THE WATER.

ARE YOU SURE THIS IS WHAT YOU WANT?

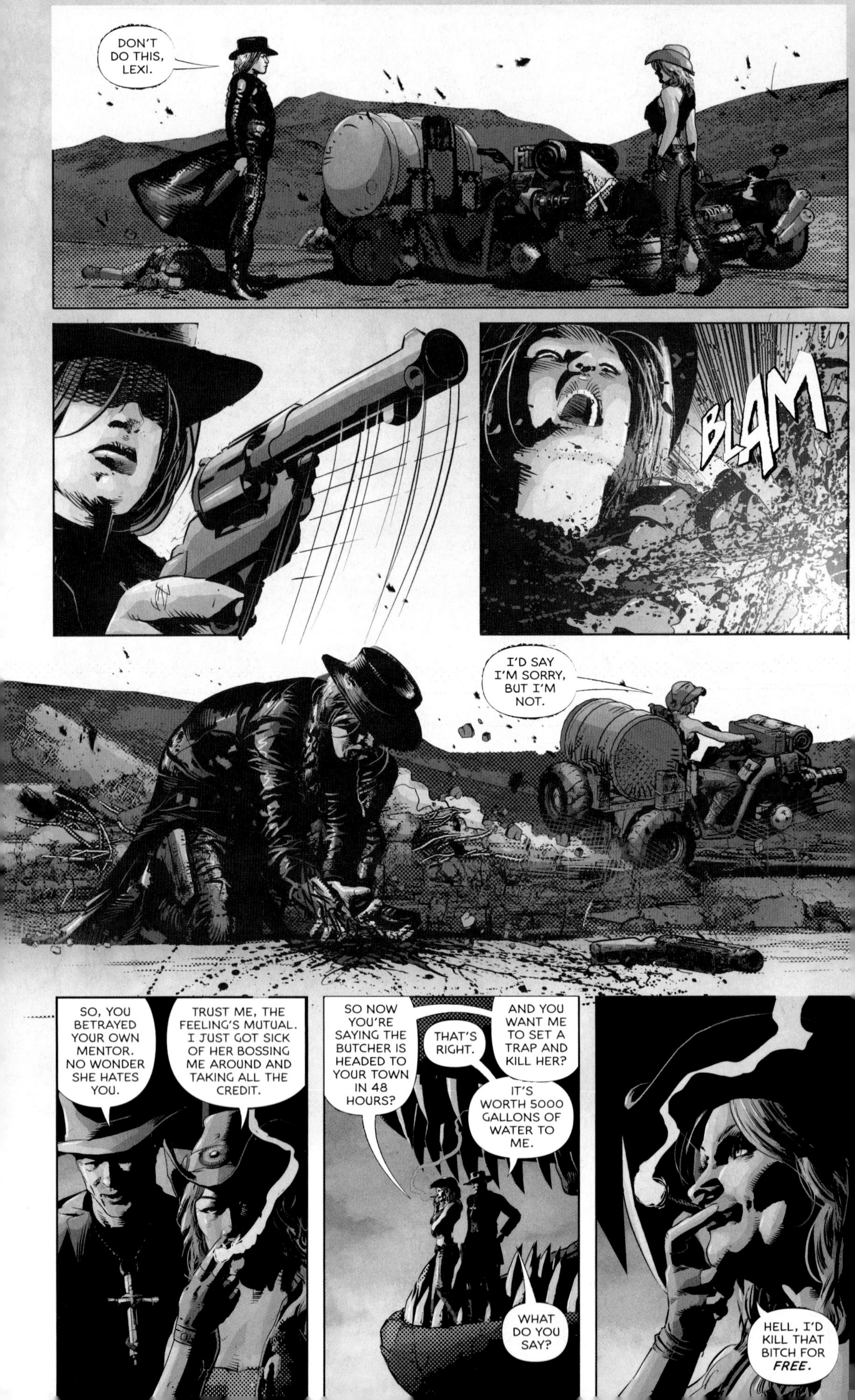
DON'T DO THIS, LEXI.
BLAM
I'D SAY I'M SORRY, BUT I'M NOT.
SO, YOU BETRAYED YOUR OWN MENTOR. NO WONDER SHE HATES YOU.
TRUST ME, THE FEELING'S MUTUAL. I JUST GOT SICK OF HER BOSSING ME AROUND AND TAKING ALL THE CREDIT.
SO NOW YOU'RE SAYING THE BUTCHER IS HEADED TO YOUR TOWN IN 48 HOURS?
THAT'S RIGHT.
AND YOU WANT ME TO SET A TRAP AND KILL HER?
IT'S WORTH 5000 GALLONS OF WATER TO ME.
WHAT DO YOU SAY?
HELL, I'D KILL THAT BITCH FOR *FREE.*

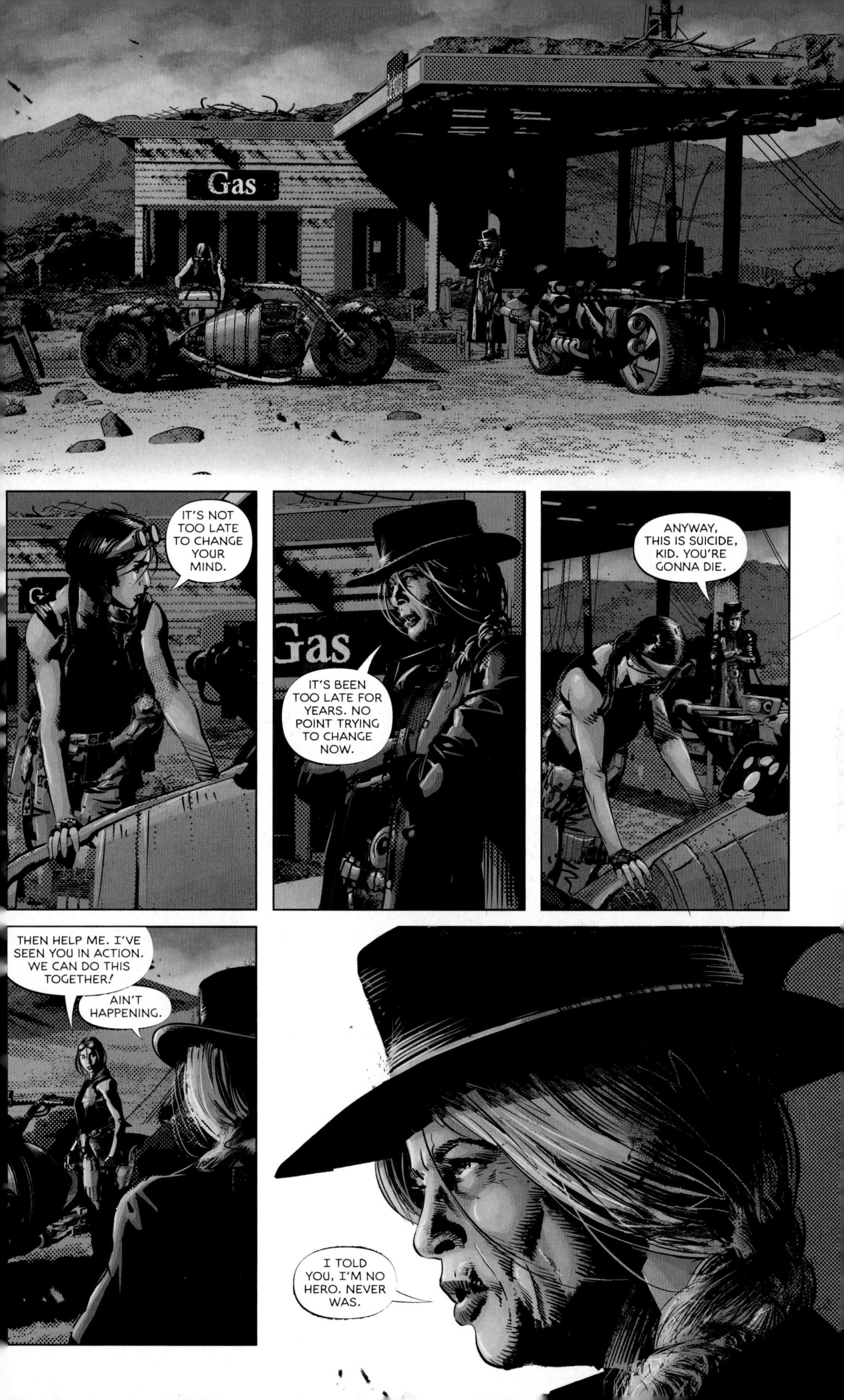
Gas
IT'S NOT TOO LATE TO CHANGE YOUR MIND.
Gas
IT'S BEEN TOO LATE FOR YEARS. NO POINT TRYING TO CHANGE NOW.
ANYWAY, THIS IS SUICIDE, KID. YOU'RE GONNA DIE.
THEN HELP ME. I'VE SEEN YOU IN ACTION. WE CAN DO THIS TOGETHER!
AIN'T HAPPENING.
I TOLD YOU, I'M NO HERO. NEVER WAS.

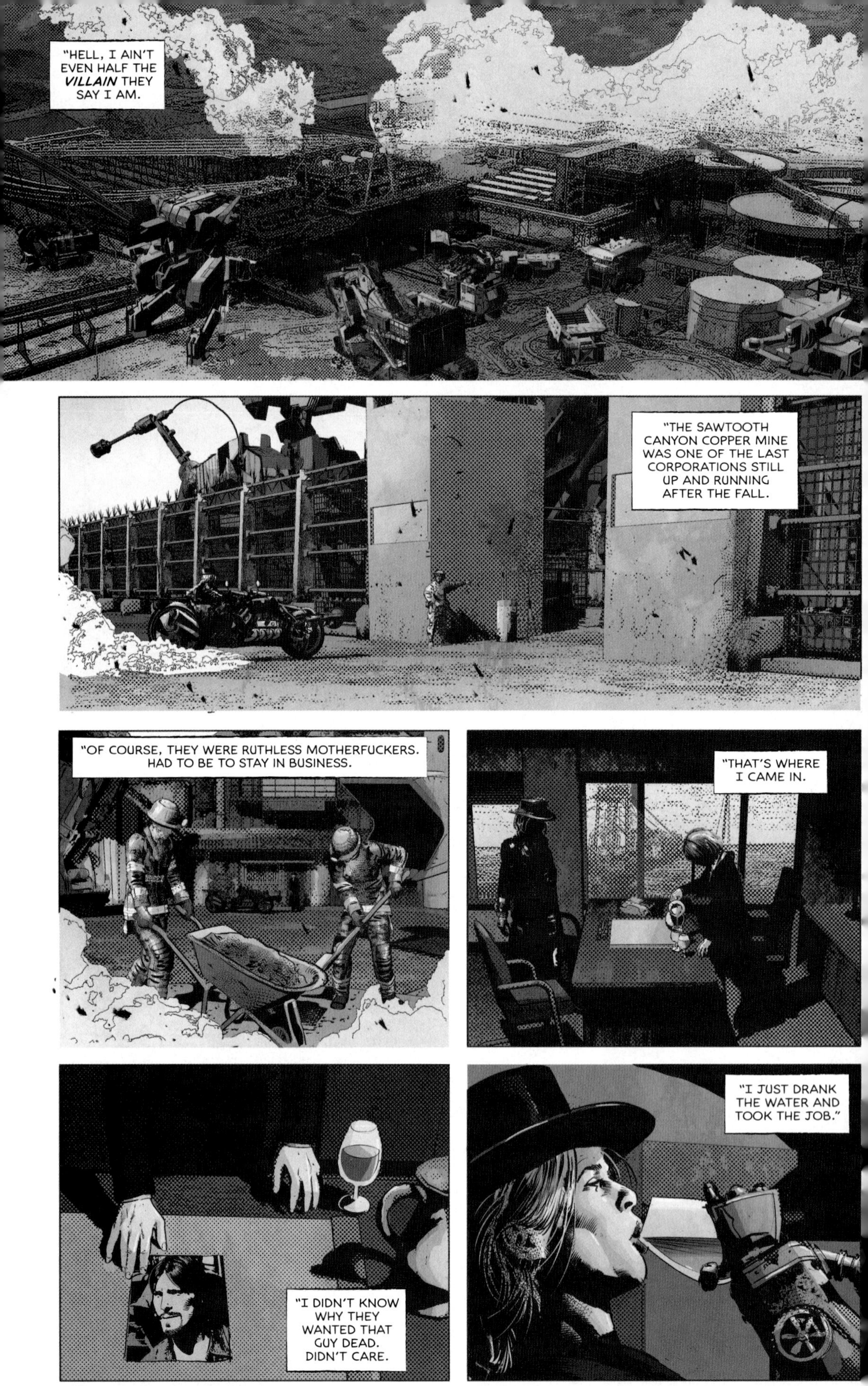
"HELL, I AIN'T EVEN HALF THE *VILLAIN* THEY SAY I AM.
"THE SAWTOOTH CANYON COPPER MINE WAS ONE OF THE LAST CORPORATIONS STILL UP AND RUNNING AFTER THE FALL.
"OF COURSE, THEY WERE RUTHLESS MOTHERFUCKERS. HAD TO BE TO STAY IN BUSINESS.
"THAT'S WHERE I CAME IN.
"I DIDN'T KNOW WHY THEY WANTED THAT GUY DEAD. DIDN'T CARE.
"I JUST DRANK THE WATER AND TOOK THE JOB."

"THEY WANTED A SILENT KILLING AND WERE WILLING TO PAY EXTRA FOR IT. NO GUNS.

"THEY TOLD ME WHERE AND WHEN TO FIND HIM. NOT IN THE MAIN PART OF THE BAR LIKE THE LEGEND SAYS, BUT IN A PRIVATE ROOM IN THE BACK.

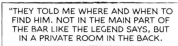

"BUT THEY DIDN'T TELL ME WHAT HE WAS DOING THERE.

UNITED WE BARGAIN! POWER TO THE WORKERS!

WHUMP

PRIVATE

"PAY WAS FOR ONE KILLING."

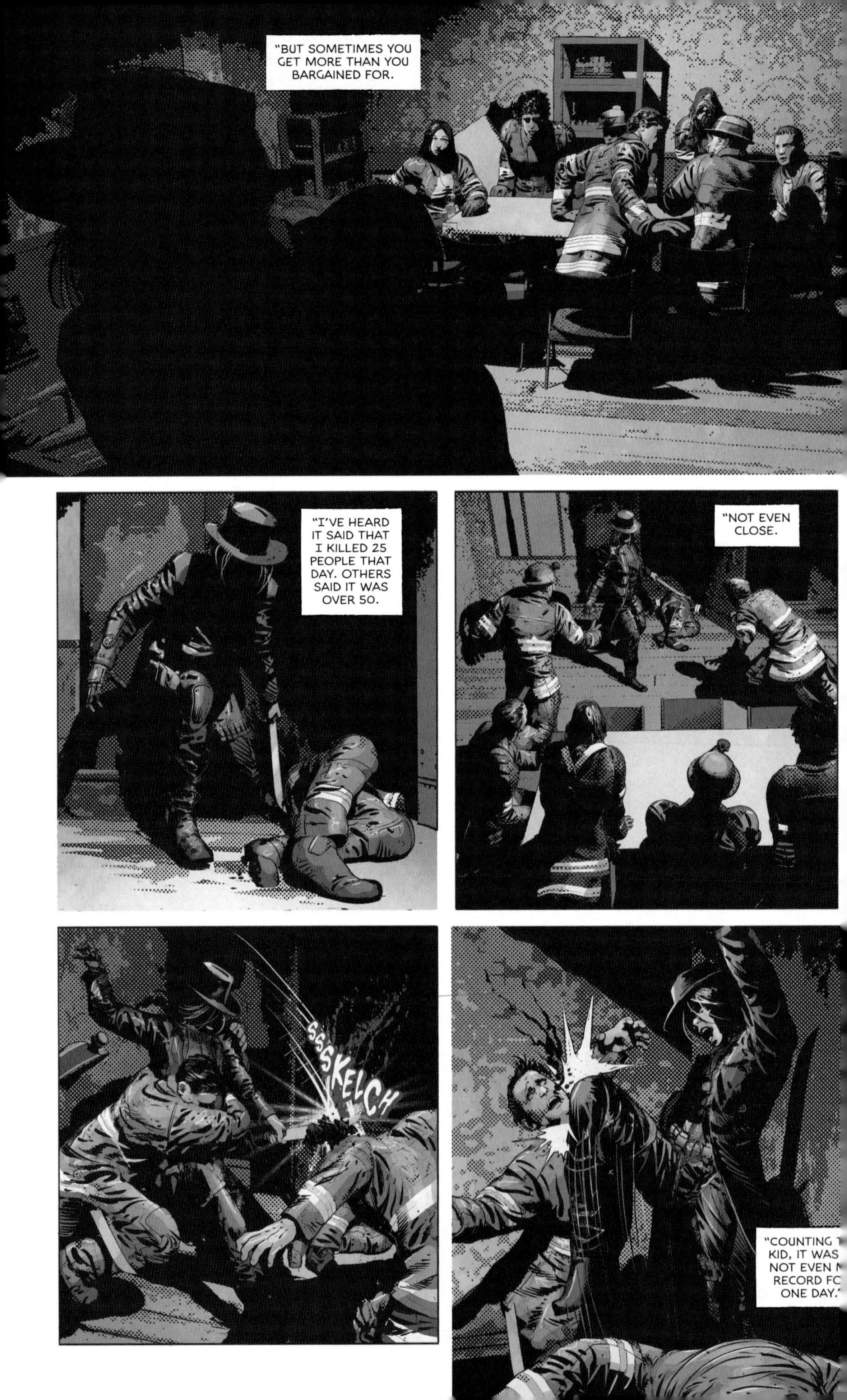
"BUT SOMETIMES YOU GET MORE THAN YOU BARGAINED FOR.
"I'VE HEARD IT SAID THAT I KILLED 25 PEOPLE THAT DAY. OTHERS SAID IT WAS OVER 50.
"NOT EVEN CLOSE.
SSSKELCH
"COUNTING T KID, IT WAS NOT EVEN M RECORD FO ONE DAY."

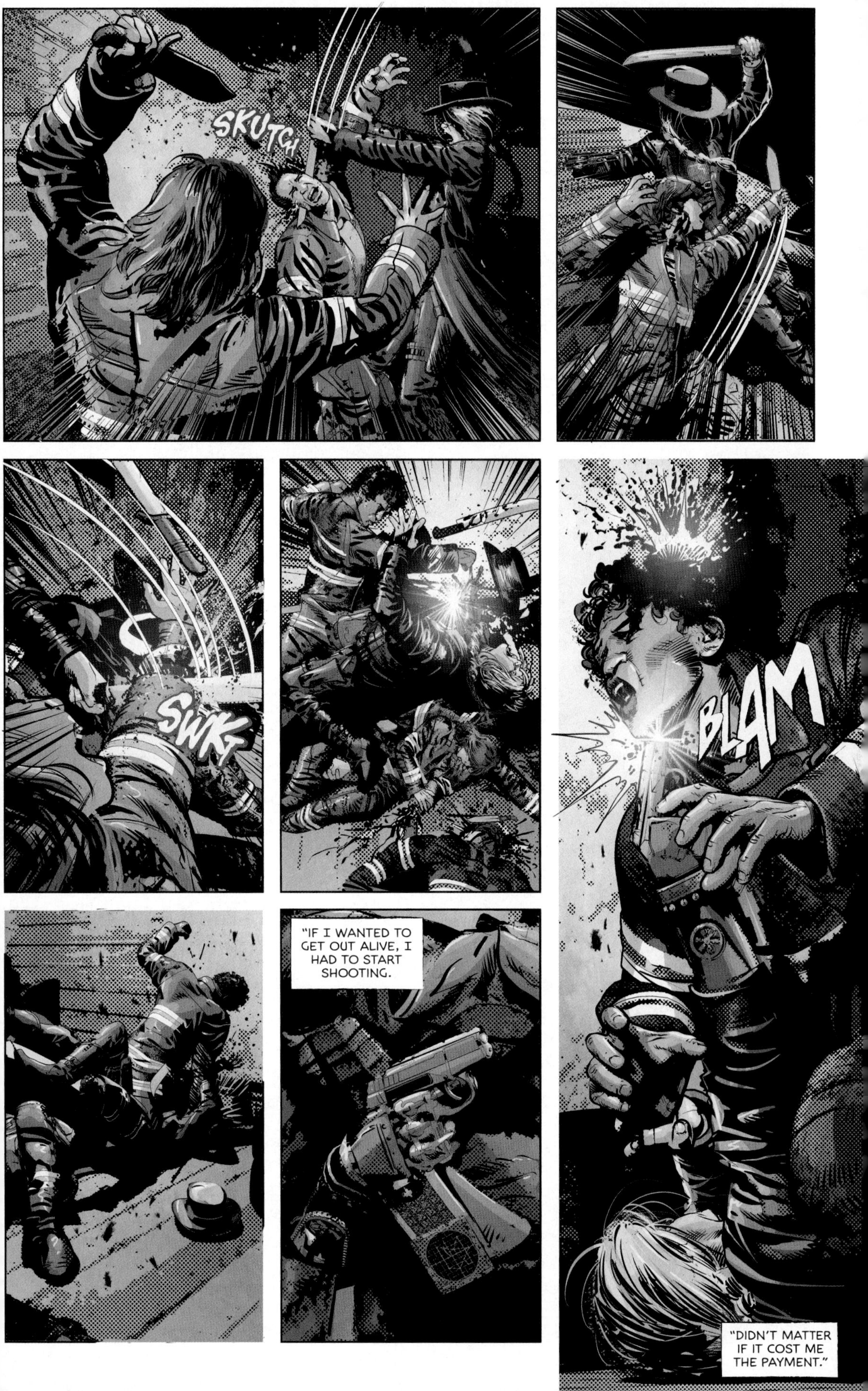
SKUTCH
SWKT
BLAM
"IF I WANTED TO GET OUT ALIVE, I HAD TO START SHOOTING.
"DIDN'T MATTER IF IT COST ME THE PAYMENT."

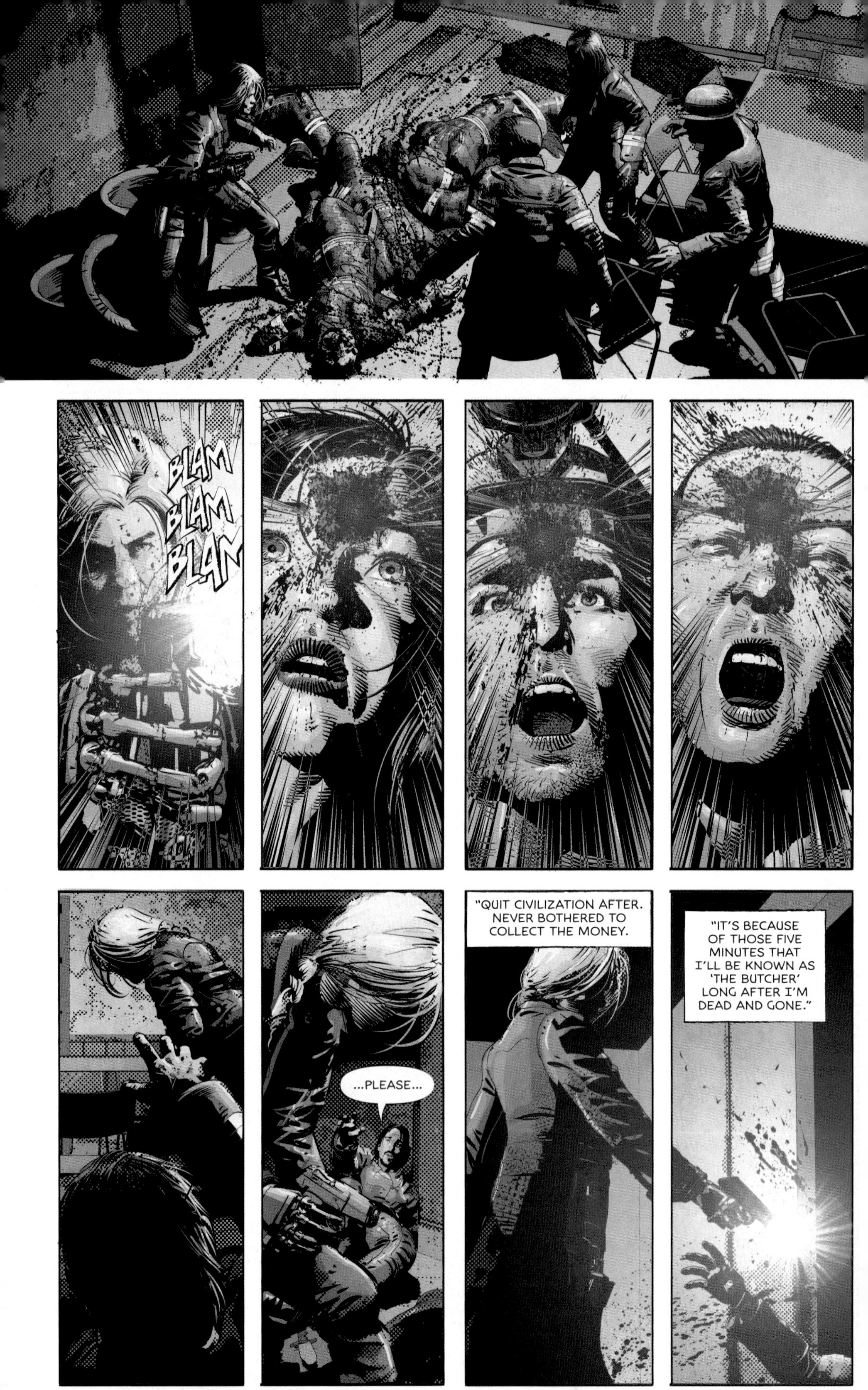
BLAM
BLAM
BLAM
"QUIT CIVILIZATION AFTER. NEVER BOTHERED TO COLLECT THE MONEY.
...PLEASE...
"IT'S BECAUSE OF THOSE FIVE MINUTES THAT I'LL BE KNOWN AS 'THE BUTCHER' LONG AFTER I'M DEAD AND GONE."

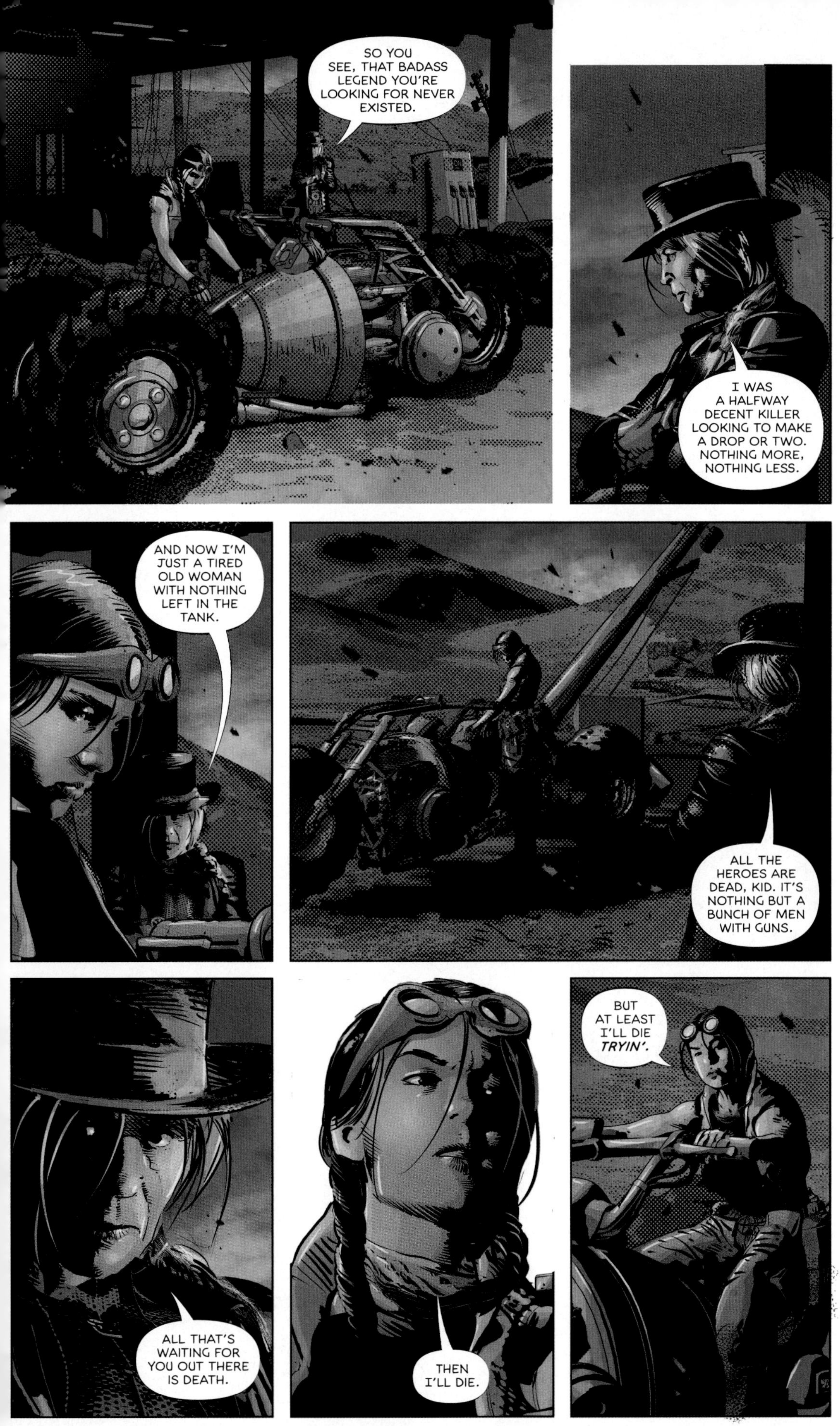
SO YOU SEE, THAT BADASS LEGEND YOU'RE LOOKING FOR NEVER EXISTED.
I WAS A HALFWAY DECENT KILLER LOOKING TO MAKE A DROP OR TWO. NOTHING MORE, NOTHING LESS.
AND NOW I'M JUST A TIRED OLD WOMAN WITH NOTHING LEFT IN THE TANK.
ALL THE HEROES ARE DEAD, KID. IT'S NOTHING BUT A BUNCH OF MEN WITH GUNS.
ALL THAT'S WAITING FOR YOU OUT THERE IS DEATH.
THEN I'LL DIE.
BUT AT LEAST I'LL DIE *TRYIN'*.

VRQOOOOOM

"ALL THE HEROES ARE DEAD.

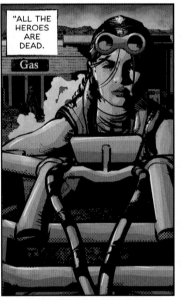

"ALL THE HEROES ARE DEAD.

Gas

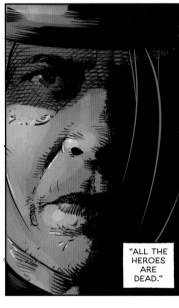

"ALL THE HEROES ARE DEAD."

...DAMMIT...

VRZOOOM

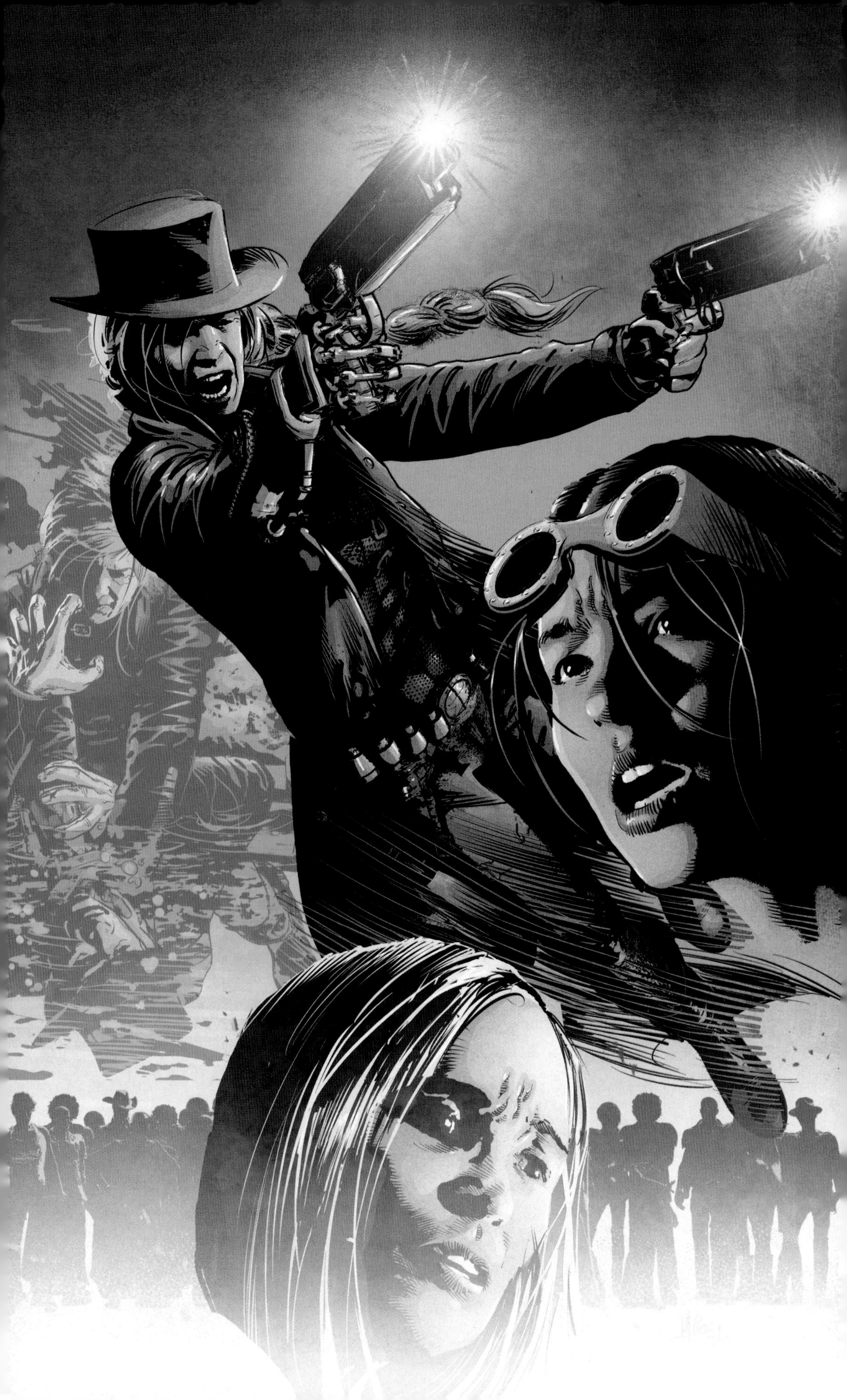

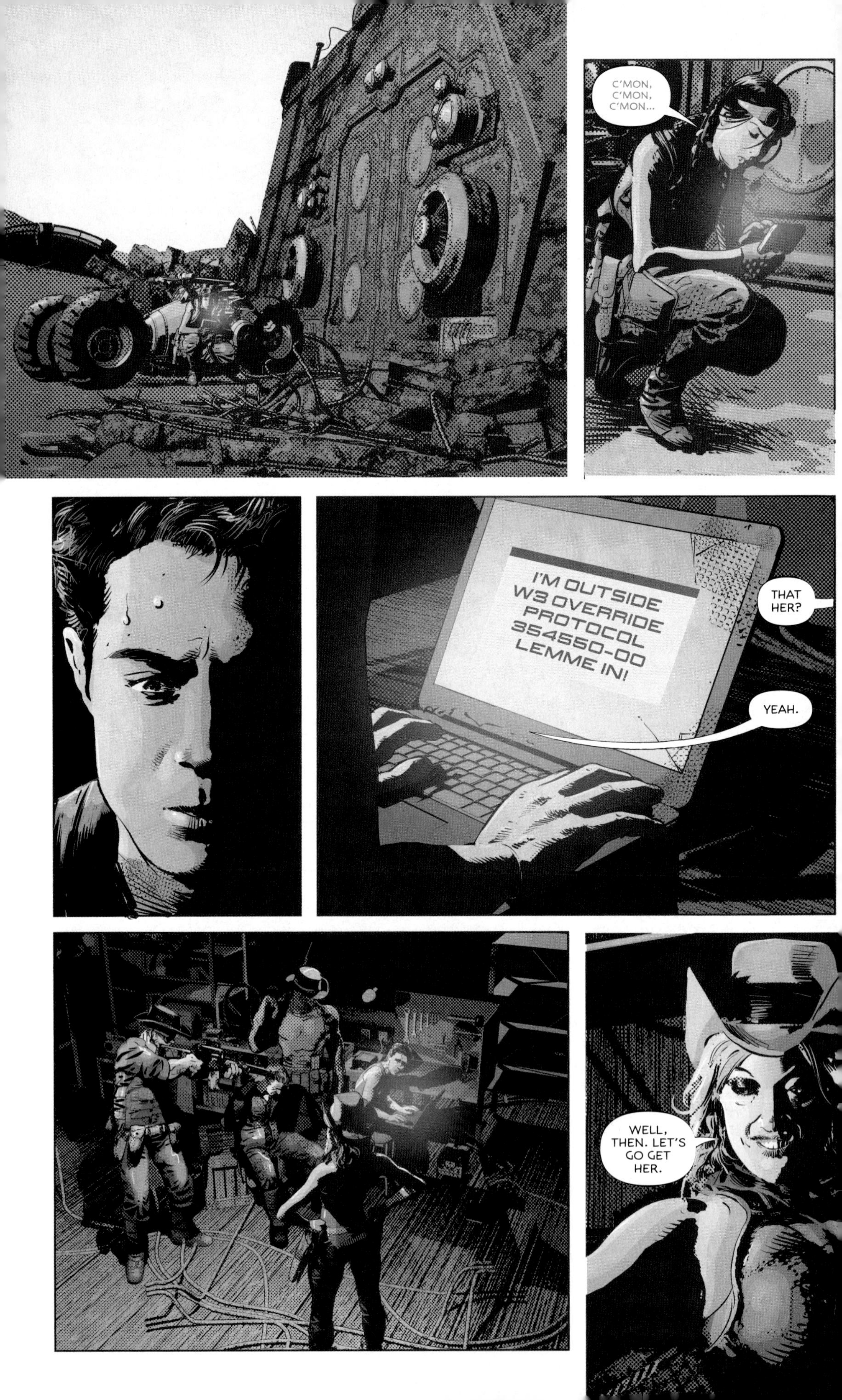
C'MON, C'MON, C'MON...
I'M OUTSIDE W3 OVERRIDE PROTOCOL 354550-00 LEMME IN!
THAT HER?
YEAH.
WELL, THEN. LET'S GO GET HER.

DAMN, ZEKE, TOOK YOU LONG...

...ENOUGH...

THEY WERE GONNA KILL MY WHOLE FAMILY! I'M SORRY, ROSE.

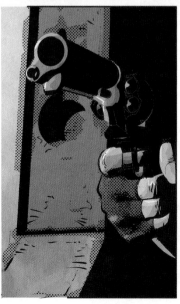

SO, YOU'RE THE NEW ME, HUH?

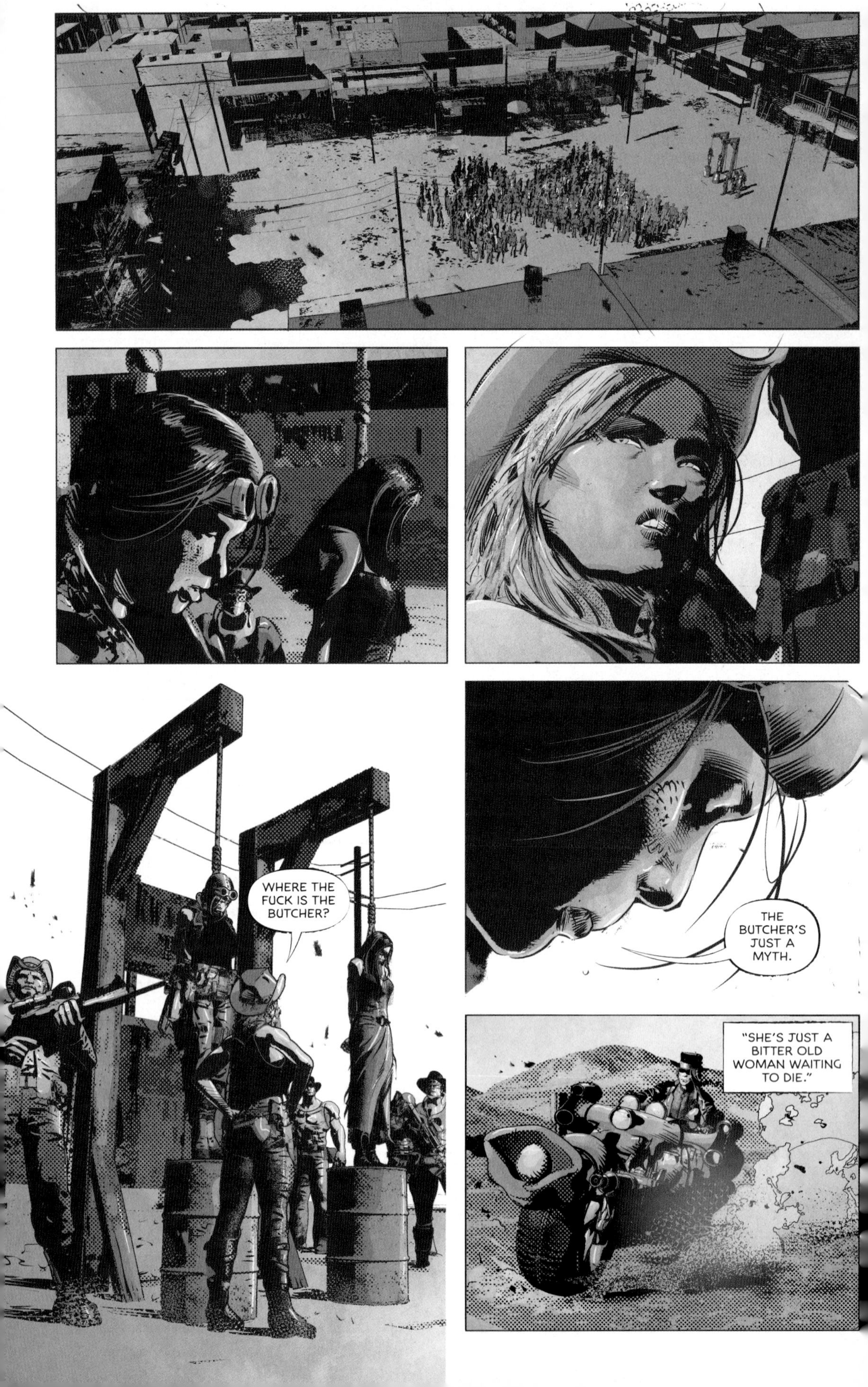
WHERE THE FUCK IS THE BUTCHER?
THE BUTCHER'S JUST A MYTH.
"SHE'S JUST A BITTER OLD WOMAN WAITING TO DIE."

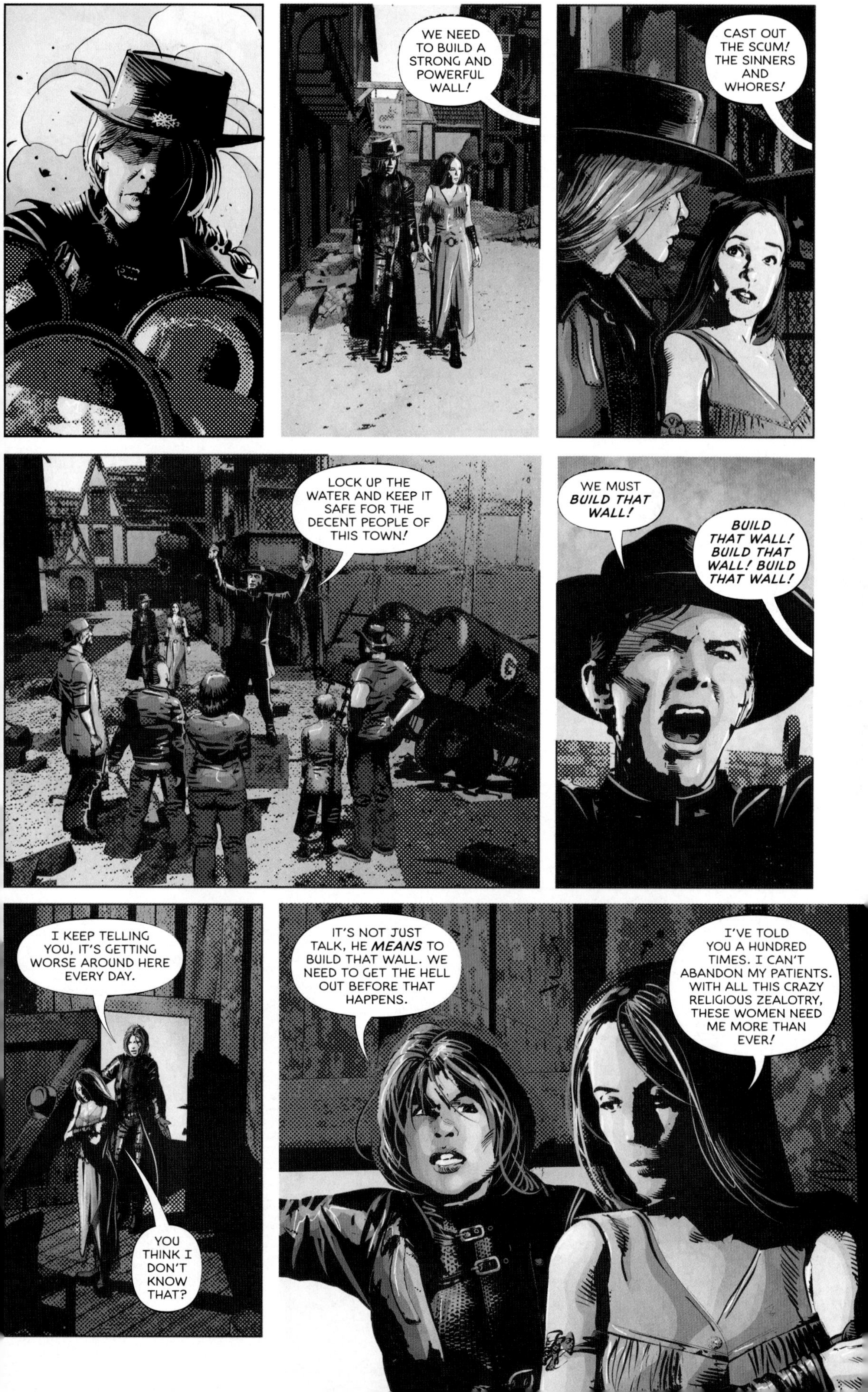
WE NEED TO BUILD A STRONG AND POWERFUL WALL!
CAST OUT THE SCUM! THE SINNERS AND WHORES!
LOCK UP THE WATER AND KEEP IT SAFE FOR THE DECENT PEOPLE OF THIS TOWN!
WE MUST BUILD THAT WALL!
BUILD THAT WALL! BUILD THAT WALL! BUILD THAT WALL!
I KEEP TELLING YOU, IT'S GETTING WORSE AROUND HERE EVERY DAY.
YOU THINK I DON'T KNOW THAT?
IT'S NOT JUST TALK, HE MEANS TO BUILD THAT WALL. WE NEED TO GET THE HELL OUT BEFORE THAT HAPPENS.
I'VE TOLD YOU A HUNDRED TIMES. I CAN'T ABANDON MY PATIENTS. WITH ALL THIS CRAZY RELIGIOUS ZEALOTRY, THESE WOMEN NEED ME MORE THAN EVER!

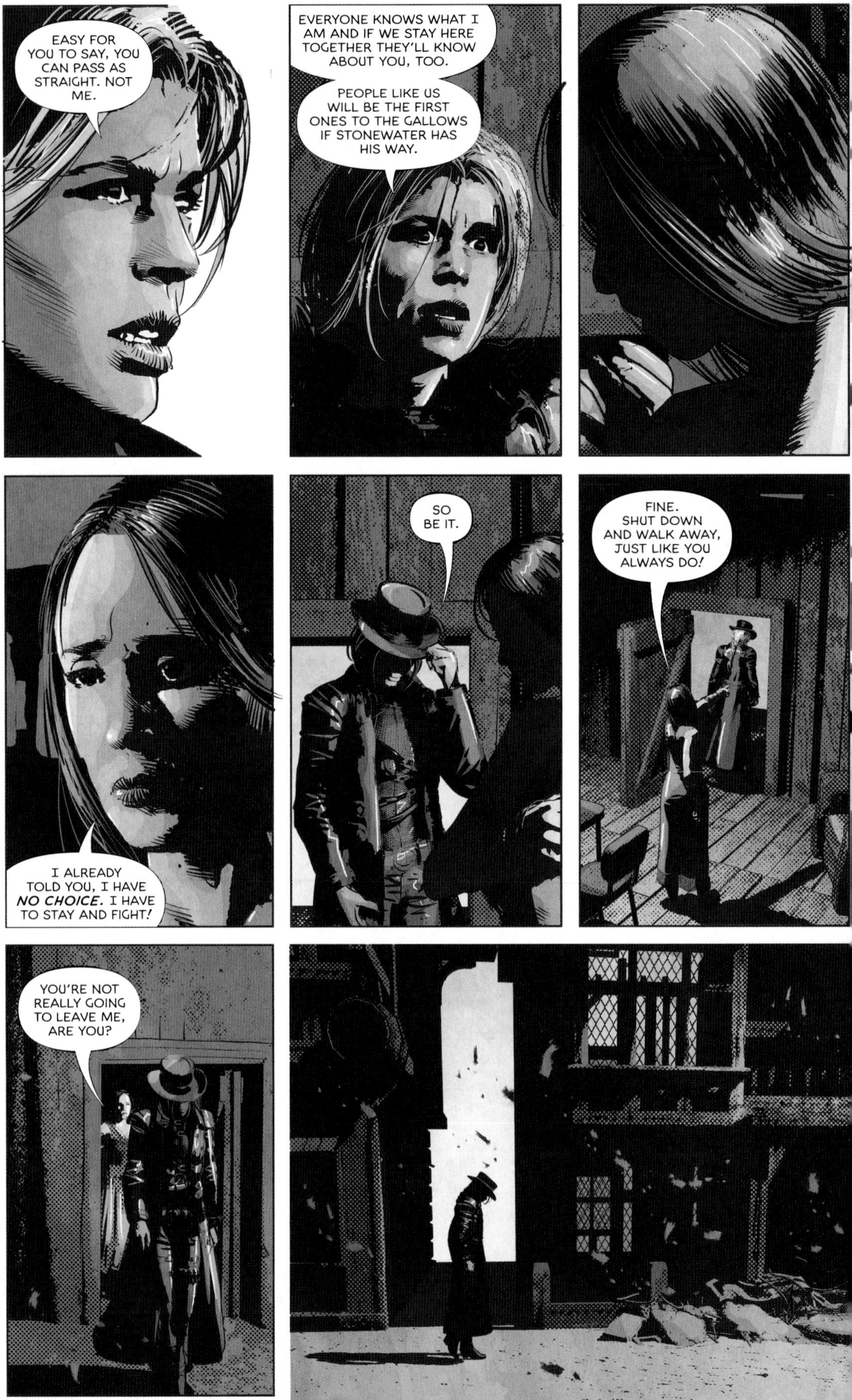
EASY FOR YOU TO SAY, YOU CAN PASS AS STRAIGHT. NOT ME.
EVERYONE KNOWS WHAT I AM AND IF WE STAY HERE TOGETHER THEY'LL KNOW ABOUT YOU, TOO.
PEOPLE LIKE US WILL BE THE FIRST ONES TO THE GALLOWS IF STONEWATER HAS HIS WAY.
I ALREADY TOLD YOU, I HAVE ***NO CHOICE.*** I HAVE TO STAY AND FIGHT*!*
SO BE IT.
FINE. SHUT DOWN AND WALK AWAY, JUST LIKE YOU ALWAYS DO*!*
YOU'RE NOT REALLY GOING TO LEAVE ME, ARE YOU?

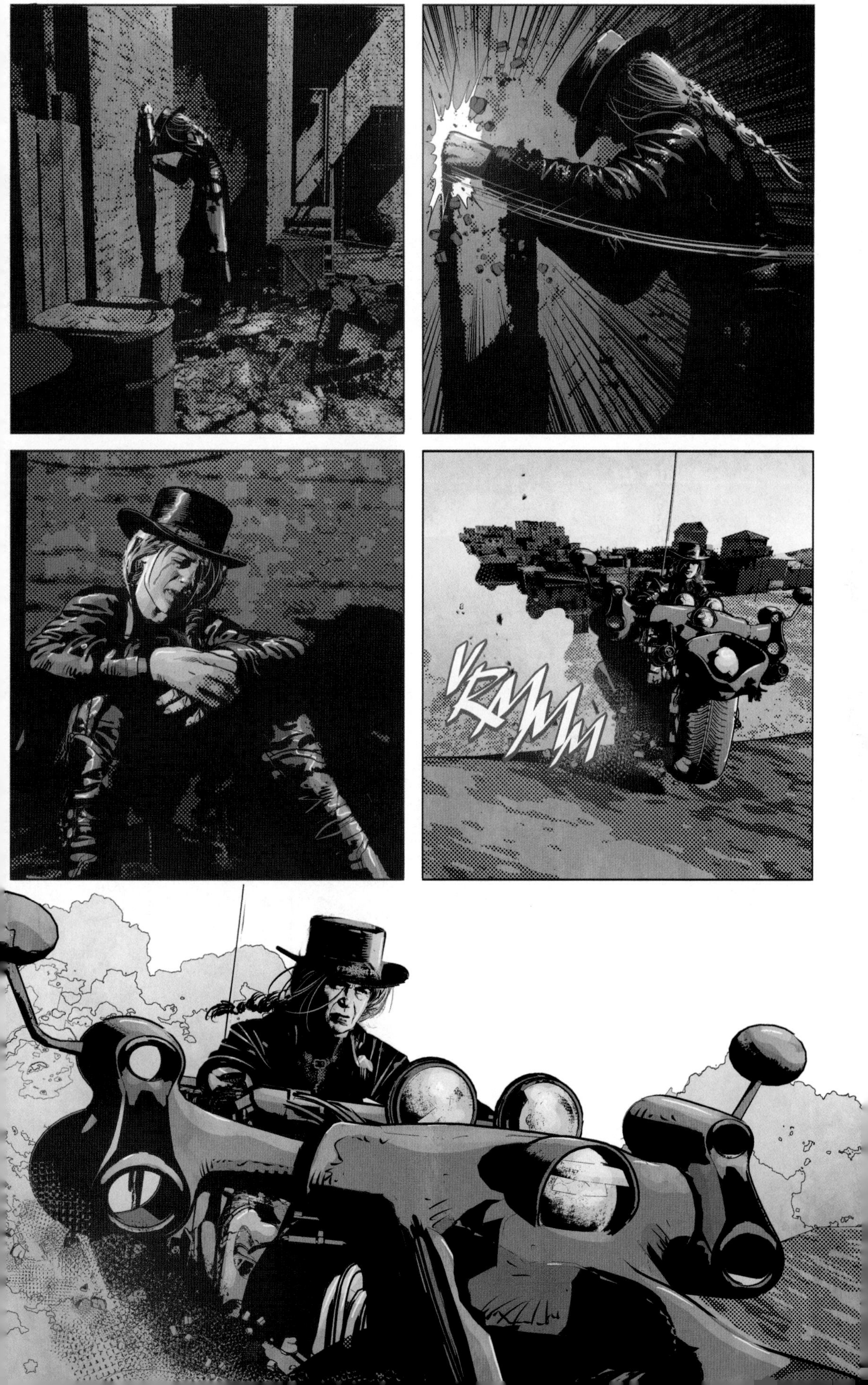
VRMMM

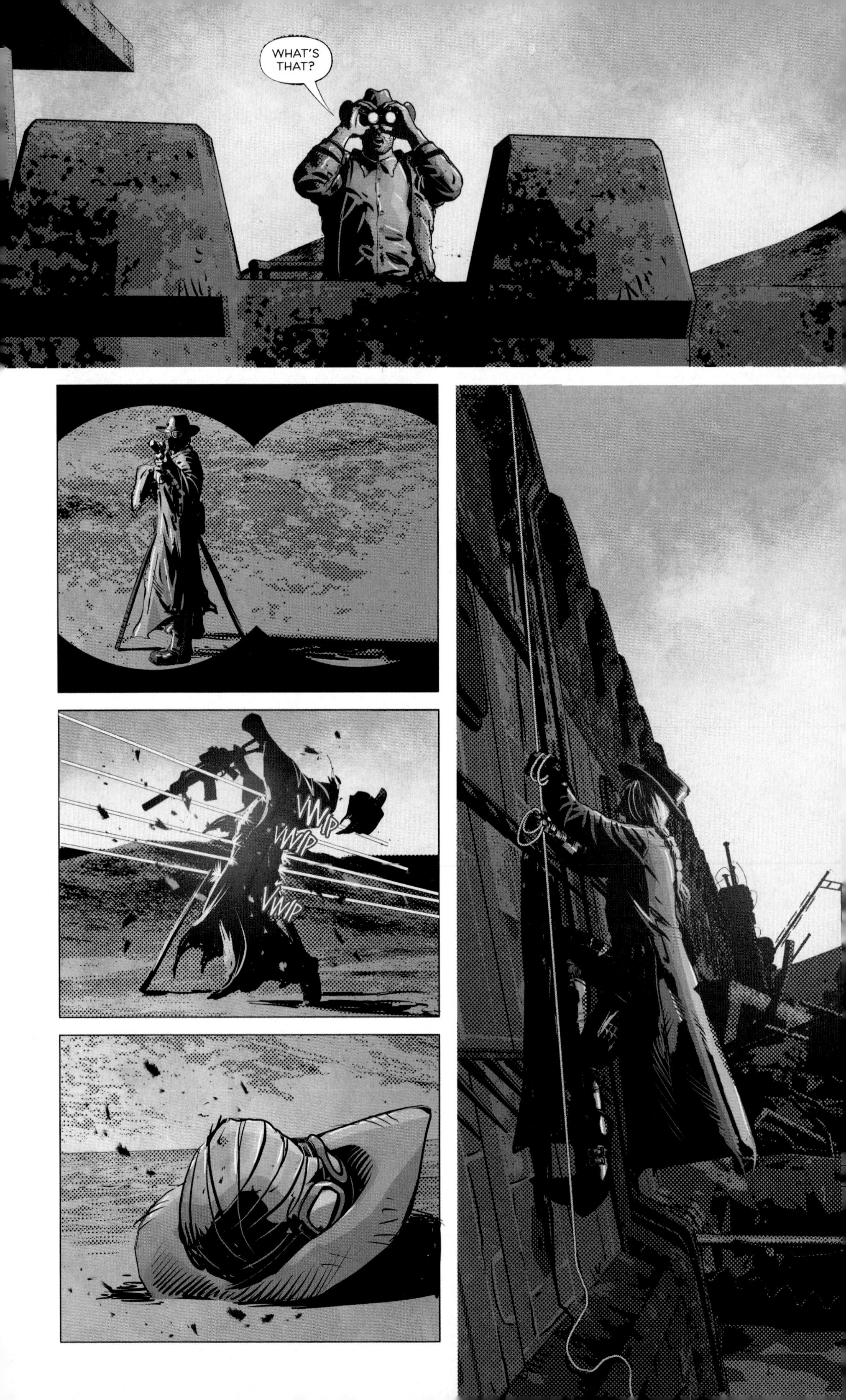
WHAT'S THAT?
VWIP
VWIP
VWIP

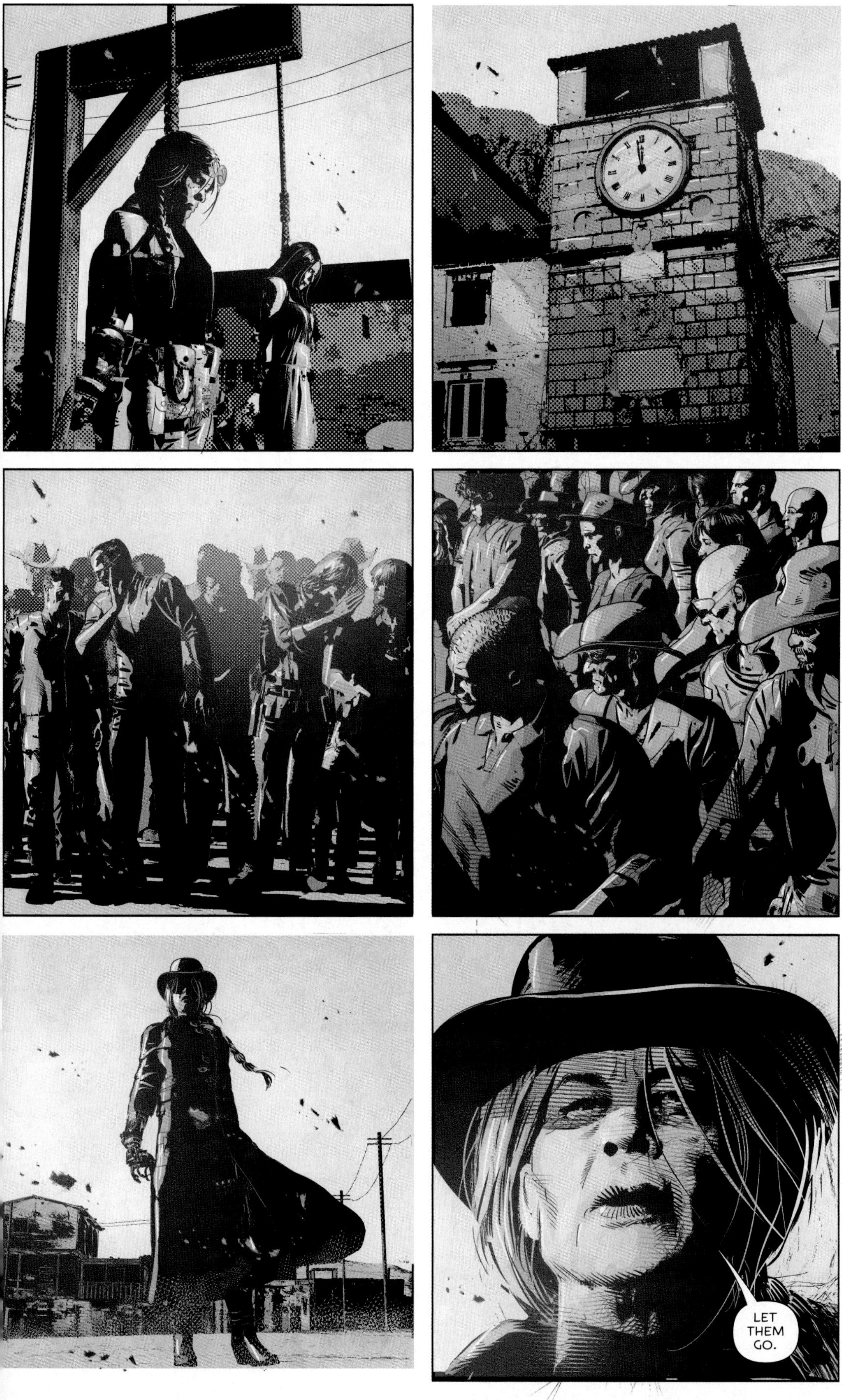
LET
THEM
GO.

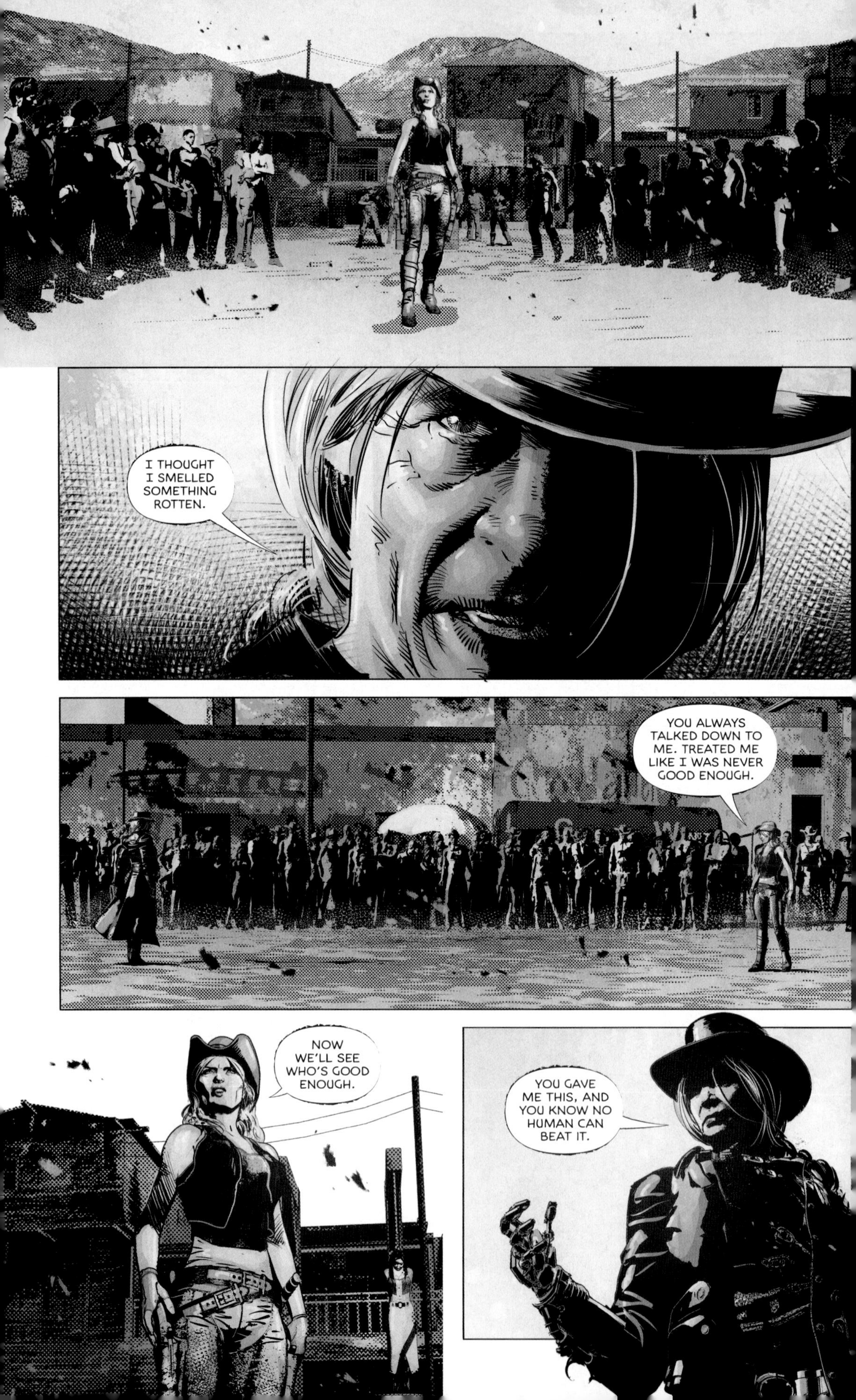
I THOUGHT I SMELLED SOMETHING ROTTEN.
YOU ALWAYS TALKED DOWN TO ME. TREATED ME LIKE I WAS NEVER GOOD ENOUGH.
NOW WE'LL SEE WHO'S GOOD ENOUGH.
YOU GAVE ME THIS, AND YOU KNOW NO HUMAN CAN BEAT IT.

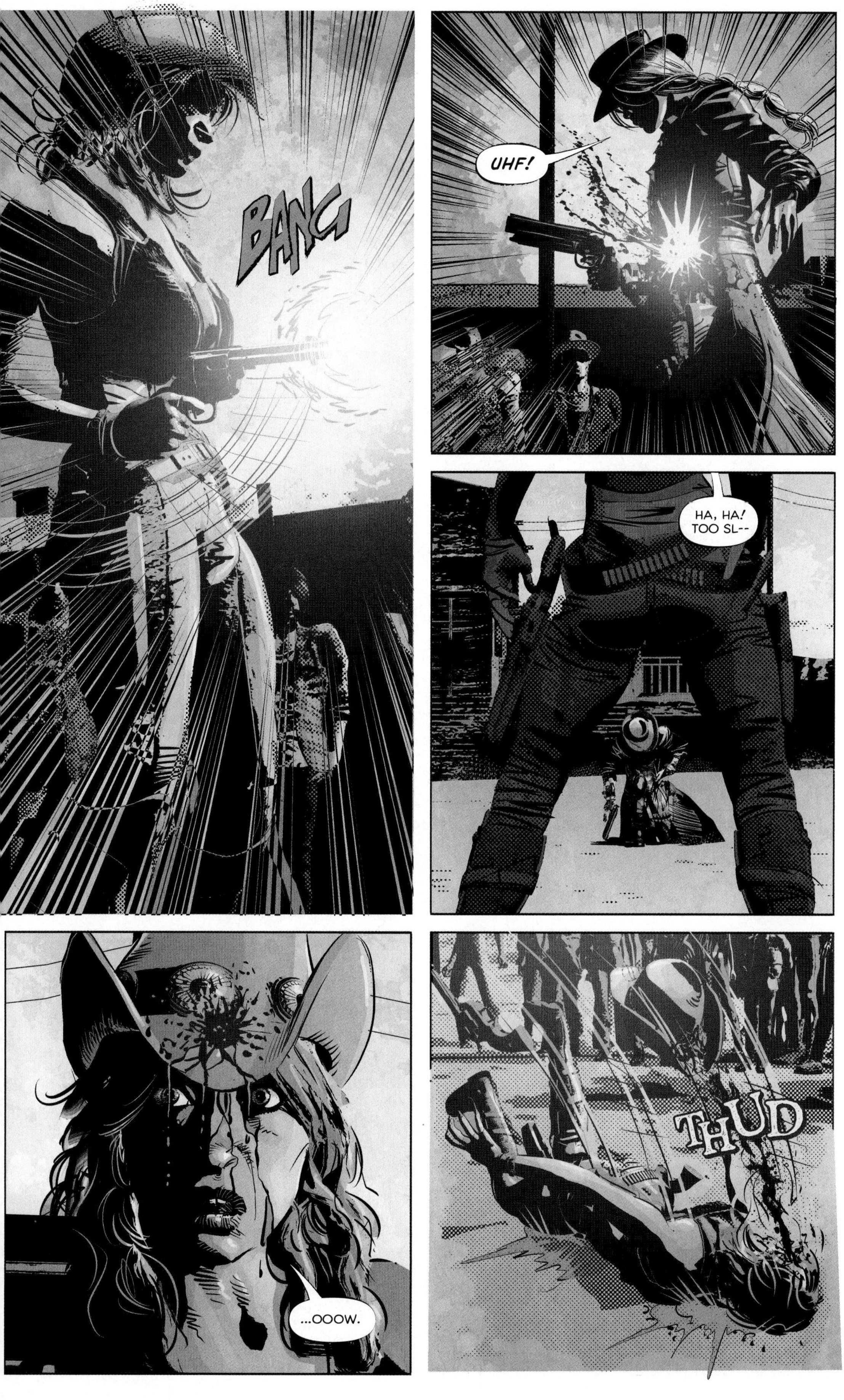
BANG
UHF!
HA, HA! TOO SL--
...OOOW.
THUD

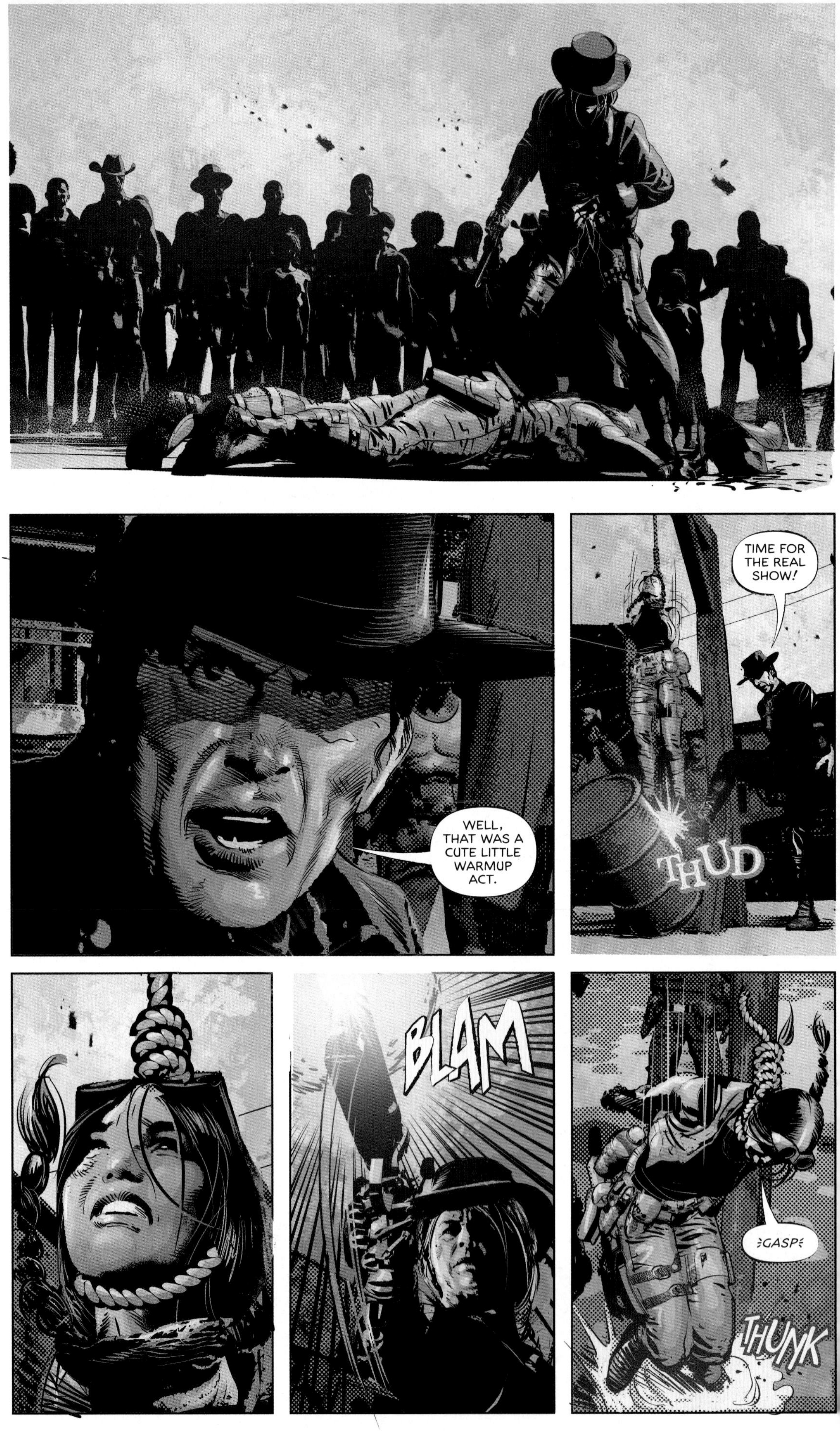
WELL, THAT WAS A CUTE LITTLE WARMUP ACT.
TIME FOR THE REAL SHOW!
THUD
BLAM
GASP
THUNK

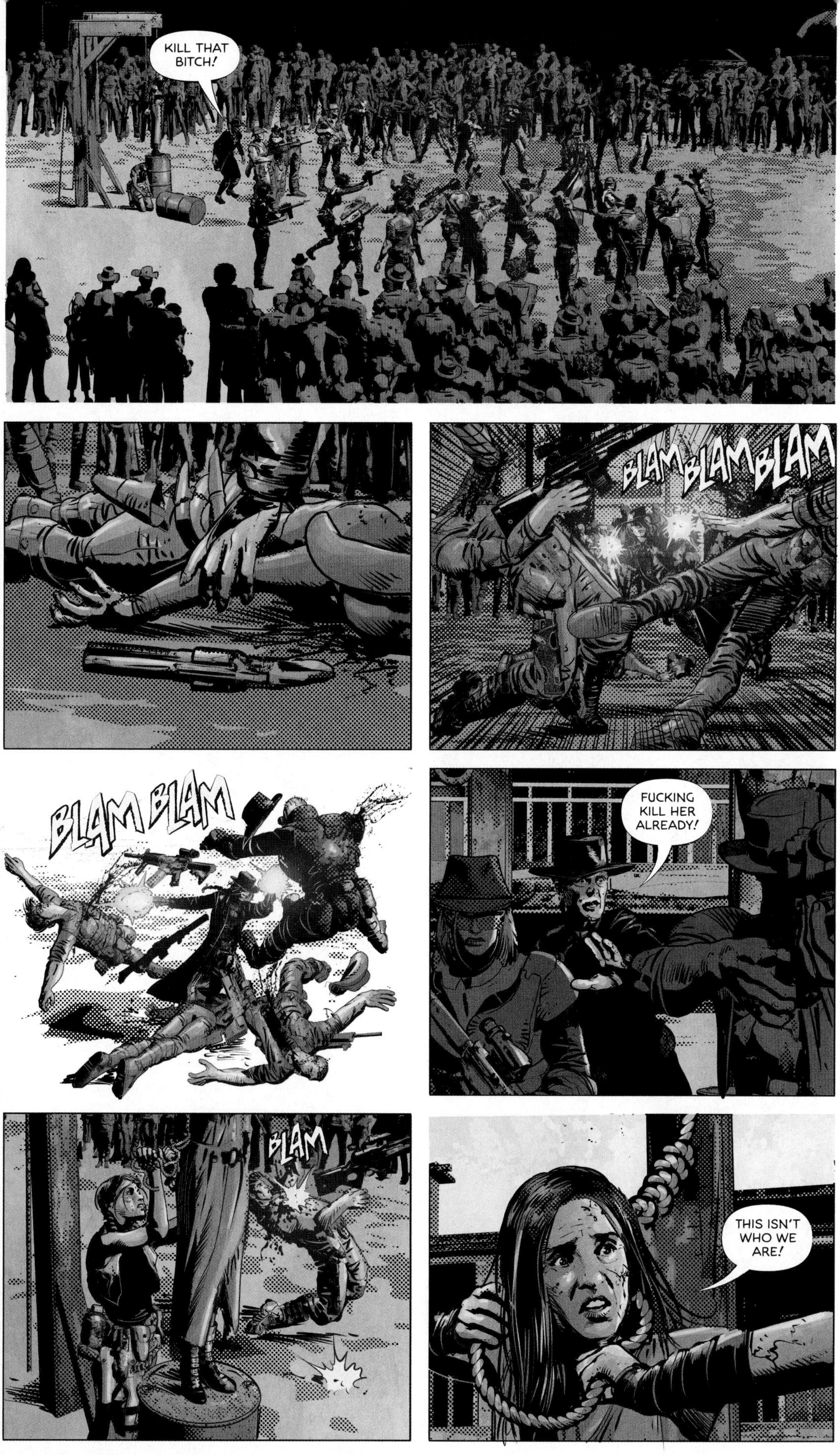
KILL THAT BITCH!
BLAM BLAM BLAM
BLAM BLAM
FUCKING KILL HER ALREADY!
BLAM
THIS ISN'T WHO WE ARE!

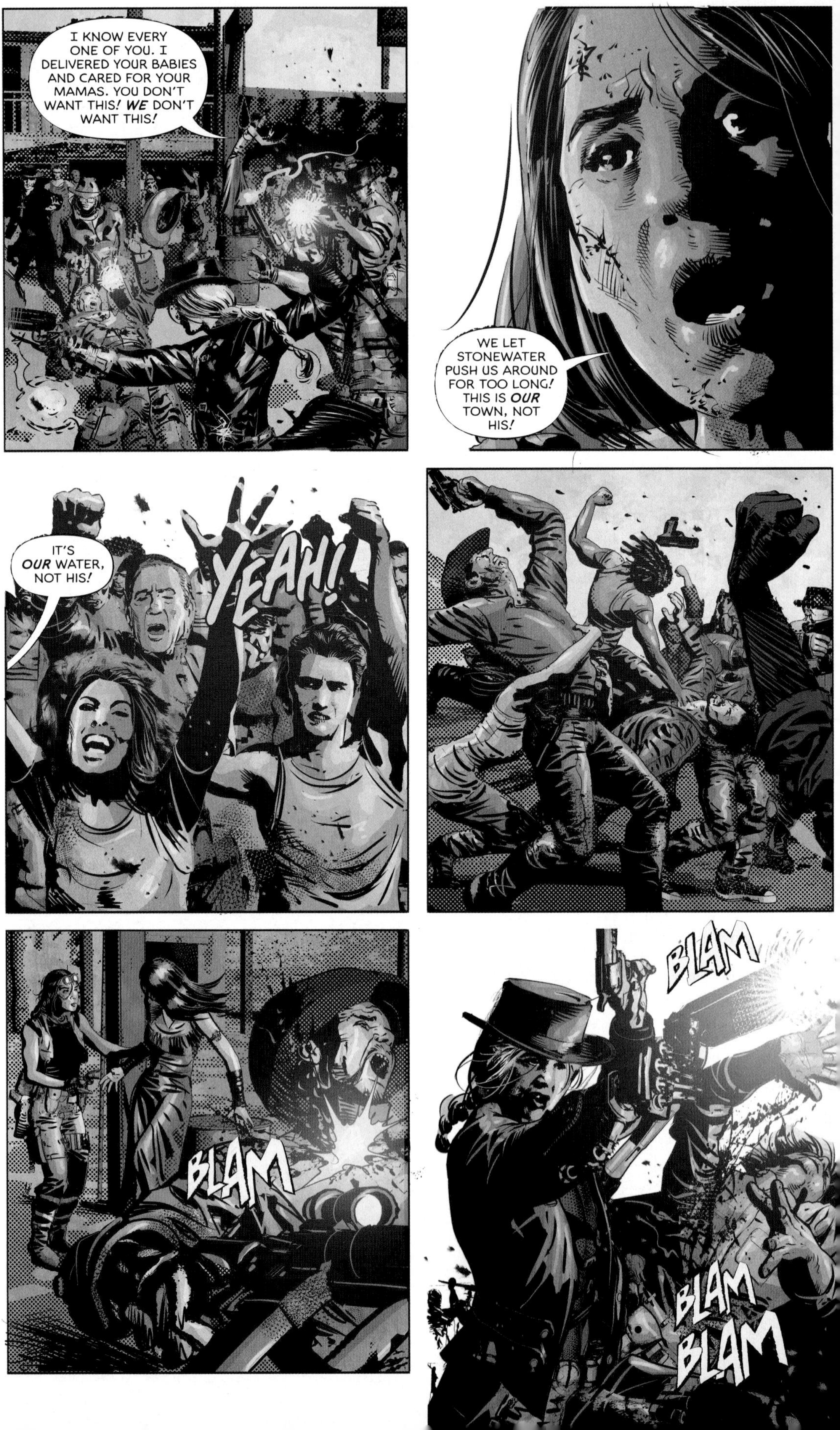
I KNOW EVERY ONE OF YOU. I DELIVERED YOUR BABIES AND CARED FOR YOUR MAMAS. YOU DON'T WANT THIS! *WE* DON'T WANT THIS!
WE LET STONEWATER PUSH US AROUND FOR TOO LONG! THIS IS *OUR* TOWN, NOT HIS!
IT'S *OUR* WATER, NOT HIS!
YEAH!
BLAM
BLAM
BLAM
BLAM

BLAM

BLAM

HE'S RUNNING FOR THE VAULT! IF HE LOCKS THAT DOOR BEHIND HIM, WE'LL NEVER GET HIM! HE'S GOT THE ONLY KEY.

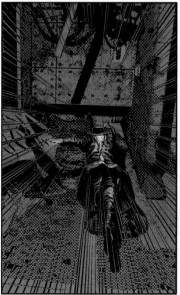

WHAM

VZZZZZZZZZZT

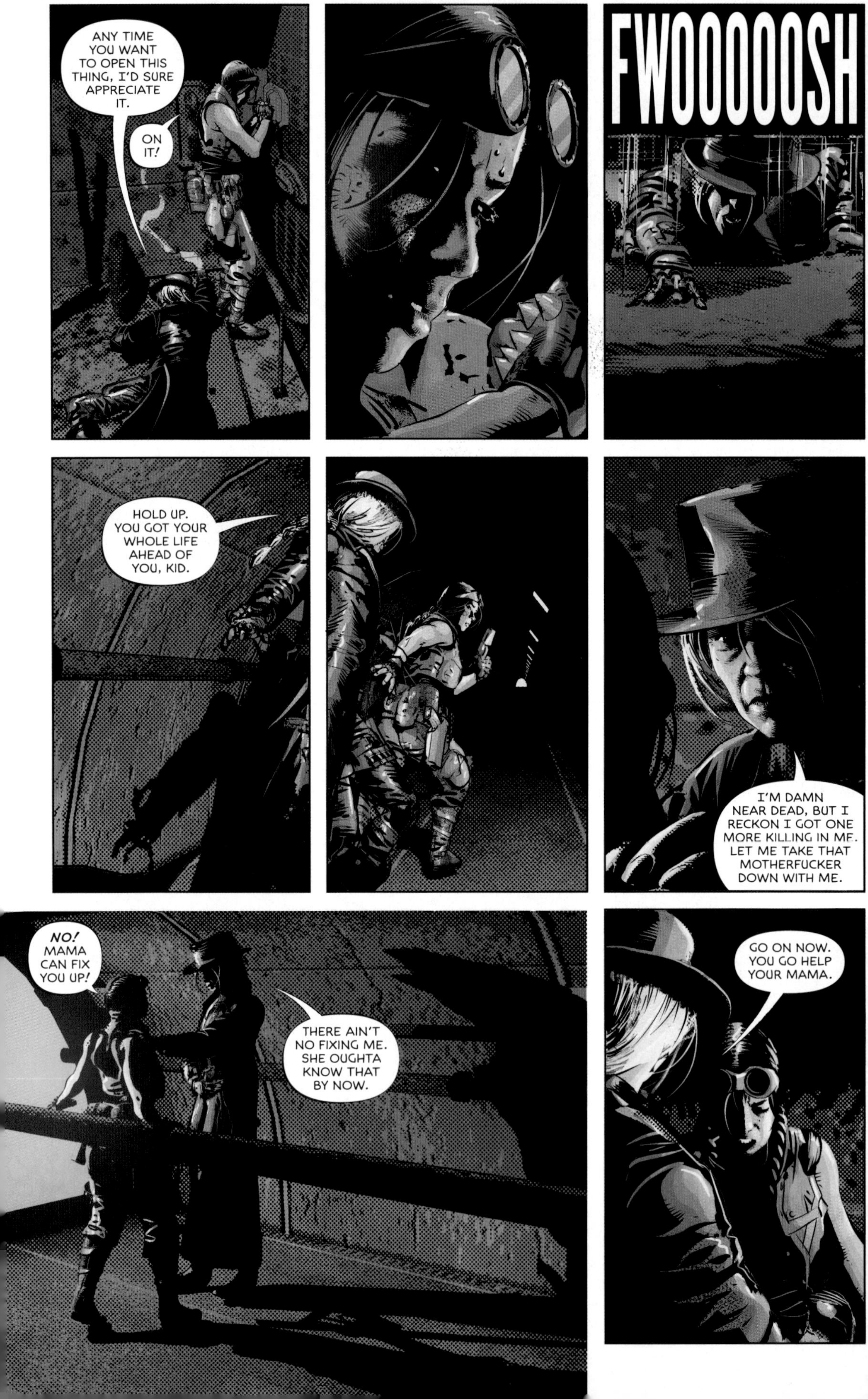
ANY TIME YOU WANT TO OPEN THIS THING, I'D SURE APPRECIATE IT.
ON IT!
FWOOOOOSH
HOLD UP. YOU GOT YOUR WHOLE LIFE AHEAD OF YOU, KID.
I'M DAMN NEAR DEAD, BUT I RECKON I GOT ONE MORE KILLING IN ME. LET ME TAKE THAT MOTHERFUCKER DOWN WITH ME.
NO! MAMA CAN FIX YOU UP!
THERE AIN'T NO FIXING ME. SHE OUGHTA KNOW THAT BY NOW.
GO ON NOW. YOU GO HELP YOUR MAMA.

ZING

WHAT THE--?!

YOU KNOW WHAT YOU ARE?

YOU'RE A FUCKING STAIN ON THIS TOWN.

I'M HERE TO CLEAN UP.

UHF!

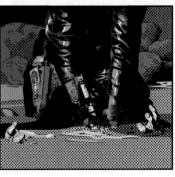

I'M SORRY, BABY.

DON'T YOU FUCKING LEAVE ME AGAIN, DO YOU HEAR ME?

DON'T LEAVE ME...

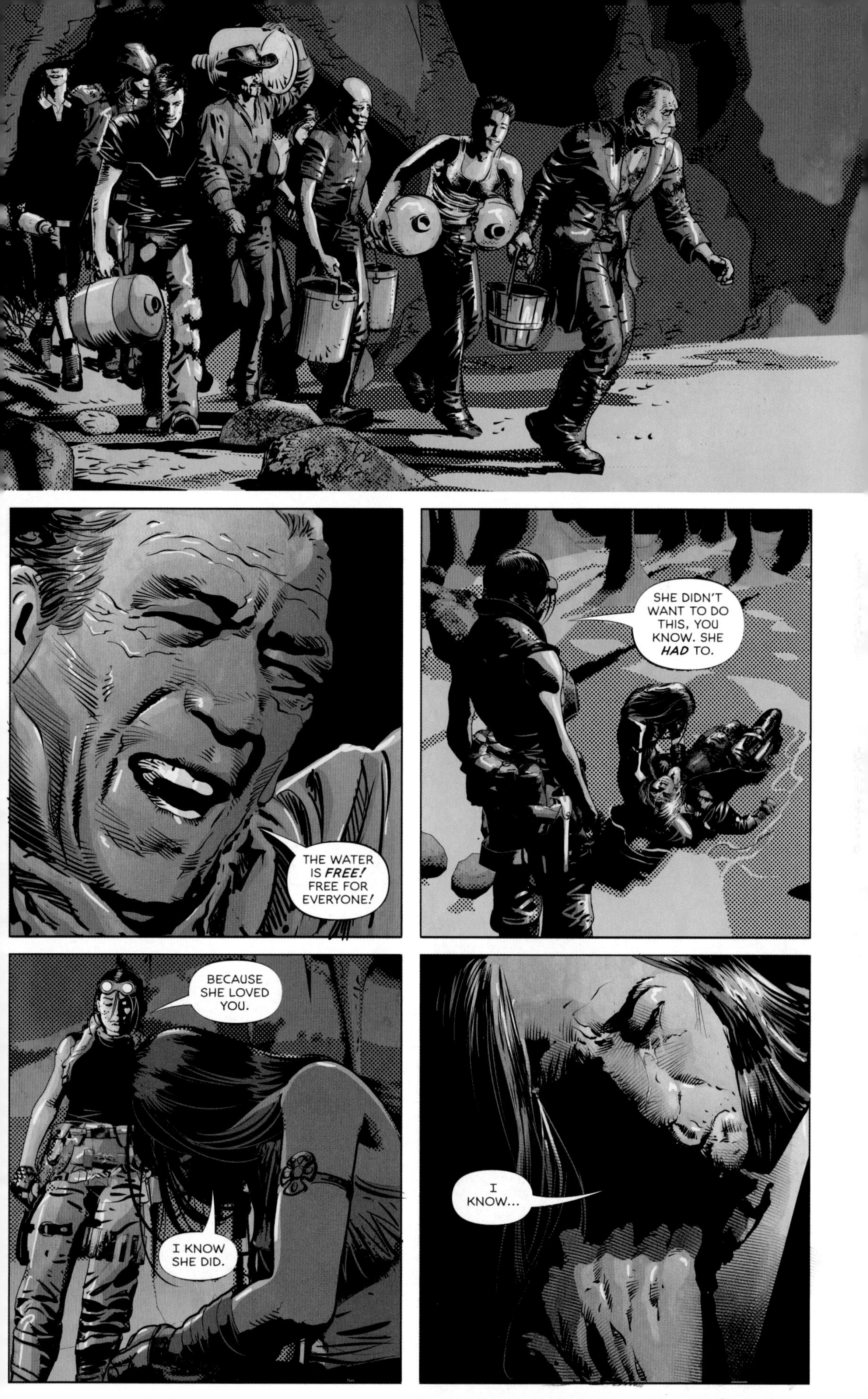
THE WATER IS FREE! FREE FOR EVERYONE!
SHE DIDN'T WANT TO DO THIS, YOU KNOW. SHE HAD TO.
BECAUSE SHE LOVED YOU.
I KNOW SHE DID.
I KNOW...

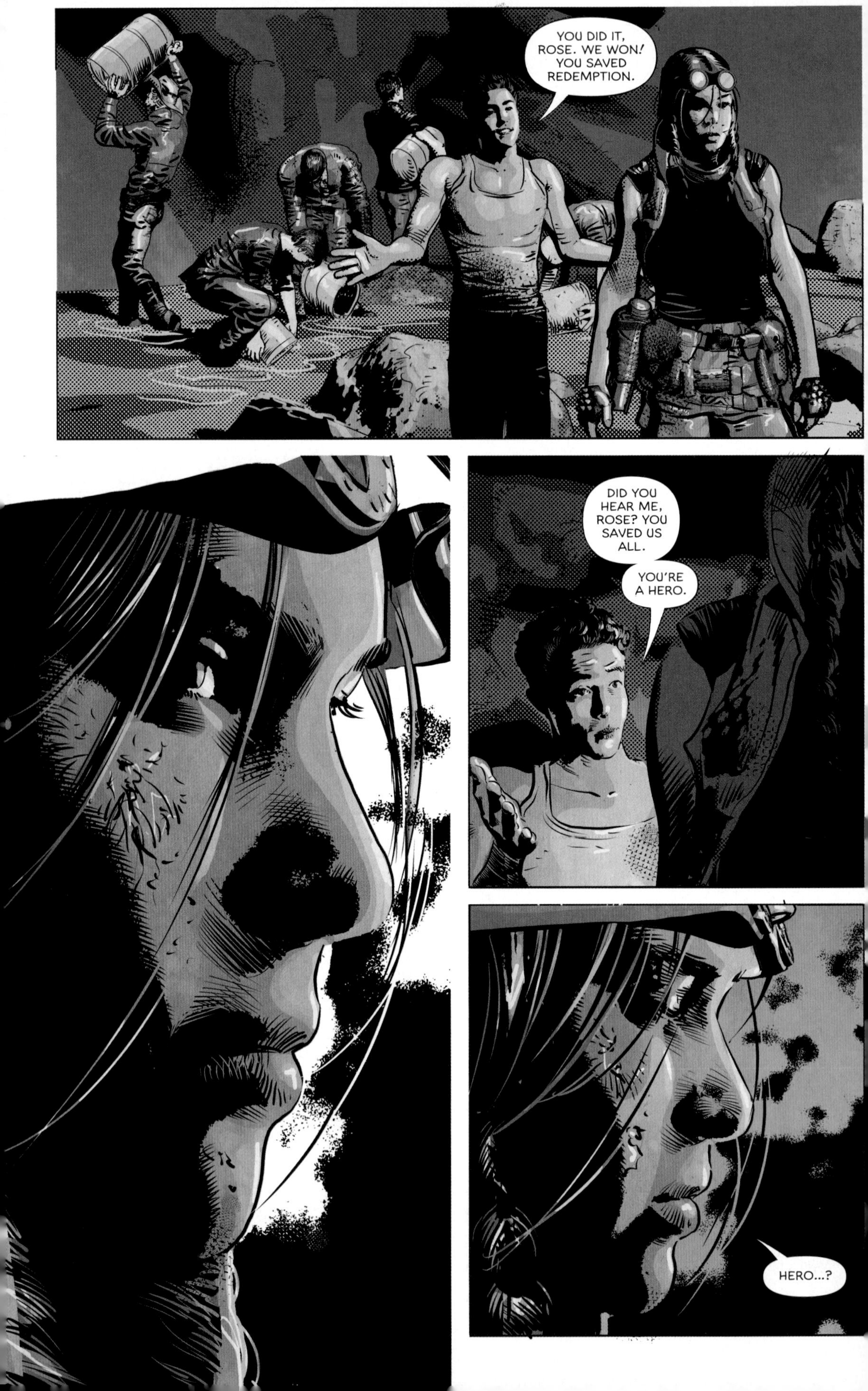
YOU DID IT, ROSE. WE WON! YOU SAVED REDEMPTION.
DID YOU HEAR ME, ROSE? YOU SAVED US ALL.
YOU'RE A HERO.
HERO...?

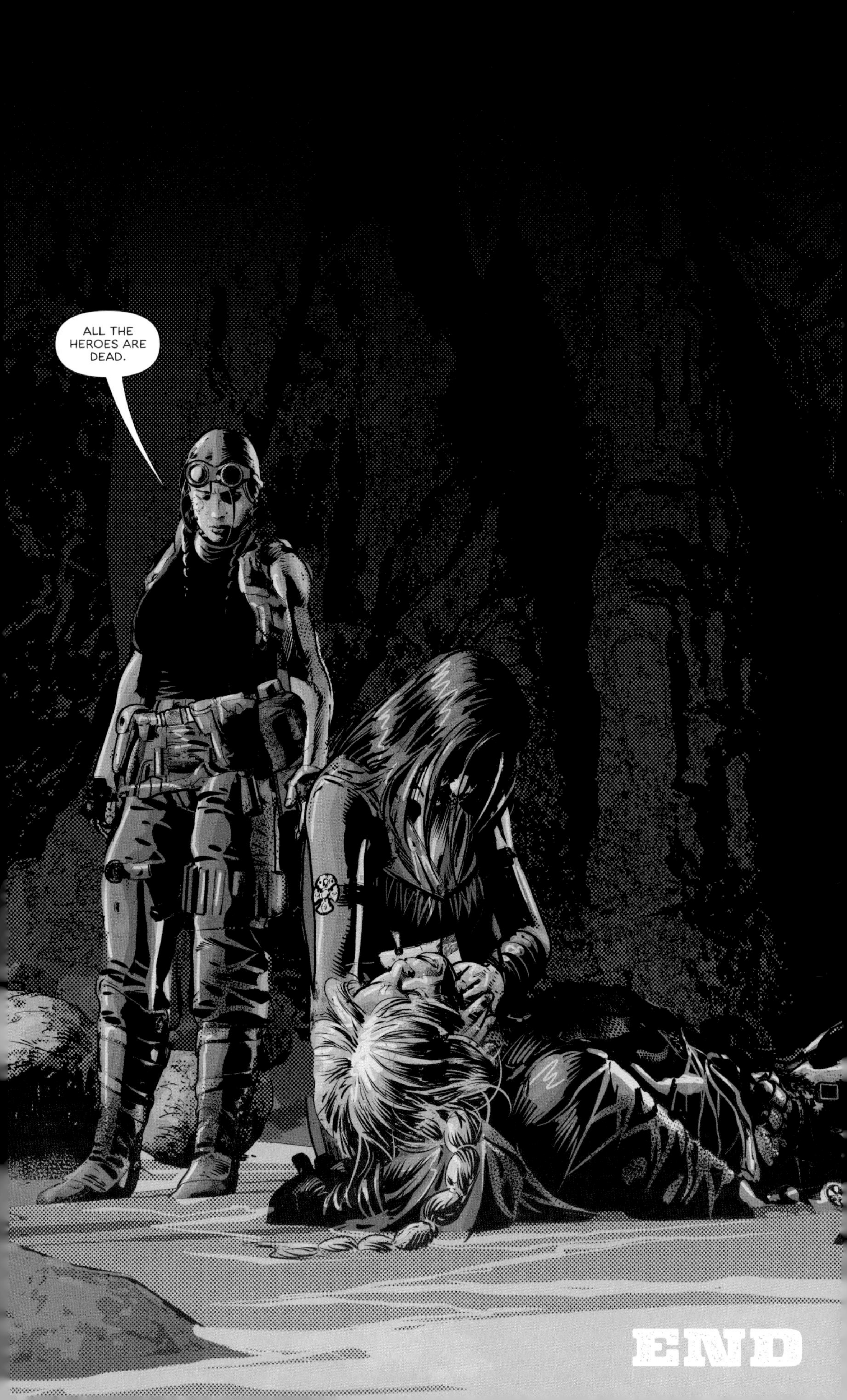
ALL THE HEROES ARE DEAD.
END

LETTERS FROM THE CREATORS OF
REDEMPTION

2020 was a long, strange year for all of us. An apocalyptic time to be writing a post-apocalyptic tale.

Christa Faust

There's a classic storytelling tradition that celebrates the grizzled old cowboy. The scarred and hardboiled outlaw with a steely squint and a bad reputation. He (and it's always a he) is usually paired with a wiseass young gun or a sexy girl half his age who somehow falls for him anyway. Because male characters are allowed to remain both tough and virile as they age. Older female characters, not so much.

That goes double for queer female characters. There's a kind of running joke about the straight man who supports gay rights, as long as both of the chicks are hot. I think this is true of a lot of readers too. They are fine with stories about queer women that at least pay lip service to the male gaze. But what about the rest of us?

That's where The Butcher comes in.

When I was approached with the concept for *Redemption*, I was all in. I loved the idea of being able to write about an older queer woman who was tough

> **For me, character always comes first with all the other details falling into place from there.**

and complicated and didn't give a shit what men thought of her even before she passed her Last Fuckable Day. An outlaw in every sense of the word.

At the heart of this series is a trio of complex, unconventional female characters. Dangerous and subversive women who defy cliches and refuse to play by the rules. Women who can fight and fix things and rescue themselves. For me, character always comes first with all the other details falling into place from there.

Of course, the world was intriguing too. I'm fascinated by post-apocalyptic stories, and I loved the idea of combining that concept with classic Western tropes and imagery. I took inspiration from films like *The Rover* and *Death Rides a Horse* as well as *Unforgiven* and the *Mad Max* movies. I was also inspired by William Gibson's concept of "The Jackpot" from his novel *The Peripheral*. The apocalypse isn't caused by a single big catastrophic event, like a nuclear war, but by a cascade of global comorbidities and contributing factors like climate change and civil unrest and disease all lining up like a row of cherries in a Vegas slot machine.

Mike Deodato really nailed it with his beautiful and evocative art and character design. I love the way he brought our bleak, gritty world and its inhabitants to life. It's been a real pleasure working with an artist of his caliber.

2020 was a long, strange year for all of us. An apocalyptic time to be writing a post-apocalyptic tale. Here's hoping that we find a way to course-correct and steer ourselves away from that Jackpot instead of heading right into the heart of it. Meanwhile, pour yourself a nice cool glass of water and enjoy *Redemption*.

- Christa Faust

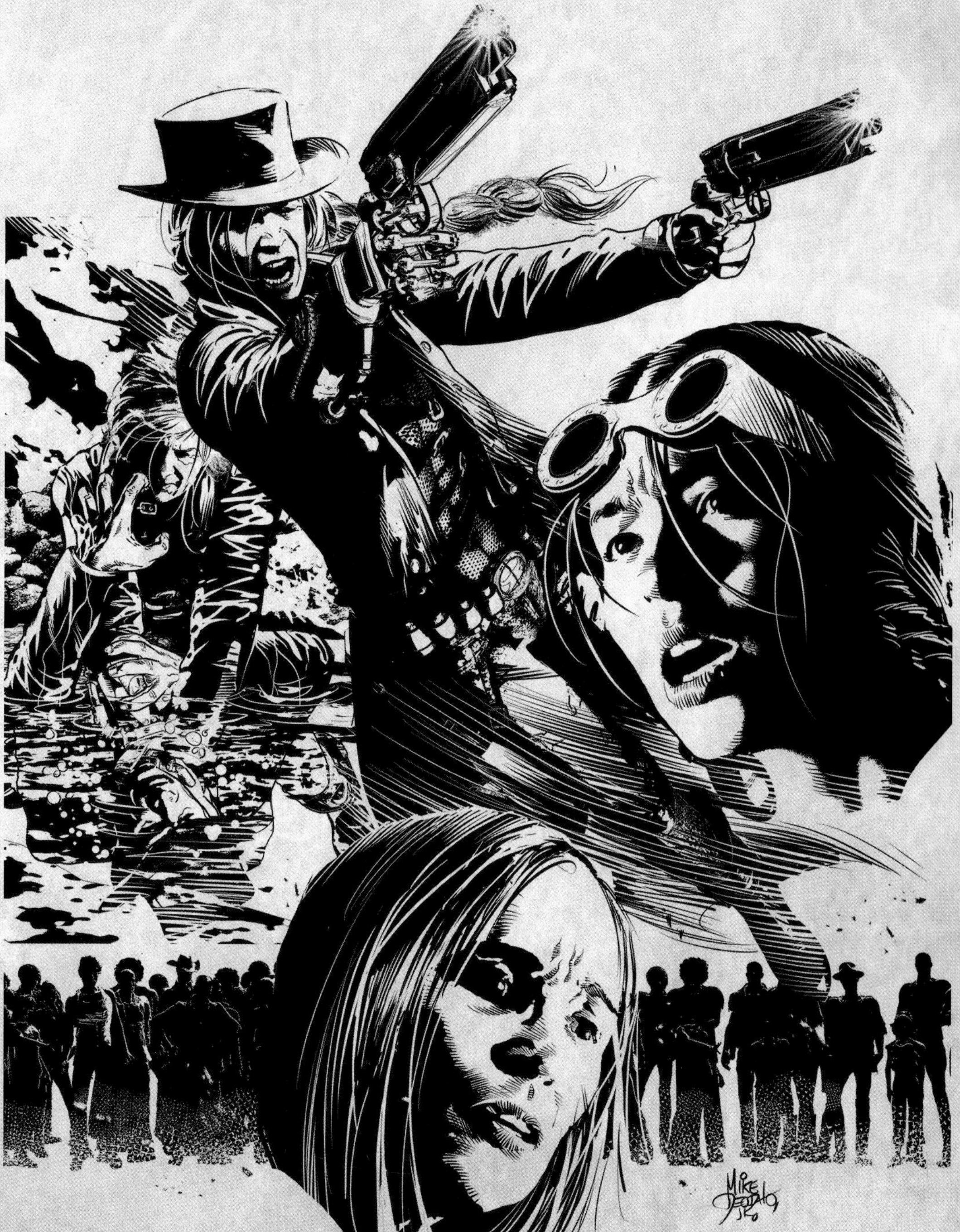
MIKE DEODATO

Mike Deodato Jr.

Howdy, partner!

There are two comics genres I am absolutely crazy about: Post-Apocalyptic and Western.

The first genre I have done plenty of in my career. Actually, one of my first independent books (when I was just 20) was called *3000 Fallout*.

As for Westerns, I hadn't had much luck. The closest I got was when I was almost hired to do a *Tex* album for Italy, but it didn't work out in the end.

One of the first things I told Axel when I came to AWA was that I would love to do a Western. I even sent him the samples I did for the Italian character.

It took some months but the waiting was worthwhile. Axel finally presented me with the perfect book: A Western placed into a post-apocalyptic world! The best part? It was written by Christa Faust, my partner in crime on *Bad Mother.* I couldn't be happier with the result.

My choice, style-wise, was to forget the experimental layout designs I had been using in *The Resistance* and *Bad Mother.* Instead, I opted for a mostly straight-forward approach to make the series look more like a classic Western. The halftone dots were the cherry on top of the pie to give it the right retro look.

Redemption is one of my best works and I bet you will enjoy the ride with The Butcher as much as I did!

Adios amigos!

- Mike Deodato Jr.

Issue 1 Variant Cover by **Frank Cho,**
Colored by **Sabine Rich**

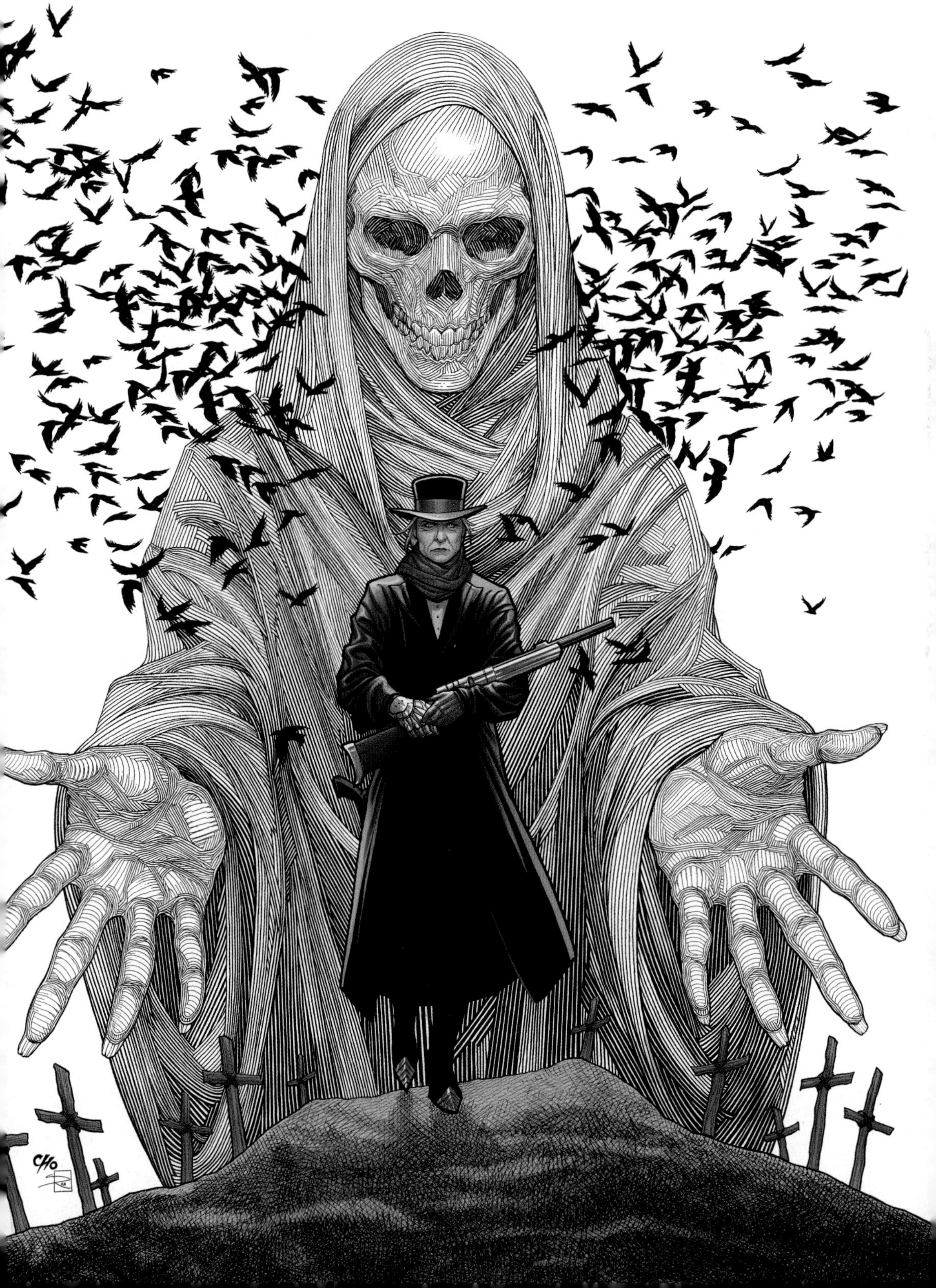
CHO

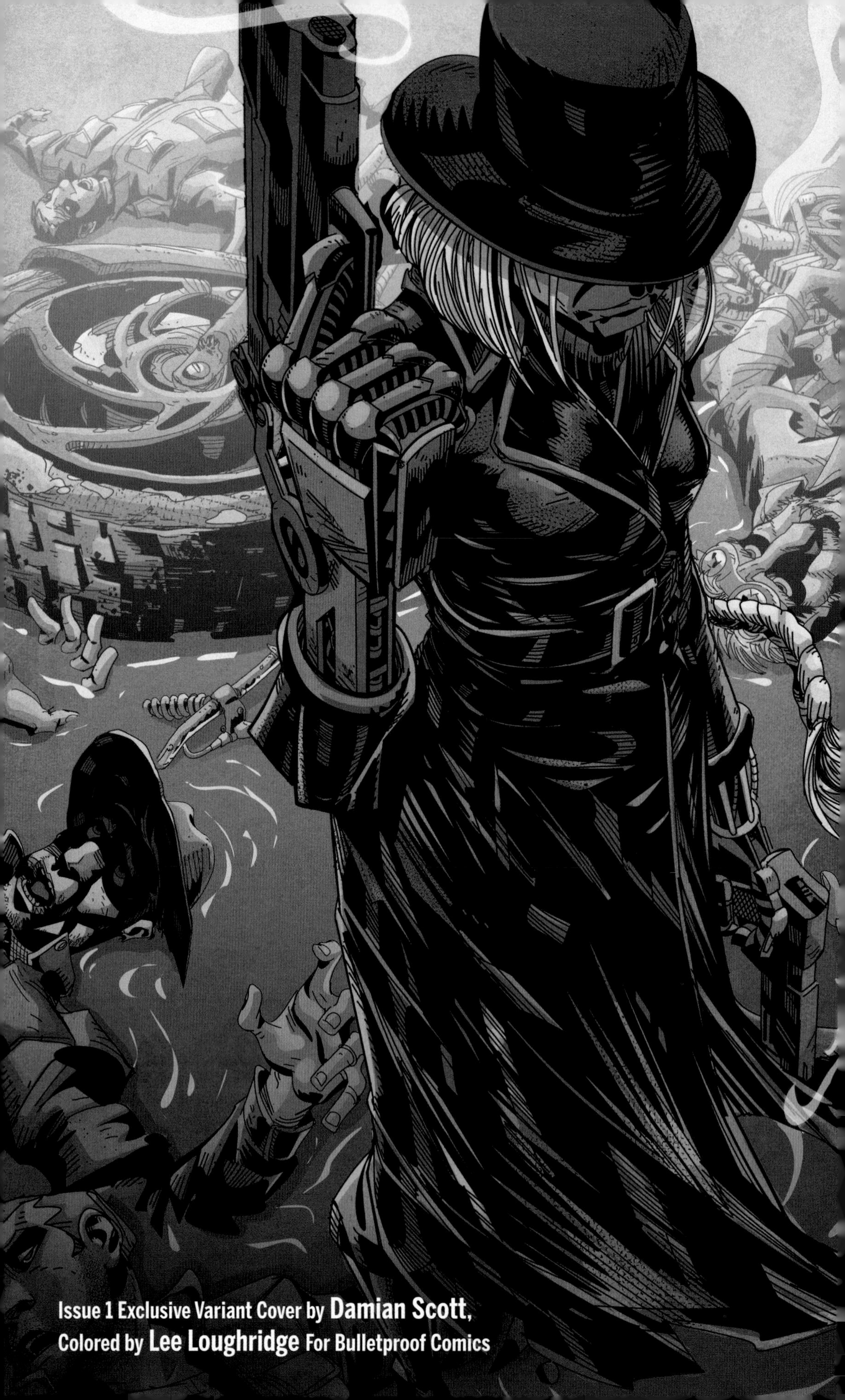

Issue 1 Exclusive Variant Cover by **Damian Scott,**
Colored by **Lee Loughridge** For Bulletproof Comics

Issue 1 Exclusive Variant Cover by **Johnny Desjardins**,
For Bulletproof Comics

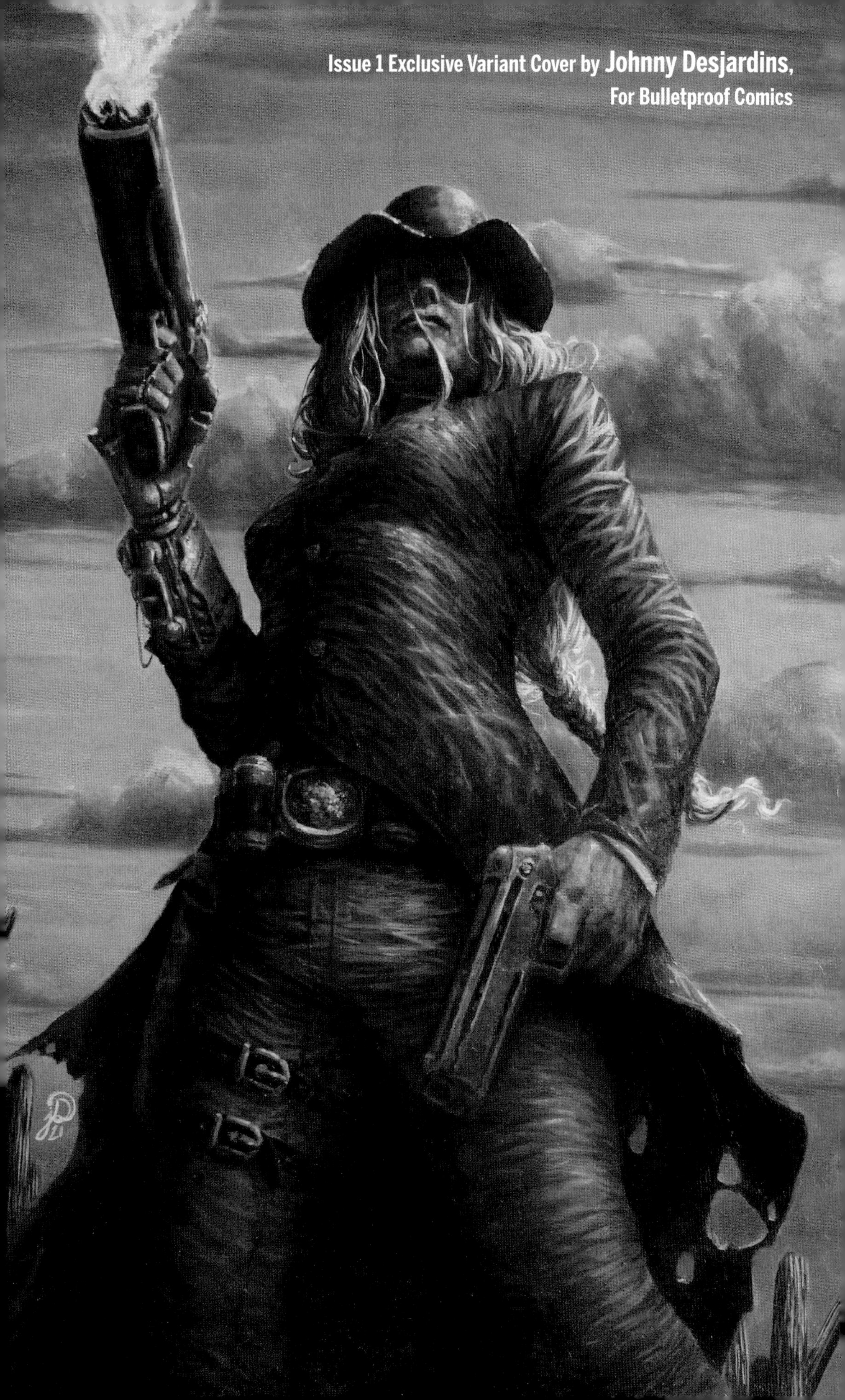

ISSUE #3 PAGE EIGHT (six panels)

Panel 1:
Cut to: Down in the bunker, Cat and Rose sit at the table. Hatless Cat is playing solitaire with a deck of cards so old and faded that the suits are barely visible. Rose is working on the cybergun.

1 ROSE   Do you think I'm ready?

2 CAT   You'd better be. Execution's just two days away.

Panel 2:
Close on Rose, scared and trying to cover it with bravado.

3 ROSE   You think I don't know that?

Panel 3:
Close on Cat, her face showing a brief flash of heartbreak and longing.

4 CAT   You remind me so much of your mother sometimes.

Panel 4:
Close up. Sharp Rose has picked up on the emotional undercurrent here.

5 ROSE   You and her were more than friends, weren't you?

Panel 5:
Two shot. Cat is stony and silent as the truth slowly dawns on Rose.

6 ROSE   You loved her.

Panel 6:
Close on Cat, trying to keep her emotions in check.

7 CAT   That was a long time ago.

ISSUE #3 PAGE NINE (six panels)

Panel 1:
Two shot

ROSE   Then why won't you go with me? Help me save her?

CAT   I'm a killer, kid. Not a savior.

Panel 2:
Close on Rose.

ROSE   But you haven't always been The Butcher.

Panel 3:
Two shot.

ROSE   You didn't kill those all miners until after whatever went down between you and my mother, right?

CAT   You shouldn't believe every tall tale you hear.

Panel 4:
Close on Cat, face cold and closed off now.

CAT   Anyway, it don't make no difference now. This is your problem, not mine.

Panel 5:
Tight on Rose, tears glistening in her angry eyes.

ROSE   You don't give a shit about…

Panel 6:
Match cut to a flashback of young Inez, same expression, same tears. She and Rose really are so much alike, and we should really see that here.

INEZ   … anyone but yourself!

ISSUE #3 PAGE TEN (six panels)

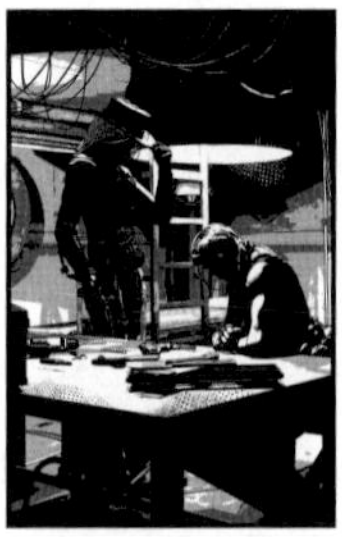

Panel 1:
Cat is standing now, putting her hat back on her head and fixing to walk out.

1 CAT	You're right. I don't.

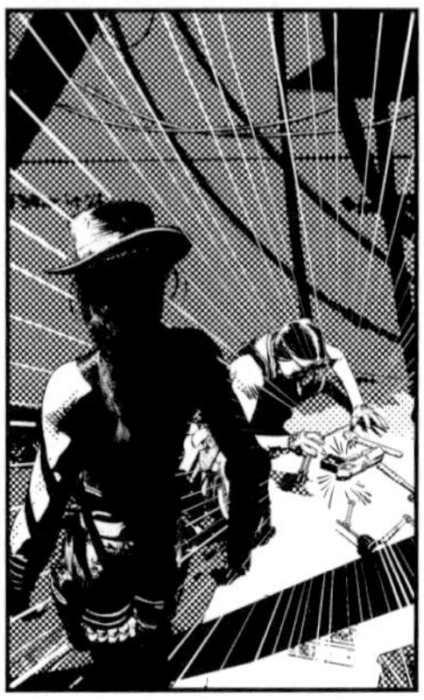

Panel 2:
The cybergun Rose was working on starts flashing and beeping on the table. Cat looks back and frowns, wary.

2 FX	beep beep beep
3 CAT	The hell is that?
4 ROSE	Somebody tripped the long-range weapon sensor.

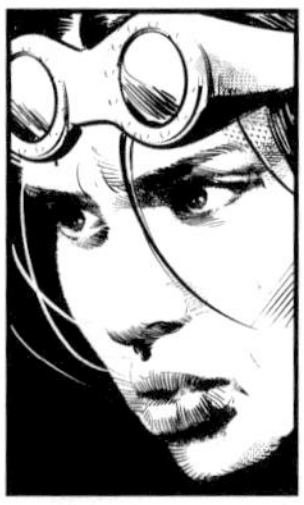

Panel 3:
Tight on worried Rose.

5 ROSE	Several somebodies.

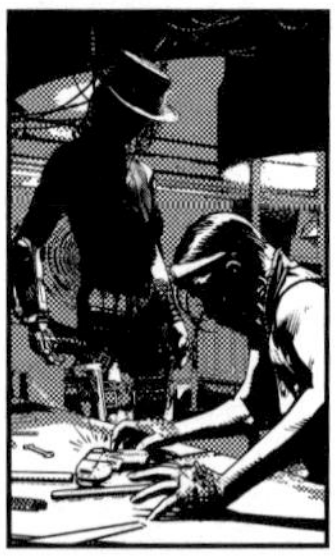

Panel 4:
Tighter on Cat and Rose.

6 CAT	How many?
7 ROSE	Signal is pretty janky. Eight? Maybe ten?

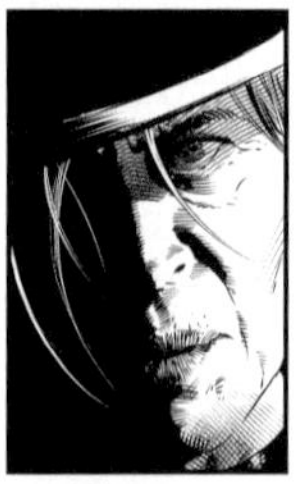

Panel 5:
Close on Cat.

8 CAT	Well, you wanted to know if you're ready.

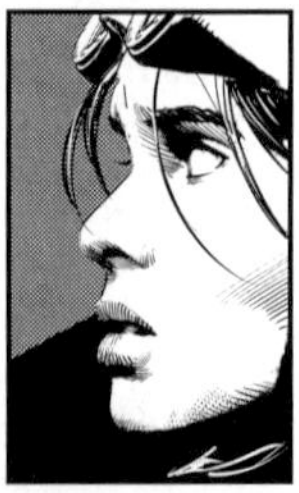

Panel 6:
Close on Rose, the danger and gravity of the situation weighing heavily on her.

9 OFF/CAT	Now's your chance to find out.

Panel 1:
Wide shot of Gage and his posse in front of the gas station. One of his guys is coming out of the building, flashlight in hand and shrugging.

GUY   There's nobody here, boss.

Panel 2:
Tighter on Gage. He's not happy with this news.

GAGE   Shit.

Panel 3:
A woman in the posse comes up beside Gage with a hand held scanner. Let's call her Ana.

ANA   I got a single vehicle headed west at high velocity.

GAGE   That's got to be them.

Panel 4:
Gage calls out to his gang.

GAGE   Let's go!

Panel 5:
The vehicles take off, burn rubber as they peel out of the gas station parking lot.

SFX   VRROOOOOOOOM

ISSUE #3 PAGE TWELVE (six panels)

Panel 1:
Follow Gage and posse as they pursue the vehicle. Wide shot of the canyon. The pass is open on one end and the first members of the posse are coming through, following the vehicle (we will later reveal that it is riderless so don't give that away yet). The other end is blocked by the massive wreck of a commercial airplane, now partially buried in the shifting sand that has accumulated over the long, dry decades since the crash. One broken wing is slanted up, blocking vehicles from passing through while the lower half of the cabin is buried, like a whale with only the top of its back visible above water. This will be important because there will be a fight down in the mostly subterranean cabin later.

Panel 2:
Zoom in on Gage and posse as they get close to the vehicle they're pursuing. Again, we can't show too much of the vehicle without spoiling the reveal (It's riderless). The lead rider has clicked on high beams, eyes wide—

Panel 3:
—starkly illuminating the riderless vehicle! Surprise!

1 LEAD No rider, sir.

Panel 4:
Close on Gage.

2 GAGE It's a trap! Fall back!

Panel 5:
Now cut to Cat and Rose, side by side on their bellies on a rocky outcrop, about ten feet high and overlooking a narrow canyon pass. Cat has chunky infrared binocs, and Rose has her own goggles on and set to infrared capacity. They are watching out for the approaching posse, not yet visible.

Panel 6:
Close on Cat, cybergun raised as she draws a bead. Rose, her own cybergun also drawn, is sweating and chewing one corner of her lip.

3 CAT Now!

Panel 1:

Overhead wide shot as three men go down, two dead and one wounded, clutching a blown-out and bleeding knee. The remaining posse members draw their own weapons as they scatter for cover behind rocks and vehicles. (Now we are down to 5 men, including Gage.)

SFX   BLAM BLAM BLAM BLAM BLAM

Panel 2:

Tight on Gage, crouching behind a rock formation, gun up and eyes wide. He is steeling himself, as a female posse member (not Ana) gets taken out in the background. (Now we are down to 4 men, including Gage)

GAGE   Cover me!

Panel 3:

Gage makes a run for a closer rock formation, firing the whole time not at the currently invisible shooters but at the loose stones and dirt just below their presumed position.

SFX   BLAM BLAM BLAM BLAM BLAM

Panel 4:

Close on Cat and Rose, hands thrown up to protect their faces from a spray of flying gravel and dirt as the outcropping starts to crumble beneath them.

CAT   FUCK!

Panel 5:

Wider as the outcropping gives way beneath them and they tumble to the canyon floor in a spill of jagged rocks and sand.

SFX   RRRRRRUMBLE

ISSUE #3 PAGE FOURTEEN (five panels)

Panel 1:
Bullets hit the sand and rocks all around them as Cat instinctively rolls towards Rose, grabbing her by the collar. Both are battered and dirty and scraped up from the fall but not seriously injured.

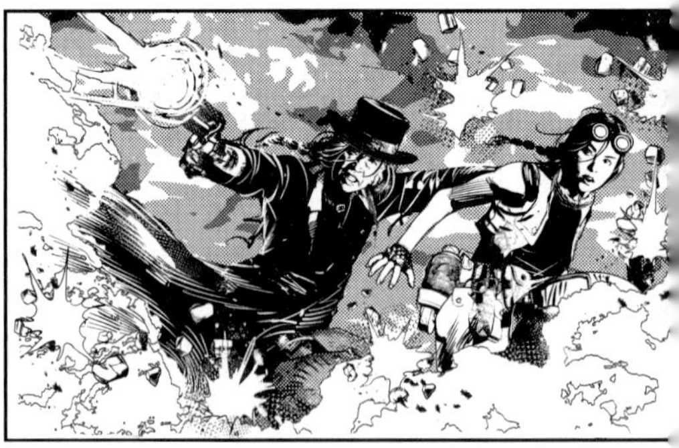

1 CAT MOVE!

2 SFX (RICOCHETS) ZING ZING ZING

Panel 2:
Cat and Rose are on their feet now, Cat providing cover fire with one hand, taking out yet another unlucky posse member (now we are down to 3, including Gage) while pushing Rose towards a nearby tipped over vehicle. Rose's dropped gun is on the ground beside her.

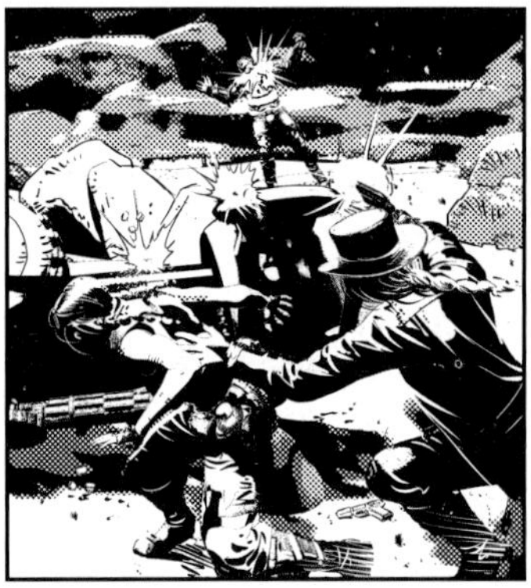

3 CAT Hunker down. I'll draw their fire.

Panel 3:
Rose is running for cover, looking back over one shoulder.

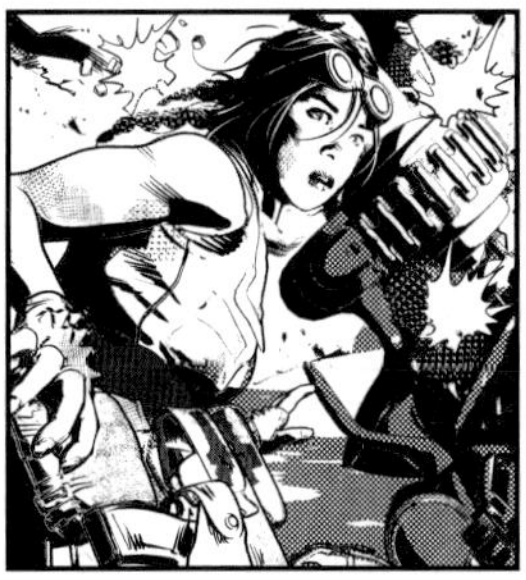

4 CAT (OP) Hey, kid!

Panel 4:
Two shot as Cat tosses Rose's modded cybergun towards her.

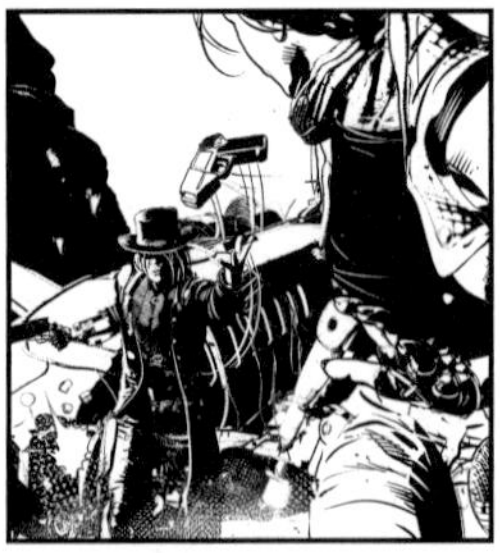

5 CAT You might want this.

Panel 5:
Rose catching the tossed gun against her chest as she dives behind the vehicle.

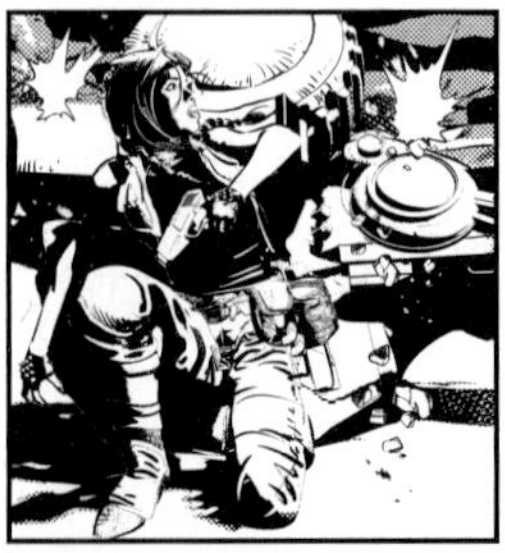

6 SFX (RICOCHETS) ZING ZING ZING

ISSUE #3 PAGE FIFTEEN (eight panels)

anel 1:
lose on Cat, calling out from her new posi-
on behind a large rock.

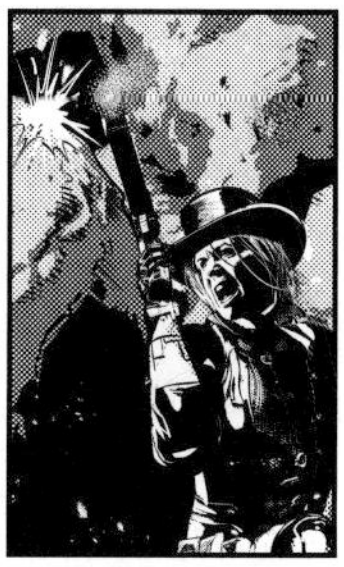

SFX (RICOCHETS) ZING

CAT That you, peeping tom?

anel 2:
lose on Gage's face, reacting.

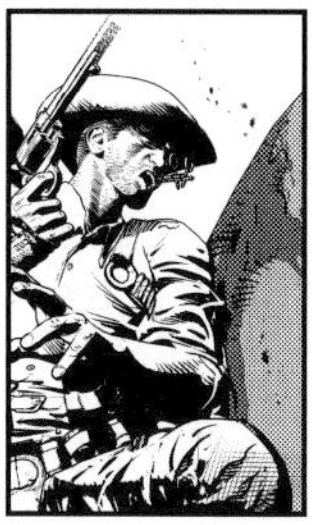

GAGE Fuck you, dyke.

anel 3:
ose watches as Cat makes a run for the
rashed plane, shooting as she goes.

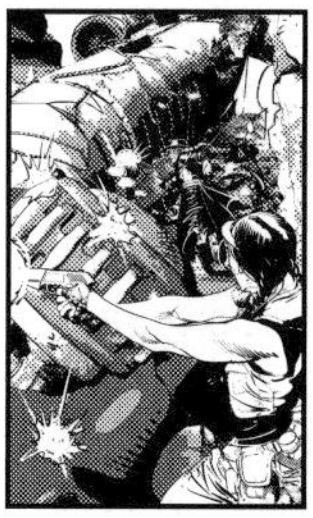

SFX BLAM

anel 4:
age follows as his remaining 2 remaining
osse members cover him. One of them is
na. Let's call the last man Billy.

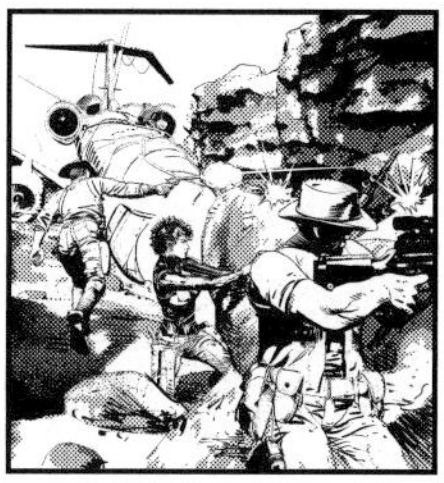

SFX BLAM BLAM BLAM BLAM

anel 5:
ose takes aim and shoots

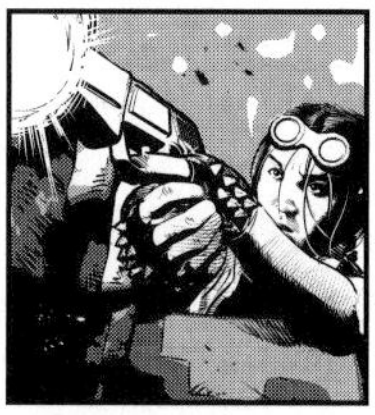

SFX BLAM

anel 7:
illy howls in pain and drops to his knees,
leeding heavily and clutching his stomach.

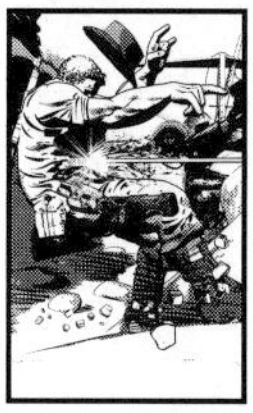

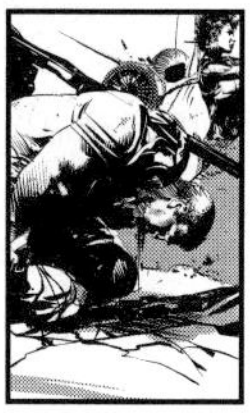

BILLY URGHK!

anel 8:
loser on Rose. This is super intense for her
nd she is not yet able to shut off her emo-
ons. She is horrified and scared and con-
cted and we should see that in her face.

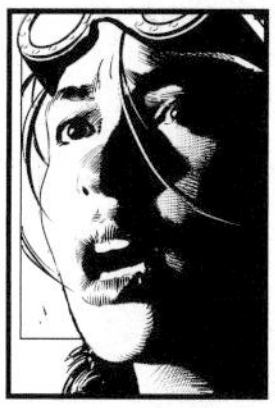

ISSUE #3 PAGE SIXTEEN (six panels)

Panel 1:
Cat has climbed up onto the humpback of the plane cabin sticking out of the sand. She is facing off against Gage, who is standing on the other end of the cabin. He is finally confronting his demon.

1 GAGE I've thought about this day for years, you know. What I would say. What I would do.

2 CAT Well you'd better get to it. I haven't got all night.

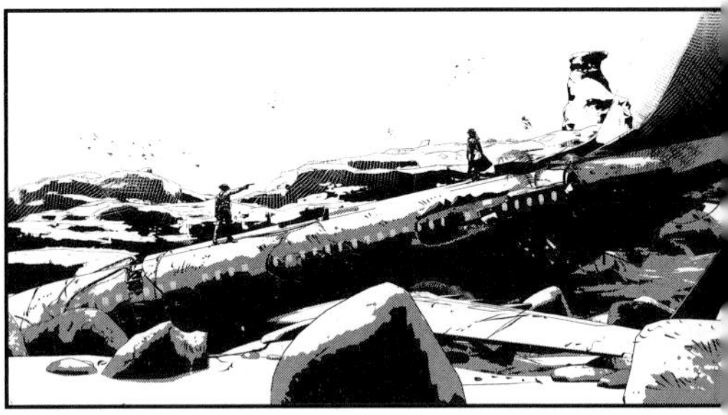

Panel 2:
Cat takes a step towards him and the old, rusted hull of the plane gives out beneath her boot.

3 SFX KREAK

4 CAT WHAT THE—?

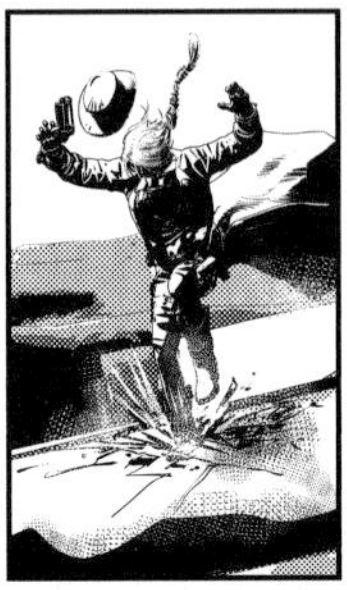

Panel 3:
Inside the dark, dilapidated plane full of mummified corpses and broken open suitcases revealing the sad, mundane belongings of long dead passengers. There is a massive crack in the ceiling and Cat is dropping in from above, surrounded by a swirling spill of rusted metal fragments and dust and sand.

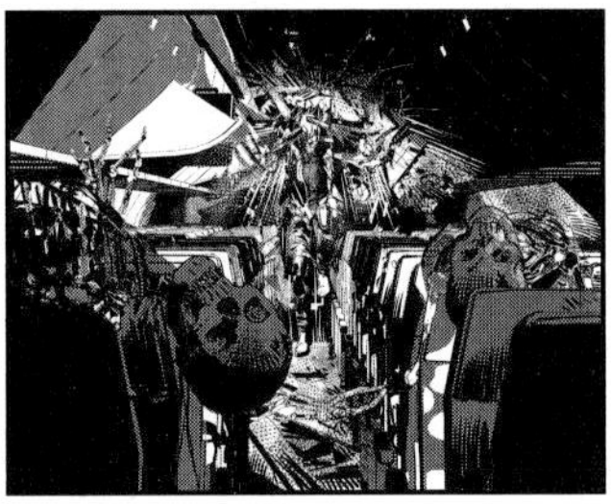

Panel 4:
Cat is crouched in the aisle, activating a light on her cybernetic hand that illuminates the creepy interior in harsh, shadowy film noir style.

5 SFX – rattlesnake rattle! RATTLE-RAT
TLE-RATLE

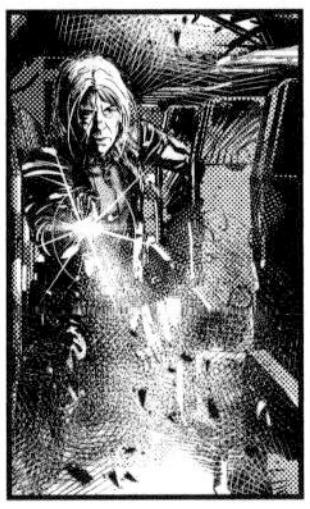

Panel 5:
Cat whirls around to throw her spotlight on a coiled, pissed-off rattler who had been sleeping peacefully in the lap of a corpse before this big, noisy interloper violated the sanctity of its lair.

6 OFF/CAT Aw, hell.

7 SFX rattlesnake rattle!: RATTLE-RATTLE-RATLE

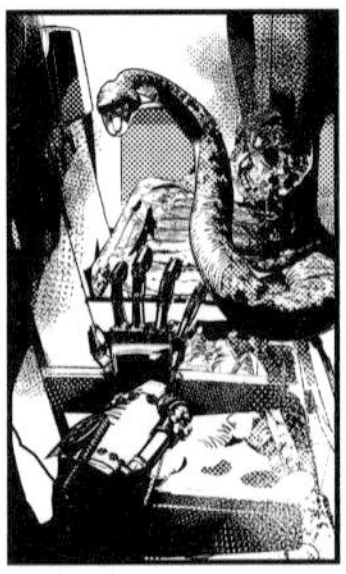

Panel 6:
The snake strikes at Cat as she dodges to one side and catches it in midair, gripping its neck with a thumb pressing down on the back of its chunky, triangular head.

8 SFX – hssssssss

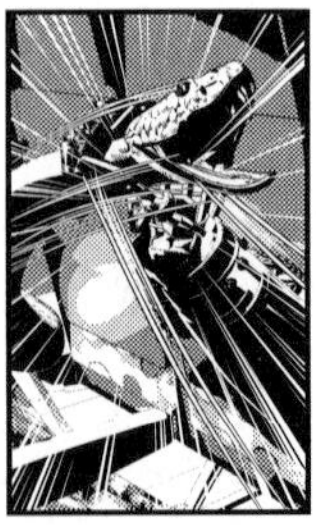

ISSUE #3 PAGE SEVENTEEN (seven panels)

anel 1:
at is still holding the squirming, coiling, and ery much alive snake when Gage comes flying own through the shattered roof, shooting at Cat s he falls.

SFX BLAM BLAM BLAM

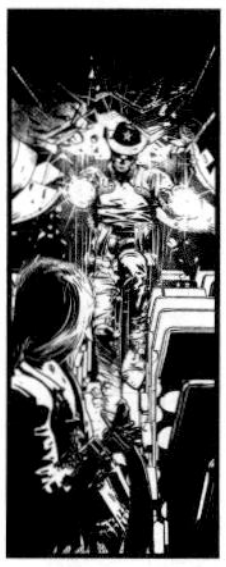

anel 2:
at flings the snake in Gage's direction.

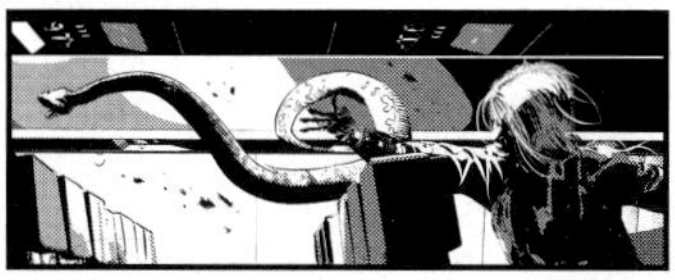

anel 3:
s Gage lands, we see the snake sink its fangs to his wrist.

GAGE Motherfucker!

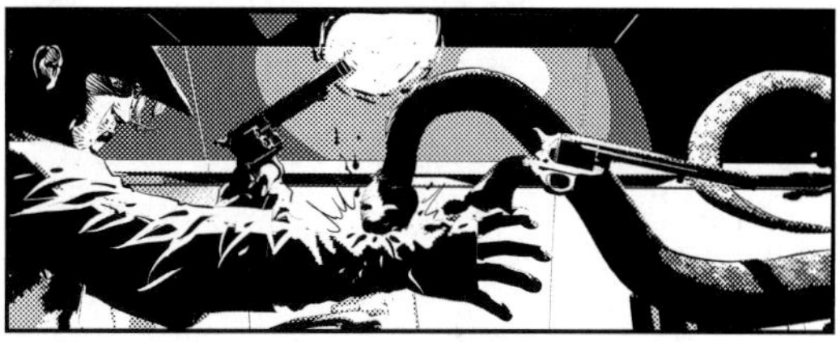

anel 4:
at shoots Gage in the chest.

SFX BLAM

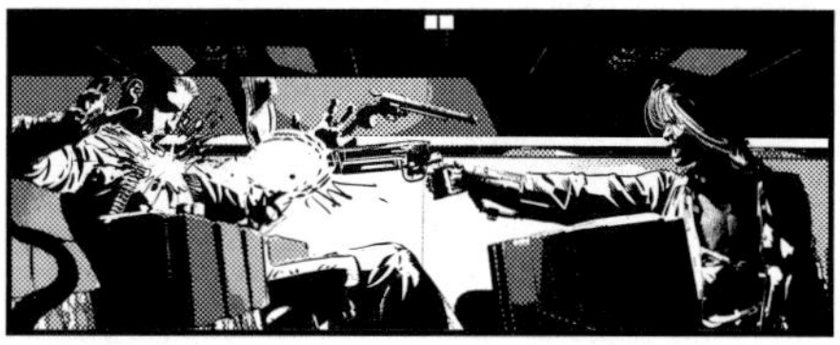

anel 5:
at steps on collapsed Gage's bloody, bitten rist, causing his gun to drop from his rapidly welling hand as she draws a bead on his fore-ead.

OFF/CAT You got something to say to me, you'd best say it now.

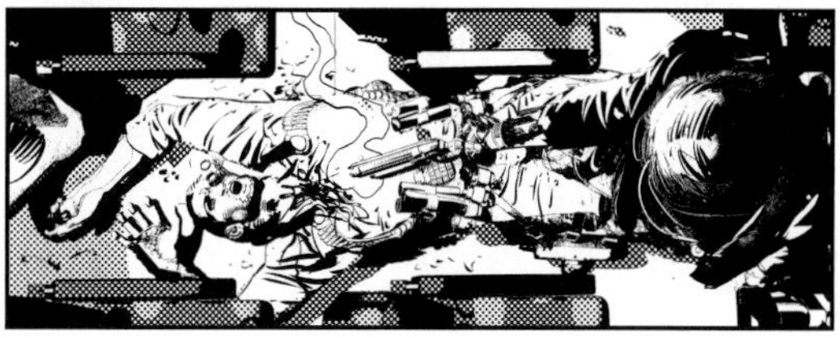

anel 6:
lose on Gage, showing blood-webbed teeth.

GAGE I fucked your girlfriend Inez last night.

GAGE She fought me at first, but once she got a taste of real dick, I had that bitch speaking in tongues.

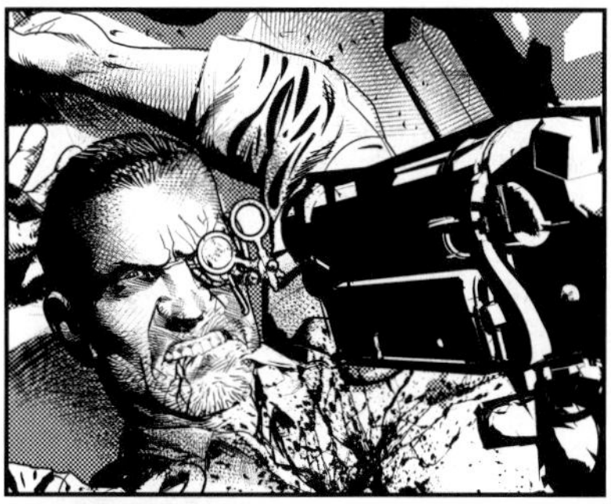

anel 7:
lose up on Cat, an expression of cold, grim fury s blood flies.

SFX BLAM

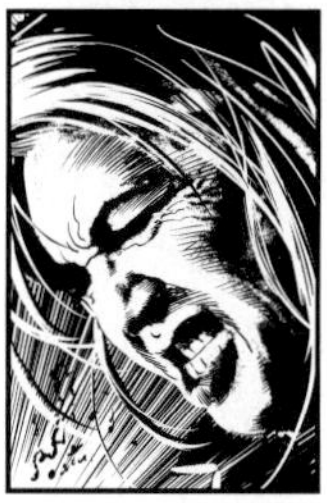

ISSUE #3 PAGE EIGHTEEN (nine panels)

Panel 1:
Rose peeks around the rock to see that Billy, the man she shot, is trying to crawl towards his dropped gun.

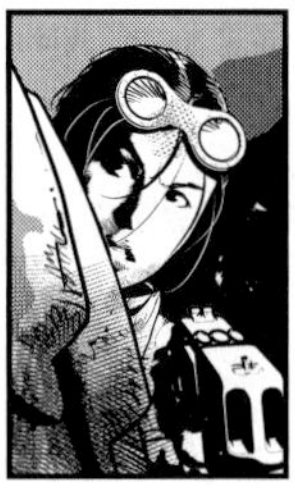

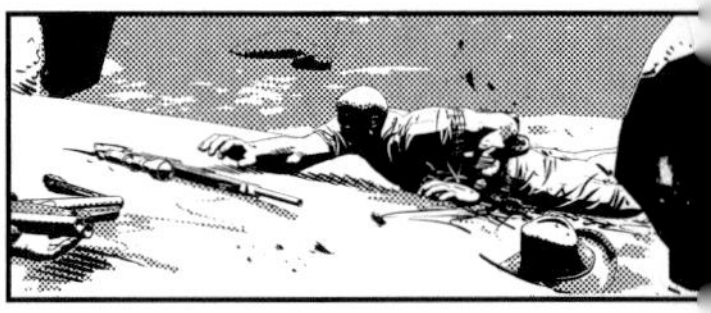

1 ROSE Fucking hell!

Panel 2:
Rose fires at him again, hitting him in the hip this time. He shrieks in agony.

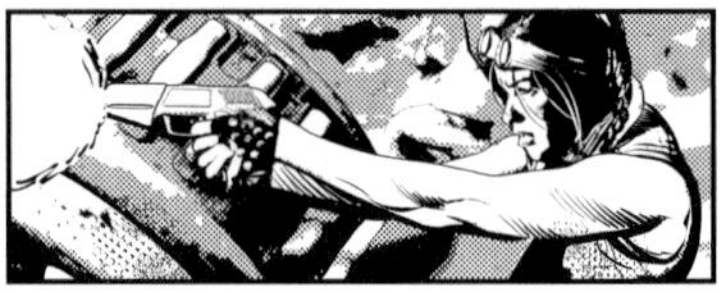

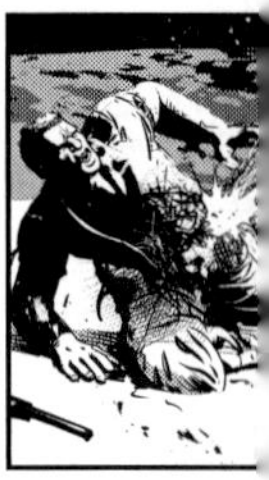

2 BILLY Noooooooooooo! Please!!!!

Panel 3-4:
Tight on Rose. Eyes wide and wild as she shoots.She's losing her shit a little here. The crawling man in the background is crying now.

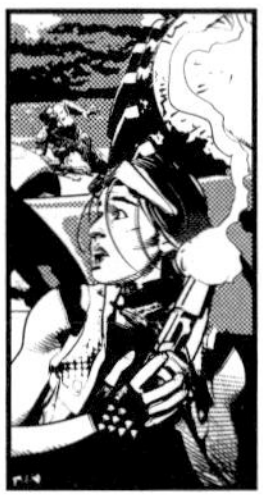

3 SFX BLAM

Panel 5:
SILENT

Panel 6:
Suddenly, Ana tackles Rose. As they fall together to the dusty ground, Rose drops the cybergun.

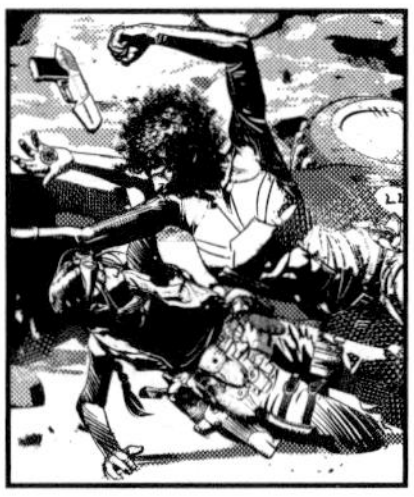

4 ANA Got ya!

Panel 7:
Ana grabs the cybergun, pressing it to Rose's head—

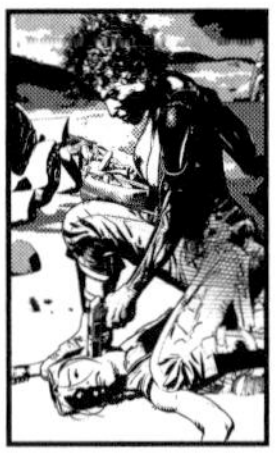

5 ANA Say your prayers, bitch.

Panel 8:
—and pulling the trigger. Rose flinches, but nothing happens.

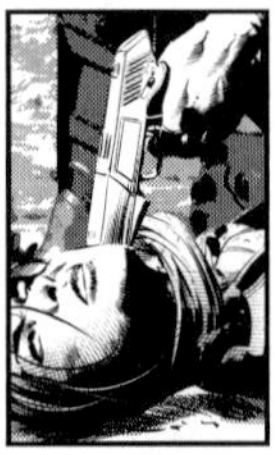

6 FX - klik

Panel 9:
Rose and the woman face to face. Rose smirks.

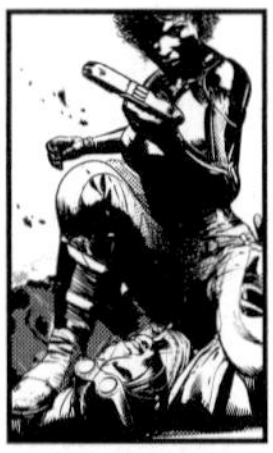

7 ANA What the fuck?

8 ROSE Voice command override. Alpha Ten Seven Tango.

ISSUE #3 PAGE NINETEEN (six panels)

anel 1:
ose's cybergun is suddenly electrified in na's hand, creating a taser-like effect that ause her to fly backward, dropping the gun nd screeching.

SFX ZZZZZZZZZAT

ANA Arrrrrrrrrrrrgh!!!

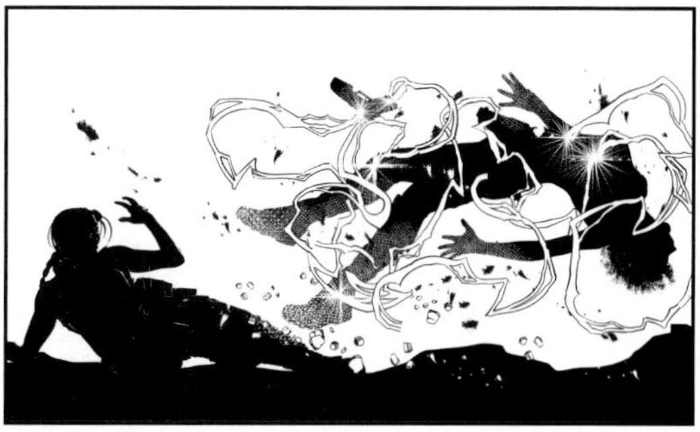

anel 2:
ose grabs the cybergun—

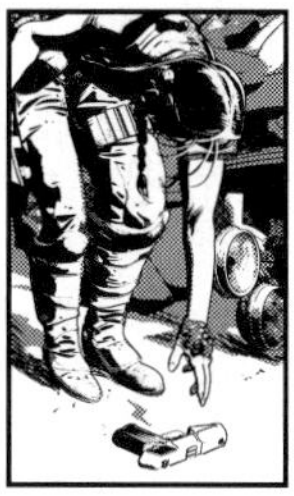

anel 3:
-and fires, hitting the woman in the neck.

SFX BLAM

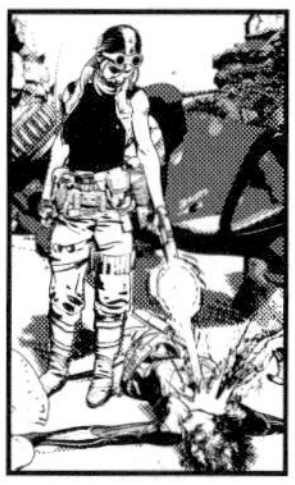

anel 4:
ose stands over the dying woman with a housand yard stare. Behind her, Cat ap-roaches.

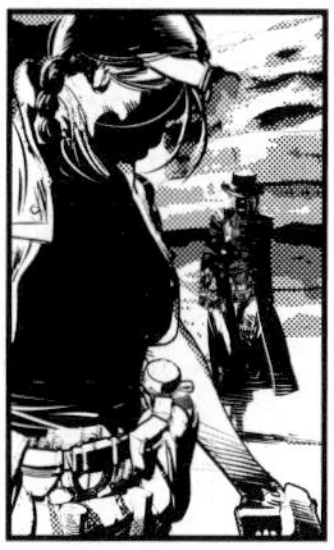

anel 5:
lose on Cat, hiking her thumb at Billy, who still trying to crawl away behind her be-ind her.

CAT That your guy, too?

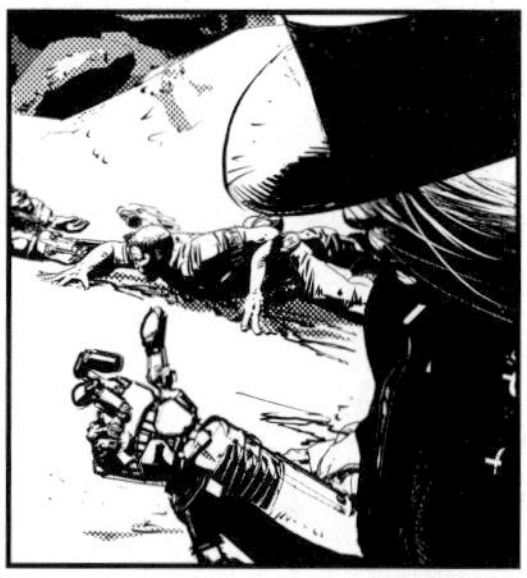

anel 6:
wo shot. Rose, nodding.

ROSE Yeah.

CAT Well then, you better finish the job.

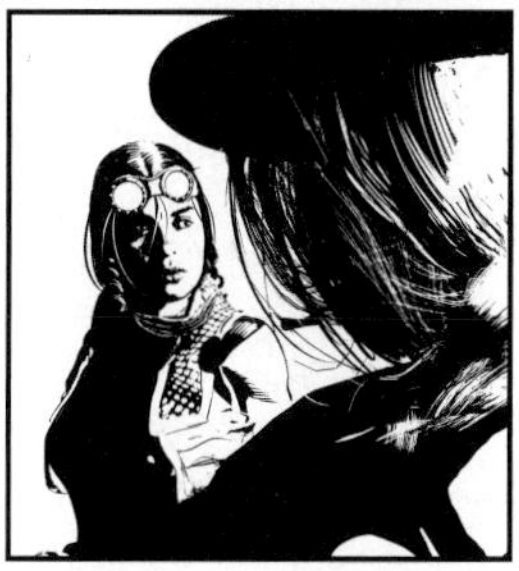

ISSUE #3 PAGE TWENTY (five panels)

Panel 1:
Rose stands over Billy, cybergun aimed his head.

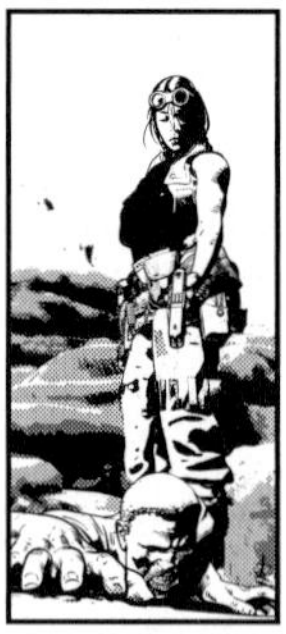

Panel 2:
On Billy, He knows what's coming and has his eyes squeezed closed and teeth bared in a fearful grimace. We want to feel the profound weight of the moment and really see the humanity of the man who she is about to kill.

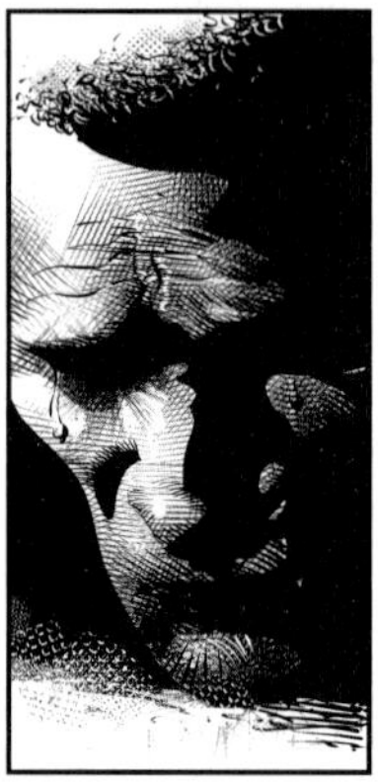

Panel 3:
On Rose, cool, as she shoots.

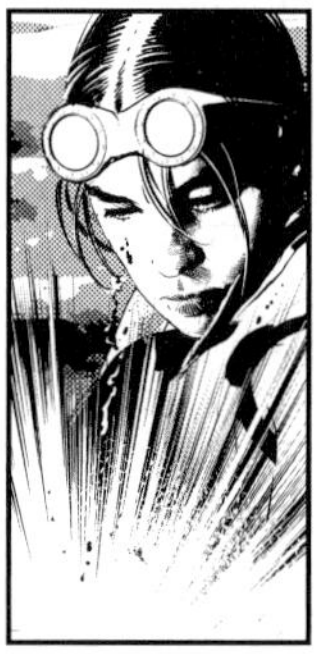

Panel 4:
Tight on Rose, eyes hard and narrow, a light spatter of blood across her cheek. Behind her, Cat has a hand on Rose's shoulder. Her face is also grim and serious. She knows the significance of this moment.

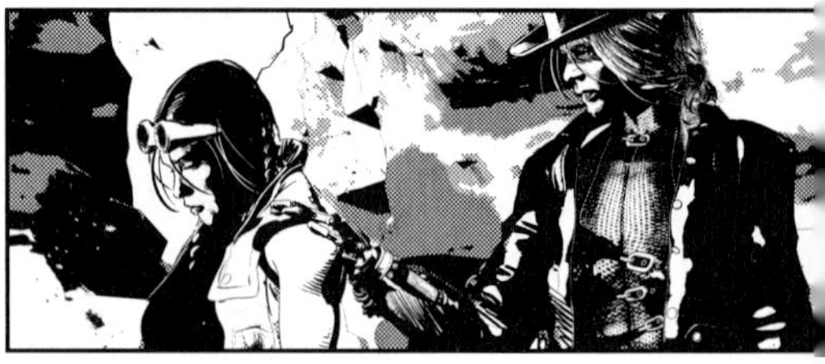

Panel 5:
Pull out to a wide shot of the canyon full of corpses, Rose and Cat in the middle of it all.

1 CAT Good job, kid.

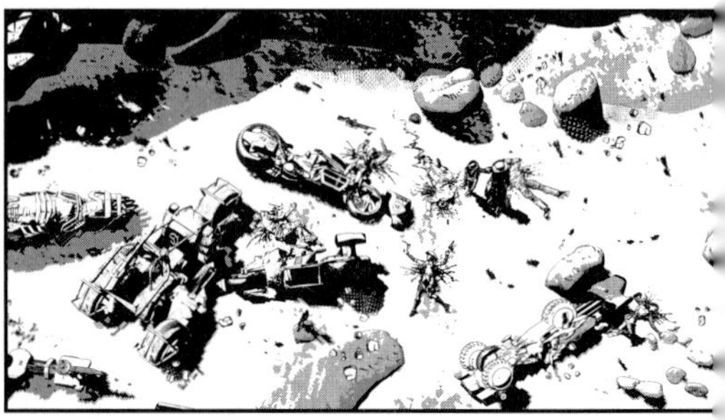